---

STUDIES IN THE HISTORY OF SCIENCE

General Editor: L. Pearce Williams

---

# ROBERT BOYLE AND THE ENGLISH REVOLUTION

Valentine Greatrakes—ambiguous and disturbing symbol in the dialogue between rival natural philosophies of the period—legitimate spiritual healer, popish imposter, or crypto-republican magus?

# ROBERT BOYLE
# AND THE
# ENGLISH REVOLUTION

*A Study in Social and Intellectual Change*

by J. R. JACOB

BURT FRANKLIN & CO., INC.

NEW YORK

© 1977 Burt Franklin & Co., Inc.
235 East 44th St.
New York, New York
10017

**Library of Congress Cataloging in Publication Data**
Jacob, J. R.
Robert Boyle and the English Revolution.
(Studies in the history of science; 3)
Bibliography: p.
Includes index.
1. Science—History—Great Britain. 2. Science—
Social aspects—Great Britain. 3. Boyle, Robert,
1627-1691. 4. Scientists—Great Britain—Biography.
I. Title.
Q127.G4J3      530'.092'4      77-2997
ISBN 0-89102-072-1

Printed in the United States of America
Designed by Harold Franklin

*To Elmer and Justine*

# Contents

# Acknowledgments

This book began as a Ph.D. dissertation, and to those who encouraged me in that work I am deeply grateful: J. E. McGuire, Charles Webster, J. R. Ravetz, and Professors James John, F. G. Marcham, L. M. Marsak, and James Morton Smith. To Professors Marcham and Marsak, I am especially indebted for years of friendly guidance and the freedom to pursue and develop my own intellectual interests and judgment. Equally essential has been the help I have received over the years from a number of libraries: Olin Library, Cornell University; the University of Glasgow Library; the Brotherton Library, Leeds University; the British Museum; the Library of the Royal Society of London; Cambridge University Library; the Bodleian Library; Christ Church Library; the New York Public Library; Union Theological Seminary Library. In particular Cambridge University Library has proved a most agreeable place for me to work, and my special thanks are due to the rare books department for their supremely competent and kindly assistance. To the staff of the Royal Society Library and to T. Wragg, librarian of the Devonshire Collections, Chatsworth, I owe particular debts of gratitude. It is also a pleasure to acknowledge those friends and colleagues whose support, advice, and conversation helped in one way or another to produce this book: Ruud Kemperink, Professor Helli Koenigsberger, Dorothy Koenigsberger, Dr. Ernst Wangermann, María Wangermann, Professor L. Pearce Williams, Drs. John Biddle, Gavin Lewis, Daniel Gasman, Richard Andrews, and Tina Stiefel. Professors Richard Schlatter and J. G. A. Pocock read the entire manuscript and offered wise counsel that saved me from committing the worst excesses.

For permission to quote from manuscripts in their collections I am obliged to His Grace, the duke of Devonshire; the president and fellows of the Royal Society of London; the trustees of the will of J. H. C. Evelyn; and the Historical Library of the Yale Medical

1

Library. I also wish to thank the editors of *The Journal of European Studies* for permission to quote from my article "The Ideological Origins of Robert Boyle's Natural Philosophy," 2 (1972): 1-21; the editors of *Albion* for permission to quote from my "Robert Boyle and Subversive Religion in the Early Restoration," 6 (1974): 175-93; the editors of *History of Science* for permission to quote from my "Restoration, Reformation and the Origins of the Royal Society," 13 (1975): 155-76; the editors of *Social Studies of Science* for permission to quote from my "The New England Company, the Royal Society and the Indians," 5 (1975): 450-55; and the editors of the *Journal of the History of Ideas* for permission to quote from my "Boyle's Circle in the Protectorate" (January 1977).

For financial assistance toward the research and writing of this book I thank the American Philosophical Society for a grant in 1969-70 from the Penrose Fund and the Research Foundation of the City University of New York for a stipend in 1972-73. The typing of the manuscript has been expertly performed by Carol O'Connor.

Finally, this book has been an intellectual adventure of the first importance to me principally because it was shared every step of the way by a fellow scholar of the seventeenth century, M. C. Jacob, who, happily for me, is my wife.

# Preface

Robert Boyle has been the subject of much useful scholarship in the last four decades. Historians of science have shown the important role he played in the evolution of physical theory, chemical practice, and scientific method.[1] Others have been interested in the relationship between his science and his religion and have made notable attempts to show how his natural philosophy integrates the two;[2] how, indeed, his scientific ideas[3] and interests[4] are partly the product of his faith. Finally, thanks to the labors of R. E. W. Maddison and J. F. Fulton, we now know much more about Boyle's life,[5] correspondence,[6] and bibliography.[7] I am heavily indebted to all of these efforts. But even so I have tried to throw fresh light on our common subject, and if I have succeeded it will be because my debt is not to Boyle scholarship alone but to seventeenth-century studies in general and especially to the rich historiography of the English revolution. In my book, whatever I have to say that is original and suggestive comes from the connections I hope to have established between Boyle's natural philosophy and his experience of the revolution, and in these matters I could not have proceeded if it had not been for the important work produced by students of the profound constitutional, social, economic, and intellectual changes that occurred in mid-seventeenth-century England. Sometimes I cite this work; all too often there are no citations, and this must serve, however lame, as a general acknowledgment. But at least it allows me to say at the start what I am about.

My thesis is that in order to arrive at a fuller understanding of Boyle's thought, we must see it in the context of the world in which it evolved, the world of the English revolution and counterrevolution—civil wars, interregnum, and Restoration. This is not to say that one cannot understand Boyle's philosophy without reference to this environment. But this has been accomplished before, while, until now, no one has made a systematic attempt to re-

3

late the development of Boyle's thought to his experience of events
from one year to the next. This is not surprising since we have
only recently learned enough both about his life and thought and
about the revolution. What now emerges is a clear correlation between Boyle's thinking and experience. Not only are Boyle's ideas
defined by his intellectual heritage, his reading, and the internal
development of his thought; they are also partly the product of the
challenges posed and opportunities created by social and political
upheaval—they constitute his response to revolution. Two results
follow from this discovery.

First, the social medium and his participation in it offer a new
means of integrating his science and religion. His involvement in
the larger world produced in him a new kind of piety defined
largely by the necessities, real and supposed, of revolution, and his
natural philosophy grew partly out of and conformed altogether to
this piety. For Boyle, the question of a conflict between his science
and his faith scarcely arose because the latter bred the former and
the grounds for both were a common social matrix and his responses to it. Where he did see conflict between faith and science,
it was not between *his* faith and *his* science but between *his* science
and *other* faiths or between *his* faith and *another* kind of science
which for him was not as valid as his own. This simply reinforces
my point because, as we shall see, these other faiths and this other
science were also in part generated by the conditions of revolution;
they represented other responses to events, responses produced by
social situations in the revolution different from Boyle's own. Nor
should it surprise us that knowledge, even scientific knowledge, is
a reflection of men's experience of social conditions or that when
these conditions change what is thought of as knowledge may and
probably will also change. A substantial literature is now
available—the work of anthropologists, sociologists, and historians
alike—which argues and establishes this point.[8] I have applied this
line of inquiry systematically to a new subject, namely Boyle, and
as a result have achieved a new understanding of an old topic—the
relationship between science and religion in seventeenth-century
England.

Second, this new way of integrating Boyle's philosophy with his
piety achieves greater historicity as regards Boyle's ideas than we
had before. It not only takes more account of the social, ethical,

economic, and political dimensions of his thought, but in doing so
it links and fuses them together with his natural philosophy and
theology in ways which he must also have done but which Boyle
scholars previously had not seen. This connecting of the social with
the religious, philosophical, and technical aspects of his biography
brings us closer to his own mental processes and to what the results meant to him in the seventeenth century as distinct from
what they have commonly meant to us in the twentieth century.
This gain in historicity will lead to a fuller understanding not only
of Boyle but also of the social relations of modern science in what
was one of its most formative moments. What is thus gained in
historicity may, ironically, awaken us to the deeper social meanings
of science in our own time, which is still the heir in so many ways
of the seventeenth century—and in none so much as in science and
politics and the relations between them.

Boyle is the perfect subject for my sort of inquiry. Not only was
he at the center of scientific developments in England, he was also
the son of an important family and involved with them in the
changes England underwent at the time. His position made him
more than a scientist; he was also a landed gentleman, a leading
churchman, and a confidant of his brother Roger, baron Broghill
(later earl of Orrery), who was a principal adviser to Oliver and
Richard Cromwell and active in the government of Charles II.
Boyle was also active in the government after the Restoration. He
was Clarendon's councillor, a member of the Council for Foreign
Plantations, a founder of the Royal Society and president of the
New England Company. His involvement in science, church, and
state drew to him a large circle of friends, made him a patron of
writers and thinkers whose views reflected his own, and caused
him to confront and deal with some of the central issues of the day:
the relations between church and state; the nature of government;
the purpose of empire; and the relations between religion, science,
and the state. Boyle's public role makes it easier than it otherwise
would be to examine his response to the revolution. As a result,
we know more not only about his personal biography and the integration of his thought and experience but also about the larger
social and cultural ramifications of his natural philosophy and religion.

There is, finally, one more help in this enterprise. Like many leading thinkers of the seventeenth century, Boyle assumed the underlying unity of reality, an assumption resting in turn on the universal Christian doctrine of the oneness of God and of God's creation. Every sphere of reality—physical, moral, political, and spiritual—is invested with divine meaning and purpose, and there is a consistency and harmony throughout. It was not enough for Boyle that the universe is fraught with discernible truth; he set out on a quest to unravel that truth and apply it both to his own situation and to the world at large. This endeavor provides yet another basis for integrating his science and religion. It also allows me to argue that his response to revolution is essential to understanding his thought. He saw history like everything else, as a part of God's plan. Because events changed his life and reordered his attitudes and values, they also significantly affected his natural philosophy. He read the same meanings into nature that he learned from the revolution. Such were the dictates of the assumption of providential order in terms of which he thought. By interpreting nature in light of the lessons of experience, he arrived at a new comprehension of divine providence, God's acting in the world, the harmony of nature and history.

I have attempted to place Boyle's adoption of a mechanical and corpuscular theory of the physical universe, his experimental method, and his faith in this method in their larger cultural and biographical context. I hope in this attempt to have shed more light upon, and broken new ground for, further exploration of old questions: Why, at this particular juncture, did a handful of English thinkers discard peripatetic explanations and become what we may collectively but only loosely describe as atomists and experimentalists, and why did they go on to found the Royal Society for the promotion of their new knowledge? I have by no means exhausted these topics, but I hope I have made a substantial contribution to them.

Spelling and punctuation have been altered where the original would prevent or seriously impede comprehension. Dates conform to modern usage as to year.

# Chapter 1

---

# Conversion

# and Commitment

---

Robert Boyle, born January 25, 1627, was the youngest son of Richard, the first earl of Cork. In the late sixteenth century, Richard, one of Queen Elizabeth's adventurers, had struck out for Ireland to find his fortune. In time he built up a land empire in Munster that made him one of the most powerful men in the country, earned him a peerage, and gave him ready access to the king and the government at Whitehall.[1] He was the founder of a dynasty that would be important in English and Irish affairs for a century. Not only did he lay the economic foundations of his family's fortune, he also attempted to prepare his sons for their roles as heirs and bearers into the future of the family name.

He had worked hard, even ruthlessly, to get what he had; he did not intend to give his children the opportunity of wasting and losing it. Rather, he had masterfully initiated the family's fortunes and expected his sons to carry them forward. In a letter in 1635, he says, "all the rarest that this world can lay upon me, are farr inferior to my Study and endeavors which I have, to give my Sons a religious, learned and noble breeding. . . ."[2]

The earl of Cork wished his sons to grow up to be gentlemen in the full meaning of the term in the currency of the time—ardent in the service of their family, caste, faith, and monarch. He took pains to see that they should turn out as he wished even when they went abroad. Typically, he instructed their tutors to send him reports of his sons' progress, and on the basis of these, as well as anything his sons' own letters might reveal, he would write long

replies in which he praised or cajoled, as he felt the occasion demanded. In a directive to his most recalcitrant son, Lewis, he
shows how committed he was to making his sons gentlemen and
how fearful he was that they might become anything less:

> Lewis, remember that as our gracious Majesty, the king, hath
> given you honor, so it beholdeth you to carry yourself honor-
> ably and nobly lest by the contrary you should dishonor his
> Majestie, me and yourself, with all the rest of my children.
> And therefore above all things serve God devoutly and reli-
> giously day and night and spend no hour unprofitably but
> employ your whole time to the bettering and increasing of
> your learning and knowledge. . . .[3]

The earl's desires for Robert were only a little, if any, different
from those for his older sons. The difference, if any, stemmed from
the fact that "until his father's death, he ever continued very much
his favourite."[4] Perhaps it would be truer to say that the father
noticed early what a clever boy Robert was and gave particular attention to his upbringing. Whatever the reason, Robin, as his
father called him,[5] enjoyed all the advantages of a superior education. When he was eight years old, his father, "ambitious to improve his early studiousness," shipped him and his brother Francis
off to England "to be bred up at *Eton* college near *Windsor,* whose
provost at that time was Sir *Henry Wotton,* a person, that was not
only a fine gentleman himself, but very well skilled in the art of
making others so. . . ."[6] Robert's removal to Eton at the tender age
of eight accorded with the earl's notion that "great men's children
breeding up at home tempts them to nicety, to pride, and idleness,
and contributes much more to give them a good opinion of themselves, than to make them deserve it. . . ."[7] Robert was thus to be
spared a young life of ease. He stayed off and on at Eton for several years and, according to his own account, made good progress
in his studies.

He eventually left the college. His father then sent him and
Francis, under the tutelage of one Isaac Marcombes,[8] to the Continent to finish off their education. So began one of the formative
periods of Robert's life.

The three sailed at the end of October 1638. They crossed France and made their way to Geneva, Marcombes' home and the city where the young Boyles lived during most of their time on the Continent.

The record Robert has left of the years spent abroad is fragmentary, but still informative. Among his most remarkable experiences were ones deeply inward and spiritual. Robert set down his account of his early religious experiences a few years after he got back from his sojourn on the Continent.[9] The account forms one continuous part of his autobiography. He relates the separate experiences one after another. There is no way of telling for sure whether or not they appear on paper in chronological sequence, but they seem to have constituted a unit in Boyle's mind when he wrote. The question of the significance of their forming such a unit seems to have more to do with what was going on in Boyle's mind when he was writing the autobiography than it does with the experiences themselves. The question then will await treatment until the narrative reaches the point where Boyle sat down and wrote about his early life.

For the moment, the concern is with the experiences themselves. The two worthy of notice, occurring as they did at the onset of Boyle's adolescence, made an immediate and powerful impact upon him. In the first, he records that a storm woke him one night in Geneva probably in the summer of 1639. Even before the storm, he seems to have believed that the Judgment Day was close at hand. So the storm first of all "confirmed" him "in his apprehensions." Second, it jolted him, presumably for the first time, into "the consideration of his unpreparedness." Finally, this "consideration" led him to imagine "the hideousness of being surprised," should judgment come while he was still living "in an unfit condition" to receive it. These things together "made him . . . vow, that if his fears were that night disappointed, all his further additions to his life should be more religiously and watchfully employed." The next day, his fears settled, "he ratified his determination so solemnly, that from that day he dated his conversion. . . ."[10]

Less than a year later, in the spring of 1640, as nearly as can be determined, young Boyle suffered another experience that put his conversion to the first test for which there is any evidence. He had gone with his tutor to visit the chief cities of certain eastern provinces of France. During his tour "his curiosity at last led him to

those wild mountains, where the first and chiefest of the Carthu-
sian abbies does stand seated." There, everything in him and in
"so sad a place" went to suggest to him "such strange and hideous
thoughts, and such distracting doubts of some of the fundamentals
of Christianity, that . . . nothing but the forbiddenness of self-
dispatch hindered his acting it." Although he stopped short of
suicide, he was still to endure a "tedious languishment of many
months in this tedious perplexity." Only later did it please God "to
restore unto him the withdrawn sense of His favor." Not again,
however, was he to be as he had been before his months of "tedious perplexity." The effects of the experience, he says some years
later, were to be lasting. "Never after did these fleeting clouds
cease now and then to darken the clearest serenity of his
quiet. . . ."[11] Suffice it to say for the time being that with his recovery and—one would think—as part of it, he came more and
more to see reality in spiritual terms, until in time he had evolved
a personal faith—a piety all his own—which had spread itself
through the whole fabric of his thought.

Marcombes continued to teach the Boyles the whole time they
lived abroad. Robert's principal studies were divinity, mathematics,
languages, and history, and these seem to have stood for him in
that order of importance. He showed at one point a burst of enthusiasm for mathematics. In fact, he wrote home to his father:

> We continue our Study in the Mathematickes which is (as I
> thinke) the bravest Science in the world (after Divinity,) and I
> hope to become a good proficient therein, having for scope
> therein as well as in all other studies the desire to serve God,
> to please your Lordship, and to render myselfe in some sort
> worthy to be esteemed.[12]

He had learned well his father's teaching and, indeed, that of his
age: the more skills a gentleman had acquired, the more service he
could give to family, church, and king; and the greater his service,
the worthier was he to be, and to be called, a gentleman.

In 1641 something happened to change the course of Boyle's life:
the Irish rebellion broke out and drastically altered the family's fortunes. On March 9, 1642, the earl wrote to Marcombes, describing

in graphic terms "the dangerous and poore estate"[13] to which the Irish troubles had reduced the family and telling him in view of the circumstances what had to be done with Francis and Robert. According to the earl,

> the Conspiracy to roote out all the Protestants in this Kingdome was generall, and every Irish and English Papist was publiquely or privately infected with the Poyson of this rebellion, and had vowed or received the Sacrament to roote us all out of Ireland, both roote and branch. . . .[14]

This being the case, his financial losses had been heavy. He was, for instance, collecting no rents or revenues of any kind. Yet, only the previous October he had "receaved in penny rent (besides my houses, demeasnes, parks, fyshings, yronworkes, and other royalties) at least twenty thowsand pounds sterling per annum."[15] Even worse, whereas his properties, he writes,

> heretofore . . . yealded me liberall rents, now instead thereof, they draw upon me great charge to ward and defend them, for all these places are kept at my owne charge, and there are aboue 200000 in armes and rebellion, against that poore handfull of British Protestants, that are yet alive. . . .[16]

So Richard's fortunes diminished fast. "When this generall torrent of rebellion broke forth," continues the letter, "I did not know that subject in his Majesties three Kingdomes, with whom I would have changed fortunes, all things duely considered."[17] But things had so changed that he wrote, "I know I am the greatest looser of any man in this kingdome, for I am deeply indebted, and have neither money, revenue, nor stock left me, nor can longer subsist for want of meanes; which true Complaint I did never feare, I should have taken upp. . . ."[18]

In view of the circumstances, the earl sent Marcombes £250, which was to be given to the young Boyles to do one of two things—either to make their way home to Ireland, or to go "into Holland, and putt themselves into entertaynement under the service and conduct of the Prince of Orange. . . ."[19]

Their father was newly impoverished and could no longer maintain them abroad. As younger sons of Irish aristocrats—especially
the impoverished ones—had always done, so now they were to do.
"They must henceforward maintayne themselves by such enter-
taynements as they gett in the warres. . ."[20] and in the process defend the Protestant cause against the Catholic menace. The earl
was equally explicit about what they were not to do:

> Into England I will not consent they shall yet come, till Ire-
> land be recovered, for I have neither present money nor
> meanes to defray their expences there; And for them that
> have been soe well maintayned to appeare there with out
> money, would deject their spirits, and grieve and disgrace
> me, and draw contempt upon us all.[21]

Even though from an objective point of view what had happened
to the earl was beyond his control, he nonetheless would have felt
deep shame at the thought of any of his family living in England in
straitened circumstances. Such were his pride and the mores of his
caste.

As it happened, Robert went to neither Ireland, Holland, nor
England. He wrote to his father, saying that the travel money had
not come. Besides, having only just concluded a tour of Italy, he
was too weak and weary to undertake another trip. Even if he
could reach Holland, he wrote, "I . . . have little hope by reason of
my youth [he was fifteen at the time] to be receaved among the
troopes. . . ."[22] He decided instead to accept an invitation Marcombes extended, to stay on in Geneva and pursue his studies.
This was to be a temporary measure in order to allow him time "to
gather some force and vigour to serve and defend my Relig-
[ion] . . . my King and my Country according to my little
power. . . ."[23] The letter ends in these words—all that are
legible—"I beseech . . . betweene this and the end of August to
thinke upon . . . I may honorably gain my living. . . ."[24] But an ar-
rangement that was supposed to last only a few months drew itself
out in the end to more than three years' duration. First, father
writes to son in the late summer of 1642 to tell him "to
stay . . . with Mr. Marcombes till the Spring time. . . ."[25] By mid-

summer, 1643, Richard was dead. After this, nothing is known of Robert's life until he decided to leave Geneva for England in 1644.

Boyle went because "being unable to subsist any longer, I was forced to remove thence. . . ."[26] He lacked the means to afford the trip. But on Marcombes' credit he bought some jewels which he sold along the way. He reached England in the middle of 1644 and made for London. He must have lost touch with his family after his father's death, since he apparently did not know that his sister Katherine, viscountess Ranelagh, was living in London; he met her quite by accident.

As a youngster, Robert had left the shelter of the family seat for school and then again for the Continent. When his father died, he was thrown back even more rudely on his own devices. Finally, he went to England in the humblest fashion at the most inauspicious time. He was without employment or any prospects. The family's treasure was spent, and the older sons were fighting to the very death against the Irish rebels.[27] England itself was in the throes of civil war. Once more Robert was robbed of the almost effortless plenty that would otherwise have been his. The earl had raised him to be industrious and independent. And what father and tutor had not taught him, circumstances did.

His fortunes, however, were only low, not desperate. By his father's will, he was heir to the manor of Stalbridge in Dorsetshire. The evidence seems to suggest that before he met his sister, he may not have known this. Had he not run into her, he says, he would have become a soldier,[28] the one fit calling for a gentleman in which there was no shortage of places. But he would probably not have decided to take up arms if he could have helped it. He had already begged off joining the Dutch army when his father had given him the chance. The army would now be a native one, but this did not alter the case. Though he would have had "the excellent king himself, divers eminent divines, and many worthy persons of several ranks" for his comrades, "yet the generality of those he would have been obliged to converse with, were very debauched, and apt, as well as inclinable, to make others so. . . ."[29] Only extreme necessity, it seems, would have driven him to put his soul in jeopardy by becoming a soldier. The evidence suggests that he gave up the idea as soon as he learned that he was heir to

Stalbridge.[30] It follows that he probably did not know the provisions of his father's will before he went into England.

At first he stayed with his sister in London and met her friends. Four months after arriving in England he left his sister's house, went tò Stalbridge, and began to settle into his own property. He never went off to war.

On August 25, 1645, he was in London, writing his brother Roger, baron Broghill, and telling him of a forthcoming trip to France.[31] One of his purposes in going was probably to repay Marcombes for care and maintenance after the earl's death.[32] But he did not stay long in France, as there is a record of his being in Cambridge in December 1645. By the following March, he was back at Stalbridge;[33] for a few years thereafter he moved back and forth between Stalbridge and London.

These years were not particularly easy ones for Boyle.[34] Stalbridge, no doubt, gave him a modicum of security. But times were as troubled and uncertain for property holders as for everyone else. There was an untended manor in Dorset to put right, hold on to, and maintain, and there was an Irish estate that had also fallen to him,[35] still to be claimed. Boyle had no experience in the slippery business of managing estates. His father, until his death, had relieved him of all responsibility in this quarter. Robert had been left to pursue his studies undistracted. So all he had to go on now were personal qualities acquired or strengthened in earlier trials and setbacks. He was not penniless—far from it—but his pockets were not flush. Had times been different—had there been general peace in England and Ireland—Boyle would have been much better off. He could have worked with considerably less application and probably reaped a fatter return. He might even have lived a carefree life. As it was, he had to work and scheme just to keep what he had—he had to pit his energies against men and events. The difference that Boyle must have felt, then, was not that between early wealth and subsequent impoverishment, but between what might have been a life of ease and what circumstances dictated—the necessity of self-willed effort.

To Marcombes, Boyle wrote that the time since his removal to England, "truly hath been chequered with a great deal of variety of fortune, and a great many vicissitudes of plenty and want, danger and safety, sickness and health, trouble and ease." At one point he was taken prisoner "upon some groundless suspicions, but quickly got off with advantage." For some time, it seems, Boyle was also the victim of embezzlement. The culprit was one of the earl's former servants, Tom Murray, whom Boyle kept on to manage his affairs. He found out and sent Murray away. Boyle wrote, "I thence reaped the benefit of making further discoveries into economical knowledge, than ever otherwise I should have done" and "attained to a knowledge of my own small fortune beyond the possibility of being cheated. . . ." In each case Boyle saw himself as having profited from his hardships and God as making it so.

> I were guilty of an ingratitude [as] great as the favour I have received if I did not acknowledge a great deal of mercy in God's dispensation towards me; which truly hath been so kind, as oftentimes to work my good out of those things I most feared the consequences of, and changed those very dangers, which were the object of my apprehension, into the motives of my joy.[36]

Boyle did not despair in the face of difficulties. On the contrary, he identified the terms on which he must live with the terms on which God has preordained that life is and ought to be lived. He invoked divine sanction for what he must of necessity endure. In this way the drudgery of daily living acquired a transcendental significance, and this projection of private purposes onto a level cosmic and divine comforted him in defeat and steeled him for the continuing struggle.

Such a faith was doubtless a help in a world "where I myself have been fain to borrow money of servants, to lend it to men of above 10000£. a year."[37] The civil wars were indeed difficult for men in Boyle's position. The high were brought low and the lowly raised up. The sentiment was on the lips of not a few members of the until-then privileged classes.[38] Boyle himself got caught up in events and could not come through unscathed. He writes,

> I have been forced to live at a very high rate, (considering the inconsiderableness of my income) and, to furnish out these

expenses, part with a good share of my land, partly to live
here like a gentleman, and partly to perform all that I thought
expedient in order to my Irish estate, out of which I never yet
received the worth of a farthing.[39]

But at least he sensed danger to himself and his property in the
turmoil and behaved accordingly, picking his way through the
political thicket. "I have been forced," he says, "to observe a very
great caution, and exact eveness in my carriage, . . . it being abso-
lutely necessary for the preservation of a person, whom the unfor-
tunate situation of his fortune made obnoxious to the injuries of
both parties [Parliament and the cavaliers] and the protection of
neither."[40] Boyle was successful in the pursuit of "caution" and
"eveness."

One must remember, of course, that he had his charming sister,
Lady Ranelagh, to help him. Certainly his earliest stay in her house
proved rewarding. One day he met Lady Ranelagh's sister-in-law
"who was with them in the house, and was wife of one of the
principal members of the then house of commons," Sir John Clot-
worthy.[41] Through her, he was brought "into the acquaintance and
friendship of some great men of that party, which was then growing, and soon after victorious; by whose means he got early protection for his English and Irish estates."[42]

While Boyle moved at the promptings of providence and so hus-
banded his small and precarious fortune, he still found time to
pursue matters other than the merely financial and mundane. Lady
Ranelagh had wide-ranging interests and, living in London as she
did, the friends to match them. She knew, for instance, John Milton, Lucius Cary, viscount Falkland, and Sir Edward Hyde.[43] So in
coming to her house from abroad, Boyle gained access to a remarkable circle of people. Probably through her he met the two men
who, during this period, greatly influenced his intellectual
development—John Dury and Samuel Hartlib.[44]

## Boyle, Dury, and the Hartlib Circle

Who, then, were Dury and Hartlib?[45] And what did they communicate to Boyle? They had been associates for many years when

Boyle met them. Both had been advocates of various reforms in England and on the Continent for more than a decade before the outbreak of the English civil wars. Their activities overlapped. But in general terms Dury devoted himself principally to the cause of Protestant unity in Europe while Hartlib advocated reforms in such areas as farming, education, medicine, and the law. In the 1630s they had aligned themselves with certain men in the English church and Parliament sympathetic to moderate change. When the open split between king and Parliament came, Dury and Hartlib saw it as the opportunity of the age. So they stayed on in England through the 1640s and 1650s and tried to persuade each new wave of leaders to put radical proposals into effect and so to realize the vision of a regenerate England, made fit to lead Protestant Europe. This dream seems always to have been much further from realization than Dury and Hartlib thought it was. Their vision was utopian and the revolution was not. But they left their mark on the minds of the large number of men who, over the course of several decades, entertained them. Robert Boyle was one of these men, and his debt was large.

Perhaps the clearest statement of Hartlib's aims is to be found in a tract, published anonymously in London in 1641, entitled *A Description of the Famous Kingdom of Macaria. . . .* Charles Webster has recently shown that its author was not Hartlib, as was thought, but Gabriel Plattes, a member of Hartlib's circle.[46] But Plattes' authorship aside, *Macaria* served as a manifesto for Hartlib and his group. The fictitious realm it described became their model for refashioning the English nation.[47] As Plattes says, "Why should not all the inhabitants of England join with one consent, to make this country be like to Macaria . . . ?"[48] The tract is little more than a sketch. Plattes is often cryptic and many of his proposals are fragmentary. But at least the general implications of his program are clear.

The nerve center of Macaria, and the key to the kingdom's vitality, is a "house, or college of experience." Any who feel that they have something to contribute to "the health or wealth of men" can bring their ideas before the college and by experiment demonstrate them. Should a demonstration succeed, the experiment will become a part of the fund of public knowledge and the inventor "honourably rewarded at the publick charge. . . ." Information so accumulated is to be made freely accessible to any who seek it. In

*Macaria* Plattes suggests the benefits accruing from an increase in medical knowledge and knowledge of matters of husbandry. He intends his suggestions respecting medicine to stand as alternatives to the monopoly of knowledge in the hands of English physicians. "In Macaria the parson of every parish is a good physician, and doth execute both functions; to wit, *cura animarum,* & *cura corporum;* . . . ; and the physicians, being true naturalists, may as well become good divines, as the divines do become good physicians."[49] Men who are divines or physicians alone should be both. If England were to follow the example of Macaria, the medical monopoly would come down and with it would go the lack of public access to treatment: "every parish" would have its "good physician." A knowledge of one profession is helpful in the pursuit of the other. Thus, members of each profession might, with good effect, see service in the other.

In Macaria the "college of experience," besides storing up knowledge of cures and methods of treatment accessible to physicians and divines alike, also promotes improvements in husbandry. Gentlemen-farmers come to the college for advice about the proper use of their lands and then go out and apply what they have learned with profit both to themselves and their kingdom. The more they grow, the more people they can feed. The bigger the population, the stronger the country and the harder to conquer or to defeat it in battle.[50] Landowners prosper in two ways. Not only do they increase their yield, they also pay less in taxes. The king, the biggest landowner of all, listens to the same advice as do his landed subjects and "taketh a strict course that all his crown lands be improved to the utmost, . . . by which means his revenues are so great, that he seldom needeth to put impositions upon his subjects, by reason he hath seldom any wars. . . ."[51] The king manages his estates efficiently enough to be able to live of his own. His efforts and those of his landed subjects to improve husbandry keep the kingdom strong. This very strength in turn deters enemies from making war and relieves the country of the burden of having to pay the taxes for waging war. The moral that Macaria points for the English nation is obvious.

In everything the ruler of Macaria calculates his own interests and those of his landed subjects and then pursues policies that satisfy, to the extent that this is possible, the interests of everyone.

His living of his own as he does, for example, frees his subjects from onerous taxation—and in return they are willing to pay him their allegiance. A bargain is thus struck between king and landed subjects, who speak for the rest of the nation. Obligations are reciprocal between ruler and ruled, and all for the purpose of obtaining a mutual end: a prosperous, strong, and peaceful kingdom. The result is a balance of interests. Ruler and ruled, if they wish to pursue their own interests, are bound to the conditions of the balance—this alone is enlightened. The king's actions follow from his motives, and his principal motive—enlightened as well as self-interested—is again to preserve the balance. For him to resort to treachery and deceit is highly unlikely. Thus, Plattes asks: "Who can but love and honour such a prince, who, in his tender and parental care of the publick good of his loving subjects, useth no pretences for realities, like to some princes, in their acts of state, edicts, and proclamations?"[52] The politics of Macaria are not Machiavellian. Instead they rest on a lively sense among landed subjects of what constitutes their material interests. The king is thus prevented from dealing in deceptions and must himself take those interests into account when making policy.

The state church of Macaria, like the civil polity, contributes to peace and stability. "There is no diversity of opinions amongst [divines]. . . . If any divine shall publish a new opinion to the common people, he shall be accounted a disturber of the publick peace, and shall suffer death for it." The reason for this severity is not to keep the people "in error perpetually, if they be once in it." The object is rather to prevent civil strife as was occurring in England—and all over Europe for that matter—in 1641, when Plattes published *Macaria*. If anyone conceives "a new opinion," he does not have to keep it to himself. It is just that he cannot make it prematurely public.

> He is allowed every year freely to dispute it before the great council; if he overcomes his adversaries, or such as are appointed to be opponents, then it is generally received for truth; if he be overcome, then it is declared to be false.

In summary, Plattes writes that although the religion of Macaria is Christian, it consists not in taking notice of several opinions and sects, but is made up of infallible tenets, which may be proved by invincible arguments, and such as will abide the grand test of extreme dispute; by which means none have power to stir up schisms and heresies; neither are any of their opinions ridiculous to those who are of contrary minds.[53]

This last remark suggests that a subject might be of contrary mind and still be immune from punishment so long as he keeps his opinions to himself. It also suggests that anyone who would dissent from the orthodox belief would do so not so much because of what the state church holds as because of something that the church does not hold but that the individual does. A dissenter, in other words, would tend to accept the orthodox position as far as it goes—or at least see nothing "ridiculous" in it—but would claim that it does not go far enough. The tendency here, it would seem, is to render dissent still less of a threat to the social order. The upshot of ecclesiastical polity in Macaria is to subordinate religion to civil peace. "The great council" would not be likely to admit into the body of the church's orthodox teachings any opinion brought before it for trial that it judged to have a tendency to induce dissension. Plattes is forsaking the claims that men, alone and in groups, have made in the past to exclusive possession of supernatural truth. These claims have ever led to war and destruction. So he is finding new grounds for faith. That religion is truest, he is saying, that best preserves—or least disturbs—the social order. With such a faith men can prosper, pursuing their own interests, and states can grow strong, all undistracted by religious dissension and the civil strife to which dissension has often led.

Plattes holds out his vision of society, the civil and ecclesiastical polity of Macaria, as the hope of Englishmen. On the eve of the Puritan revolution—1641—he is full of confidence. He has no room for the then current Christian fatalism: "the cause is not in God, but in men's fooleries; that the people live in misery in this world, when they may so easily be relieved. . . ."[54] He puts down what may have been a widespread belief that "no such reformation, as we would have, shall come before the day of Judgment. . . . I can show," he says, "an hundred texts of Scripture which do plainly prove, that such a reformation shall come before the day of Judgment."[55] The path to reformation is simple. Macaria shows the way. To further the public good is the aim. Men are clearly both capable and responsible. To undertake what we can accomplish, he says, "we are all bound by the law of God and nature." It is in men's own interests to do so. "Those that are against this honourable design, are first, enemies to God and goodness; secondly, enemies to the commonwealth; thirdly, enemies to themselves and their posterity."[56] Men will take up the great work almost in spite of themselves and perform it in some respects without realizing what they do. "The art of printing," for instance, "will so spread knowledge, that the common people, knowing their own rights and liberties, will not be governed by way of oppression; and so, by little and little, all kingdoms will be like Macaria."[57] To this degree, at any rate, the accomplishment of reformation has a certain inevitability about it. The work can begin tomorrow, Plattes maintains. Everyone can do his share. Divines can carry the word into their parishes and spread it from the pulpit. Men of property can apply it on their estates and instruct their servants in it. And gentlemen can meet and associate freely up and down the country, pooling their knowledge and exchanging "any secrets or good experiments."[58]

We must now show how the ideals of Hartlib and his circle affected Boyle. Boyle's deeply religious nature took over whenever he was faced with the fact of civil war. To his mind—and he was far from being alone in this—the conflict was not so much a struggle for power or the result of a breakdown in the constitution as it was God's way of punishing men for their corruptions. I "have always looked upon sin as the chief incendiary of the war," he says, "and yet have by careful experience observed the war to multiply and heighten those sins, to which it owes its being. . . ." From this he concludes, "I cannot without presumption expect a recovery in that body, where the physic, that should cure, but augments the disease."[59] The war was the price men paid for straying from the path of true religion. And just as he sought a spiritual cause for the war so he sought a religious solution. "Good God!" he would utter, "that reasonable creatures, that call themselves Christians too, should delight in such an unnatural thing as war, where cruelty at least becomes necessity, and unprocured poverty becomes a crime. . . ."[60] He saw the problem as one of bringing Christians back to reason; this entailed finding and establishing a reasonable religion. To this end, he supported Dury and Hartlib's irenic aims.

He saw, however, that the goal was far from being in sight. On February 20, 1647, he wrote from London to a friend, "few days pass here, that may not justly be accused of the brewing or broaching of some new opinion. . . ." Instead of the tame religious unity he desired, he witnessed only a proliferation of sects. He feared the consequences; in the same letter, he wrote:

> Pray God, it fare not with religion amongst those novelties, as it does sometimes with a great commander, when he is taken prisoner by a company of common soldiers, who every one tugging to have him for himself, at last pull him to pieces, and so each get a limb, but none enjoys him whole.

He then reiterated his desire: "For my part, I shall always pray to God to give us *the unity of the spirit in the bond of peace*. . . ."[61]

If he saw the danger in rampant sectarianism, he also saw a threat to religious truth and irenic aims in the opposite extreme, namely, "the punishment of many of these supposed errors. . . ." The argument on this extreme ran, he wrote to Marcombes from London, that "some established and strict discipline" was necessary in order to

> put a restraint upon the spreading impostures of sectaries, which have made this distracted city their general rendezvous, which entertains at this present no less than 200 several opinions in point of religion, some digged out of those graves, where the condemning decrees of primitive councils had long since buried them; others newly fashioned in the forge of their own brains; but the most being new editions of old errors, vented with some honourable title and moderate disguisements. . . .

But the suppression of unorthodox religious opinion is not the answer for "others, that justly pretend to a greater moderation . . . ," among whom Boyle places himself and would doubtless include Hartlib and Dury. Suppression violates the irenic spirit. It does nothing to bridge religious divisions.

> Certainly to think by a halter to let new light into the under-
> standing, or by the tortures of the body to heal the errors of
> the mind, seems to me like applying a plaister to the heel to
> cure a wound in the head; which does not work upon the
> seat of the disease.

More than this, the set of mind that condones or, what is worse, issues in a repressive religious policy actively impedes the search for spiritual truth. "Our dotage upon our own opinions make us mistake many for impostures, that are but glimpses and manifesta- tions of obscure or formerly concealed truths, or at least our own pride and self-love make us aggravate very venial errors into dangerous and damnable heresies."[62] So Boyle would neither permit religious license nor instigate per- secution. He agreed with Plattes, Hartlib, and Dury that what was needed was a broad church that would not divide men by em- phasizing the doctrinal differences that separated them but rather would unite them by appealing to the Christian tenets they held in common. As Boyle says in a letter to Dury, "It is strange, that men should rather be quarreling for a few trifling opinions, wherein they dissent, than to embrace one another for those many funda- mental truths, wherein they agree." Then he refers to his continen- tal experience to reinforce his argument for a comprehensive church and general toleration.

> For my own part, in some two or three and forty months,
> that I spent in the very town of *Geneva,* as I never found that
> people discontented with their own church-government (the
> gallingness of whose yoke is the grand scare-crow, that
> frights us here;) so could I never observe in it any such tran-
> scendent excellency, as could oblige me either to bolt heaven
> against, or open *Newgate* for all those, that believe they may
> be saved under another.

He concludes his letter to Dury by encouraging his efforts to get the sort of religious settlement that they both, with Hartlib, envisioned. "Wherefore I must confess, it would be extremely my satisfaction, if I could see, by God's blessing, your pious endeavours of twisting our froward parties into a moderate and satisfactory reconcilement, as successful, as I am confident they will be prudent and unwearied."[63]

Hartlib, Dury, and followers like the young Boyle sought a solution to contemporary religious difficulties in schemes for a church that would tread a middle course between the extremes of sectarianism and strict conformity. Complete license of religious opinion would foster dissension and might in the end lead to widespread atheism, which, defined in seventeenth-century terms, meant any belief or conduct regarded as un-Christian. So what was needed was an institution to conserve Christianity, and to seventeenth-century minds this meant setting up an established church. The church of Dury, Boyle, and Hartlib's vision, by excluding from its doctrine anything that was not essential to Christianity, would embrace all believers. But it would also leave room for the secret promptings of private conscience by refusing to enforce a rigid orthodoxy. Such narrowness, if it were to exist, would violate the true spirit of the religion that it was ostensibly defending and would be inimical to the seeking of Christian truth and the winning of men to its practice. One did not coerce men into accepting Christian doctrine; rather, one preached the doctrine and any who heard were constrained by its very excellency to believe it. This was the difference between the unreasonable religion into which men had fallen, which only led to religious conflict, and that which such men as Hartlib, Dury, and Boyle regarded as reasonable.

Their ecclesiastical and doctrinal proposals were reasonable, they maintained, not merely because they would be acceptable to all men and would, therefore, avoid the Scylla of sectarian disorder on the one hand and Charybdis of strict conformity and concomitant persecution on the other. This was not the logic of their argument. Rather men would give their consent to a comprehension along lines set out by Hartlib and Dury because this was the road to reformation, the building of a truly Christian society. Their aim was not merely outward conformity but rather, as Boyle put it, *"the unity of the spirit in the bond of peace. . . ."*[64] Comprehension in the manner they suggested was not reasonable because it was expedient to the achievement of order. From their point of view, comprehension was first of all Christian, and then, because it was truly Christian, it was therefore reasonable and would incidentally lead to the achievement of domestic peace.

Other influences operated on Boyle that led him to take up the religious position of Dury and Hartlib. Boyle's sister Katherine, as well as being the patroness of Hartlib's circle, was a friend of Lucius Cary, the second lord Falkland. He was himself the chief patron of an irenical movement in England in the 1630s and early 1640s—the Tew group, so called from the fact that its members met at Great Tew, Falkland's estate outside of Oxford. The spiritual leaders of the group were, among others, John Hales and William Chillingworth. Their irenical theology set the religious tone of the movement.[65] Boyle may have learned of their ideas through his sister's friendship with Lord Falkland. He seems to have known a great deal about Falkland,[66] but could not have known him personally in the 1640s because Falkland was killed before Boyle returned from the Continent. He knew Hales at Eton[67] and may have first come across the ideas of the Tew group through him. He was not the only possible source at Eton for Boyle's irenism. Sir Henry Wotton, the provost of Eton, had worked to establish a Protestant community in Italy when he was English ambassador to Venice in the first decade of the seventeenth century. He promoted a theology that would unite the tiny Protestant minority in Italy and if possible lure Catholics into the Protestant fold. It was a theology of fundamentals that would unite Protestants to do battle against the forces of counterreformation.[68] In this sense it was not dissimilar to the irenism of the Hartlib circle in England years later. We do not know whether Boyle imbibed irenical views directly from Wotton; nonetheless, he is an important link in Boyle's religious development.

Boyle was sent to Eton not only because Wotton was skilled in molding gentlemen, but also because he and Boyle's father were friends.[69] A part of the basis of that friendship may have been common views on religion. The evidence for the earl's religion supports this possibility. He was a close friend of Dr. James Usher, archbishop of Armagh.[70] Usher, for his part, was one of the leading advocates of Protestant unity and ecclesiastical comprehension in the 1640s and before.[71] He was also Hartlib's patron and Dury's collaborator.[72] In Ireland the earl opposed both extreme Presbyterianism and the ruthless persecution of Catholics by the English church.[73] Whether the Earl of Cork believed in irenical Protestantism or not, he sent Boyle to be educated by teachers who participated in the tradition. There was Wotton himself and through Wotton there were others. It was Wotton who recommended Marcombes to the earl as a suitable tutor for his sons, first Lewis and Roger and then Francis and Robert.[74]

Marcombes accompanied Lewis and Roger on the Continent between 1636 and 1639, and their itinerary was similar to the one Robert and Francis were to follow. Geneva was the focus of their tour but they also ventured across France. Their important contacts with continental Protestantism were with representatives of the irenical movement. In Geneva they lived in the house of Jean Diodati, a scholar and preacher of the Swiss Reformed Church who had gone to Venice at Wotton's request when he was there some thirty years before and who had worked with him to establish a beachhead for Italian Protestantism and to formulate an irenical theology that would attract as many as possible to the movement. His particular contribution to Wotton's scheme was the translation of the Bible into Italian.[75] During their continental tour, Lewis and Roger went to stay in the house of a Scots philosopher and physician in Saumur. There they had the use of the library once belonging to the famous Huguenot irenicist Phillippe Duplessis-Mornay (1549-1623). This visit probably was arranged by Diodati, who had lived and preached in Saumur between 1611 and 1614 under the patronage of Mornay.[76]

When Robert went to Geneva in late 1639, though he did not live in Diodati's house as his older brothers had done, he certainly came under his influence. Boyle probably attended the church where Diodati preached.[77] A member of Diodati's family, if not Jean himself, supplied the funds whereby Marcombes took Robert and Francis to Italy in the spring of 1641. Whoever it was, he was reimbursed by Boyle's father.[78] It was probably Jean Diodati whom Boyle acknowledges having consulted on difficult theological points while he was writing his unpublished "Essay of the Holy Scriptures,"[79] a work which is expressly irenical.[80] Robert, unlike his older brothers, never laid eyes on Saumur and Mornay's library. But this may have been because the civil war in Ireland in 1641 impoverished the earl and forced Robert's continental tour to be cut short. The money from home ran out just as Marcombes, Robert, and Francis reached Marseilles, from where they were to have set off on a tour of France which may very well have included a visit to Saumur and its academy, long an important center of Huguenot learning and irenical Protestantism.[81] Instead, Marcombes and Robert limped back to Geneva—and to Diodati. Boyle may never have seen Mornay's library, but he knew and valued Mornay's irenical thought. Boyle called Mornay's *De la Verité de la Réligion Chrétienne* "that excellent treatise" and referred to Mornay himself as one of "the 2 greatest Favorites the two last Ages have afforded me. . . ." The other was Sir Philip Sidney, the translator of Mornay's part of *De la Verité,* who worked for the union of the Protestant princes of Europe in the last quarter of the sixteenth century.[82] This reference to Mornay and Sidney was written by Boyle in the very late 1640s or early 1650s.[83] But from what we know of his older brothers' introduction to Mornay, it is not unreasonable to suppose that Robert had his earliest exposure to the ideas of Mornay and Sidney at the hands of Marcombes or Diodati or Wotton. Even Boyle's father is a candidate because he too knew something of Sidney's work.[84] Indeed, Richard Boyle as a young man probably knew of Sidney at Queen Elizabeth's court. All of this suggests that Boyle's interest in the irenical Protestantism of the Hartlib circle probably derived initially from remoter sources in his childhood—from his father in Ireland, from Hales and Wotton at Eton, or from Marcombes and Diodati in Geneva.

Questions of church polity were not the sole interests that Boyle shared with Dury and Hartlib. Rather, they kept him informed about the whole range of their activities and he reciprocated. Sometime before he met them or at least knew them well, so it would seem, he had seriously undertaken to teach himself natural philosophy. Before many years went by, he became versed in several sciences—among them, astronomy, mechanics, pneumatics, mathematics, and chemical medicine—and became familiar with the opinions of the leading contributors to these fields. In the course of his correspondence with Hartlib in the spring of 1647, he mentioned, as if he knew their work well, "the Ptolemeans, the Tycho-nians, the Copernicans;"[85] Marin Mersenne; Pierre Gassendi; and William Oughtred.[86]

If Boyle supplied Hartlib with appraisals of the work of contemporary natural philosophers, Hartlib communicated to Boyle a new enthusiasm for learning and a sense of its social purpose. Hartlib and his associates, whom Boyle was to know, also seem to have turned him toward what was to be a lifelong interest in chemical investigations. It was probably Hartlib or one of his circle who first interested Boyle in the affairs of what he describes as *"the invisible, or (as they term themselves) the philosophical college,"*[87] of which Hartlib seems to have been one of the guiding lights.[88] The "college" met in London.[89] But the surviving evidence of its business is fragmentary.[90] Boyle leaves records enough, however, at least to indicate the range of its interests and to suggest to the historian something of its effect upon Boyle himself. It seems to have fostered inquiry into nature and to have stressed Hartlib's injunction that learning be useful. Boyle writes, for instance, that besides ethics, "the other humane studies I apply myself to, are natural philosophy, the mechanics, and husbandry, according to the principles of our new philosophical college, that values no knowledge, but as it hath a tendency to use."[91] In all this, the invisible college followed the proposal in *Macaria* for a "house, or college of experience." The difference between them lay in the fact that *Macaria* had called for the setting up of a public agency, a branch of the government, whereas the invisible college was a collection of individuals, acting in a purely private capacity. The invisible college was perhaps in lieu of the college of experience. The private body in any case seems to have had the same purposes as the hoped-for public one.

To help toward achieving these goals, the college fostered a particular habit of thinking that Boyle calls "pursued Thoughts." In some notes in manuscript he indicates what this habit is, associating it with the college and making some rather large claims for its effectiveness when properly cultivated.[92] The thoughts can be about anything; the important thing is that the mind or "imagination"[93] play over the object until the possibilities of its elaboration have been exhausted—until it has been "pursued." As Boyle says, the technique can be applied to anything. But the habit has both its uses and its abuses. The habit abused, he calls "raving."[94] Raving results from the vanity of indulging in unprofitable thoughts, "which is most conspicuous in those thoughts that are built upon impossible, unlikely or useless suppositions. . . ."[95] Examples of this excess of imagination are, he says, sexual fantasies, plays and romances, and the philosophy of the schools[96]—strange bedfellows indeed. So before the habit of pursued thoughts is useful, the thoughts to which it is applied must also be useful or profitable. Should one apply it to the mode of thought Boyle calls "meditation," "I am confident," he writes, "he shall need no other Remedy to cure his unbeleefe."[97] Pursued thoughts applied to devout reflection might stem the tide of atheism. They might also contribute to intellectual advance.

> The Experiment of this I have lately seen in those I have had the happiness to be acquainted with of the Filosoficall Colledge: who all confess themselves to be beholding for the better part of their rare and newcoynd Notions to the Diligence and Intelligence of their Thoughts.[98]

Boyle presumably adopted the habit in his own pursuit of "humane studies . . . , according to the principles of our new philosophical college. . . ." At this period (1646-1647), moreover, Boyle began to write what he called "occasional reflections." These were religious meditations upon everyday occurrences.[99] The pattern of these meditations was this: first he recorded the experience that prompted his thinking; then, elaborating, he drew a moral from each detail of the episode. Three elements are assumed in this practice—first, that in raw experience is a code for godly living; second, that occasional reflection is the key to this code;[100] and third, that there is a discernible connection between the various aspects of reality, that observation of nature, for example, can elucidate questions of religion, morality, politics, or economy.[101] Boyle believed in the unity of truth and continued to do so throughout his life, using the device of the occasional reflection to discover it.[102] This device is related to "pursued Thoughts" as they are applied to what he calls "meditation" in the manuscript fragment

on such "Thoughts." "Meditation" by way of "pursued Thoughts"
works "to cure . . . unbeleefe," and occasional reflection is Boyle's
principal intellectual tool for attaining to virtue and piety. Indeed,
"meditation" as it is used in the manuscript fragment would seem
to be another word for occasional reflection. If this interpretation of
the evidence is correct, Boyle's technique of occasional reflection is
an elaboration of the habit of "pursued Thoughts" he picked up
from Hartlib and the invisible college.

Hartlib's circle was indebted for its concerns and ideals perhaps
more than to anyone else to the Czech philosopher and visionary J.
A. Comenius.[103] In 1641 Comenius had visited England[104] at the
invitation of Parliament and had associated himself with Hartlib's
group. He shared their devotion to the ideals of Macaria and communicated to them his own schemes in such works as *Via Lucis*[105]
and *A Reformation of Schooles,* translated by Hartlib and published in
London in 1642. These works convey his basic ideas. There is a
fundamental system of truths underlying all reality—physical,
moral, political, and spiritual. This system comes from God and
orders the world.[106] Men can discover it, and if and when they do,
they will be able to exploit these truths for the amelioration and
perfecting of mankind in morality, politics, and religion. The goal
was universal peace and prosperity.[107] Nor was this merely visionary; there was a certain strategy involved.

Comenius was a Protestant who espoused Protestant ideals
growing out of the Thirty Years War in his native Bohemia.
Through his writings he inspired Protestant reformers all over
Europe, not the least of whom were Hartlib, Dury, and others in
England. These reformers read his books for the plan they offered
for the fulfillment of the Protestant Reformation, when true religion
and learning would prevail throughout the world and false doctrines would have been overcome. Of course, the major false beliefs in question in the mid-seventeenth century were Roman
Catholicism and Islam. One of the chief attractions of the Comenian vision was that the tools for the triumph of Protestantism over
its enemies were to be science and learning. The warfare would be
intellectual and the victory, when it came, largely without
bloodshed. This too is what Comenius and his followers, the
Hartlib circle included, meant by "the restoration" or "reformation
of the whole world."[108]

What has any of this to do with Robert Boyle? Some of Boyle's most basic ideas are very similar to those of Comenius and, it seems fair to say, probably derived at least partly from the Comenian system as interpreted by Hartlib and the invisible college. As we have seen, Boyle's technique of occasional reflection is probably an elaboration of the habit of "pursued Thoughts" that he associated with the invisible college. Comenius also advocated the exercise of examining experience for what it might reveal about other dimensions of reality.[109] And just as this technique for Boyle was based on the assumption of the discernible unity of truth, the same may be said for Comenius. Fundamental to the Comenian vision was this belief in the interrelatedness of things, that the world is a harmony ordered by God according to a system of truths that manifests itself in every sphere.[110] For both Comenius and Boyle lessons learned in one sphere of experience might throw light on the nature of all reality. This was to be one of Boyle's most characteristic ideas and to play a part in those turning points in Boyle's intellectual development out of which would come his understanding of himself and the world. Of course, it is not completely certain that Boyle took his belief in the unity of truth and his technique of occasional reflection from Comenian ideas. But there is some evidence, as we have seen, for the transmission of the habit of "pursued Thoughts" from Comenius to Boyle via the invisible college. Boyle began writing occasional reflections during the period of his involvement in the invisible college. Was this mere coincidence or is there a case here for influence? The latter seems more probable.

The object of the invisible college, as might have been expected of one of Hartlib's projects, was a concern, broadly speaking, to improve the public good. Its members, Boyle wrote, are "persons, that endeavour to put narrow-mindedness out of countenance, by the practice of so extensive a charity, that it reaches unto every thing called man, and nothing less than an universal goodwill can content it." He reiterated: "And indeed they are so apprehensive of the want of good employment, that they take the whole body of mankind for their care."[111] One of their chief concerns seems to have been to increase the knowledge and improve the practice of medicine. This entailed the finding and publicizing of chemical medicinals. This aim of improving man's lot and, specifically, his physical health seems especially to have exercised Boyle's imagina-

tion. On April 8, 1647, he wrote to Hartlib that he had blocked out
in his mind "a little dialogue" concerning the public good but that
"unceasing domestic distractions" had thus far prevented him from
getting it down on paper.[112] This "little dialogue" may have been
the genesis of a tract that he in fact did write during the next two
years or so,[113] entitled "An Invitation to a free and generous
Communication of Secrets and Receits in Physick," but that turns
out not to be a "dialogue" at all. It is, however, a proposal for the
advancement of the public good, and Boyle did send it to Hartlib,
who published it in 1655 in a collection of *Chymical, Medicinal and
Chyrurgical Addresses.*[114] It is close in aim and spirit to the work of
the invisible college and presumably grew partly out of Boyle's association with this group at the same period as its composition.

The title of the tract gives some indication of its content. The
tract will be examined in some detail, but first let us put it into
context. In the seventeenth century, and especially before the civil
wars, the collecting of curiosities became a kind of cult among
members of the privileged classes in England.[115] With the cult of
curiosities went a certain social exclusiveness. Collecting was
restricted to those who could afford it and who had the leisure to
indulge in it. The rarity of one's specimens, moreover, was a mark
of distinction and evidence of gentle status. Curiosities might consist, among other things, of alchemical formulas or recipes for
cures. These would circulate among only a few men, each recipient
swearing to keep secret whatever he learned and divulging it to
almost no one else. Men on the inside could then fancy that they
possessed some wisdom that it was given only certain adepts to
know. Such wisdom, they thought, was the mysterious, imponder-
able key to godlike understanding. A rigidly stratified society such
a seventeenth-century England might furnish another motive
for keeping one's knowledge to oneself or divulging it only to
those at peer level or higher. Considerations of status reinforced
the feeling that secrets were not to be spread abroad and certainly
not to be put to baser mechanical or medicinal uses. These attitudes all militated against any design to put knowledge at the
service of man and against any open-ended, rigorously methodical
inquiry to attain to the object of such a design.

Bacon had inveighed against the cult of curiosities[116] and Hartlib followed in Bacon's path. Boyle in his "Invitation to a free and generous Communication of Secrets and Receits in Physick" joined battle on Hartlib's side. Men have an obligation, he begins,

> that not charity onely, but bare humanity layeth upon us to relieve the distresses of those, that derive their pedigree from the same father we are descended from, and are equal partakers with us, of the Image of that God, whose stamp we glory in.

All men are equal before God, and this spiritual but no less essential equality puts a responsibility upon men to look after one another. Traditional forms of charity do not begin to exhaust this obligation. "And can we fancy," Boyle asks, "that all the duties of charity are fulfilled with the emptying the refuse of our servants tables into the poor mans basket, and flinging a piece of market-money to a shivering Beggar?" Since Boyle's specific purpose in this tract is to persuade men to bring their medical secrets, their medicinals and cures, out into the open for the benefit of man, his next question is even more to the point:

> Why . . . should we think it a greater charity (or more our duty) to give a distressed wretch shelter from the natural cold of the air, than to protect him from the aguish icyness of the blood? or to shade him from the outward salutes of the hot Sun, then free him from the inward dog-dayes of a burning Feaver?

Just as "those Usurers" are wrong "that hoard up all their bags from all those uses, that onely can give riches the Title of a good," so are the chemical adepts who keep medical secrets out of circulation. These very adepts "must acknowledge themselves beholding unto others." Where would they be if everybody had always refused to tell? "So," Boyle concludes, ". . . a kind of interest and justice as well as charity, seemeth to oblige us to make those goods communicable, that became ours but upon that score."[117] Nobody is doing a favor by telling his secrets; he is merely repaying what was once done for him.

Boyle tries next to head off the objections he knows will be raised to his argument. Some say, he writes, "that their receipts are of mere curiosity, or at least have no relation to the cure of our Diseases." These receipts, he replies, need not be published. But "those whose secrets may any other way advantage the publick" do not get off so easily, "since 'tis not the kinde so much as the utility of our knowledge, that obliges us to dedicate it to the publick service."[118] Boyle here turns the tables on the illuminati by implying that their secrets do not meet the necessary qualifications for dedication "to the publick service." Others counter Boyle's argument by saying that they are sworn to secrecy and must break their oaths if they are to divulge their secrets. To this Boyle says first that it would be "a greater fault to violate" an oath "than it was to make it. Though," he goes on to say, "I am apt to believe that if all men declined the taking of receipts upon these terms, they might have them upon better."[119]

Finally, Boyle considers the benefits accruing from the communication of medical secrets. Everyone, of course, stands to gain from improvements in medicine—and this in a particular way. Not only does the number of remedies increase, but where there are no barriers to the availability of knowledge, the good drives out the false.[120] In the marketplace of ideas, everything is tested and the genuine alone survives. Both the public and the honest empiric are served and the charlatan is the only loser. The empiric especially benefits. By making his ideas public, he gets the praise he deserves while he is alive to enjoy it, and is provided with the opportunity "to reform his errors" and so make new advances for the public good.[121] In serving one's own interests, one also furthers the public good. Private and public advantage go hand in hand. It was the wisdom of God to make it so. "The nature of good," Boyle writes, "is to grow greater by extension, but careful providence foreseeing how inclinable frail men would be to selfishness in the dispensation of such goods as these, hath most wisely provided, that the parting with these goods should not prejudice their possession, nor liberality impoverish him that uses it." The man, or more specifically the chemical adept, who takes up his obligation to God to serve his fellow men and communicates his secrets moves through life in step with the cosmos. Such a man is one "Whom the Nature of the riches he disperses, resembles to the Sun, who though so bountifully he bestoweth his Beams on the whole universe never findeth a scarcity of them in himself. . . ."[122]

In Boyle's notion of the communication of secrets is further evidence of a connection between him and Comenius via the invisible college. No one man or group of men, Comenius held, has "had the priviledge to see all things. . . ."[123] Pansophy, therefore, must be communal—the greater the number and diversity of people contributing to science and learning the better the result. Not only does this communal effort make it possible for men to learn more than they would if learning were the preserve of the privileged, but community also increases the chances of discovering error and so elucidating truth:

> yet who knows not, that wisemen by seeing others errours, learne to avoid them? Many usefull things will be continually suggested from former errours, and their occasions, to those that will be undertakers in this worke of Pansophie, for the better trimming and polishing of it.[124]

All of this is the same as what Boyle would say in his "Invitation." Indeed Comenius may have been the principal source of Boyle's ideas. Hartlib propagated Comenian ideas about the desirability of a communal search for truth in his translation of Comenius' *A Reformation of Schooles*, published in London in 1642. And, of course, Boyle wrote his "Invitation" during his invisible college days; the tract is consistent with the aims and interests of the college; and it was Hartlib who later published it.

Comenius was not the only important continental thinker whose works Boyle came to know and value through his connection with the Hartlib circle. There were those of Johann Valentin Andreae as well. Andreae was one of the chief sources for the Comenian pansophy and the belief among the Hartlib circle in the reformation of the world through the intellectual means sketched out in *Macaria* and elsewhere.[125] Boyle knew Andreae's *Christianopolis*, a utopian tract depicting the society that would follow upon the reformation of learning and piety, and wrote to Hartlib supporting its translation into English.[126] In 1647 Hartlib sent to Boyle copies of two other tracts by Andreae, *A Modell of a Christian Society* and *The Right Hand of Christian Love Offered*. These had recently been rendered into English by Hartlib's protégé, John Hall of Durham, at Hartlib's request.[127] Andreae's *Modell* is a scheme for a society of thinkers which is said to have existed under "a Germane Prince"[128] and which is not unlike what little the records tell us about Boyle's invisible college. Andreae's society devotes itself to the study of nature, the discovery of true religion, the practice of religious moderation, and the free exchange of ideas.[129] After reading Hall's translation of the *Modell,* Boyle replied to Hartlib enthusiastically approving the sentiments expressed therein.[130] And why should it have been otherwise? The purposes of Andreae's society closely reflect Boyle's contemporary interests, which were shaped in large measure by his association with the Hartlib circle.

Boyle followed Plattes and Hartlib by recommending in "An Invitation" that empirics make their knowledge available to one another and to men at large as a means of serving the public good. The search for knowledge was not to go on in a vacuum. Rather it was to be driven by the engines of basic human need, demanding that knowledge be useful. Cosmic order and divine purpose sanctioned the whole enterprise. Well might the reformers have enlisted the aid of providence. Implicit in their view of the world was a fundamental reorientation of outlook. Knowledge, from their point of view, could no longer belong to the chosen few who held the keys. Its fruits, at least, had to be accessible to all. Nor could it be unitary and complete or come in the form of a mystical vision or divine revelation. Rather, its seekers would have to go wherever human need took them, and because needs were many, they would not soon finish their work. There is a suggestion in the "Invitation" that the process of exchanging and accumulating information will be perpetually self-correcting. The genuine drives out the false, and the honest contributor to the store of knowledge, by subjecting his contribution to the cold eye of public scrutiny, can learn from his mistakes. There is no suggestion of a consummation of the process—of man's attaining to ultimate truth. God does not reveal himself directly as a reward to the seeker. His providence merely makes it possible for the useful—not necessarily the true— to keep winning out.

This view of society, the cosmos, and divinity has import for the development of empirical method. Human needs and desires cry out for satisfaction and so call forth from man inquiry into the world around him. But the needs are so many and the field for inquiry so vast that the project cannot be accomplished single-handedly. It must be undertaken cooperatively over time. The labor is long and the results tentative. The criterion for success is the satisfaction of basic needs: utility. But not everything brought forth to serve man proves to be useful; whatever does not so prove, must be cast out or revised in the light of experience. The provisional—provisionality itself—becomes acceptable because it is the way of reaching the useful, of satisfying human need. Knowledge does not have to be complete, systematic, logically deductive, or intuitive. If it is to serve the public good, it need only be useful, and providence guarantees that in the end it will be. Provisionality then acquires a *raison d'être* in the satisfaction of human need. And both the *raison d'être* and its consequent, the way of proceeding provisionally, bear a providential sanction and guarantee: God ordains that all men should serve the public good; it follows that all knowledge should be useful and that the way to the useful is through the provisional. The divine ordinance is or can and should be self-operative—that is, built into the fabric of the universe and man's nature—as men serve themselves in serving the public interest. The germs of Boyle's way of inquiring into the physical universe, which gets fully developed in the 1650s and 1660s, lie in part in his "Invitation" of the late 1640s.

From what evidence there is, the impact of Hartlib, Dury, and of the invisible college upon the young Boyle was profound. He was fired by their schemes and adopted their aim of serving the public good. This social and religious purpose in turn gave his life and studies a new thrust. He worked doggedly during the early years of his association with Hartlib to keep his inheritance intact and gave even these efforts an aim consistent with the spirit of the college. On April 25, 1647, he wrote: "I desire Riches, more, Consider'd as meanes to do handsom things with, then for any Ease or Delight I wish for by them. More for the Good I may do with them then the Pleasures I may reape for purchases by them."[131] In general terms, his association with the college seems to have helped him crystallize his ideas about what he wished to make of his life. He would serve the public good, he decided, after his own fashion—by quietly pursuing his religious, chemical, and philosophical studies to this end.

## Piety

Hartlib's circle, however, was not the only factor shaping Boyle's interests. There was also his deep personal piety. His religious sensibility seems to have grown out of certain experiences occurring in early adolescence. At least he suggests in his autobiography that this was the case, and this is the only evidence available. These religious experiences were considered earlier, but a treatment of their larger implications was left until now. The justification for this postponement lies in the fact that their implications have more to do with the period of Boyle's life in which he set them down than with the time of their actual occurrence.

He dated his conversion, as noted earlier, from one stormy night in Geneva, when he feared that the Judgment Day was at hand. He vowed to God that if his fears proved that night to be unfounded, he would be faithful to him and try ever after to live righteously in his sight. The storm passed. "The morning came, and a serener cloudless sky returned. . . ." He renewed, "now he was past danger, the vow he had made, whilst he believed himself to be in it. . . ." He had made the initial vow in the grip of fear. Judgment was near. "The consideration of his unpreparedness to welcome it, and the hideousness of being surprised by it in an unfit condition, made him . . . vow. . . ." The next morning he saw how contingent his promise had been upon his fear. His motive for conversion and regeneration had not been pure. So, now free of danger, he vowed again. "Though his fear was (and he blushed it was so) the occasion of his resolution of amendment, yet at least he might not owe his more deliberate consecration of himself to piety to any less noble motive, than that of its own excellence."[132] He felt a disgust with himself and a revulsion from his initial weakness. Where he could, he chose to rest his belief on the most transcendental grounds and to act from the purest, most spiritual motives.

He did not take "his more deliberate consecration" lightly. He relates his conversion and then tells a story that seems to illustrate how conscientiously he kept his promise to consecrate himself to piety. Once, when he was "in company with a crew of mad young fellows," he writes, "one of them was saying to him, what a fine thing it were, if men could sin securely all their life time, by being sure of leisure to repent upon their death-beds. . . ." This cavalier attitude toward the performance of religious obligations, needless to say, rubbed young Robert the wrong way. He "presently replied, that truly for his part he should not like sinning, though on those terms, and would not all that while deprive himself of the satisfaction of serving God, to enjoy so many years fruition of the world." For Boyle religion was not doctrinal so much as experiential. So the view of one among "a crew of mad young fellows" could seem to an equally young Robert peculiarly negative. "In effect," as he put it, "it is strange, that men should take it for an inducement to an action, that they are confident, that they shall repent of it." He would have none of this.

By his own account, he did not grow up in the usual fashion. "Though his boiling youth did often very earnestly solicit to be employed in those culpable delights, that are useful in, and seem so proper for that season. . . ; yet did its importunities meet ever with denials. . . ." If he had indulged "his boiling youth," he seems to have felt, he would not have been able to keep the promise of his conversion. To his mind a consecration to piety was inconsistent with sensual gratification—and in a way that is not at all clear. He never married. Perhaps he saw marriage as being at odds, too, with the pursuit of piety. He might have given in to "his boiling youth" and still have got to heaven by repenting just before he died, as is implied that one of "a crew of mad young fellows" intended to do. But such was not Boyle's understanding of the satisfaction of religious obligation. "Piety was to be embraced, not so much to gain heaven, as to serve God with."[133] And the service of God apparently precluded pleasure of any kind other than the purely spiritual. Any less ascetic faith was personally unacceptable. His account of what his consecration to piety entailed smacks of sanctimony, but one would perhaps do better to dwell upon Boyle's evident sincerity and what his faith took to be acted out.

A third story follows in his autobiography. Sometime after his
spiritual awakening he went into eastern France. While he was vis-
iting the monastery of La Grande Chartreuse near Grenoble,[134] he
was overcome with "such strange and hideous thoughts, and such
distracting doubts of some of the fundamentals of Christianity,
that, though his looks did little betray his thoughts, nothing but
the forbiddenness of self-dispatch hindered his acting it." After the
passage of "many months in this tedious perplexity," he regained
his faith, or, as he puts it, "at last it pleased God, one day he had
received the sacrament, to restore unto him the withdrawn sense
of his favour." Such an intense and prolonged religious experience
was not without its effects. He was, he writes, never again to be
quite free of religious doubt. But he is quick to say that this ques-
tioning benefited him in the end. He invokes the providentialist
argument here, too, and writes,

> as all things work together to them that love God,
> *Philaretus*[135] derived from this anxiety the advantage of
> groundedness in his religion: for the perplexity his doubts
> created obliged him, to remove them, to be seriously inquisi-
> tive of the truth of the very fundamentals of Christianity, and
> to hear what both Turks, and Jews, and the chief sects of
> Christians could alledge for their several opinions; that so,
> though he believed more than he could comprehend, he
> might . . . not owe the stedfastness of his faith to so poor a
> cause, as the ignorance of what might be objected against it.

His doubt spurred his search for true religion. In fact he goes
further, generalizes from his own experience, and claims that anything less than such searching falls short of producing true piety.

> He said (speaking of those persons, that want not means to
> enquire, and abilities to judge,) that it was not a greater hap-
> piness to inherit a good religion, than it was a fault to have it
> only by inheritance, and think it the best, because it is gener-
> ally embraced, rather than embrace it, because we know it to
> be the best.

Religious convention is not sufficient ground for faith. True piety comes instead through a search for, and knowledge of, the truth. As in the earlier experience of conversion, only the highest motive and strictest standard of belief will do. But this time he sets the same standard for every other Christian as for himself. "There is," he says, "nothing worse taken upon trust than religion, in which he deserves not to meet with the true one, that cares not to examine whether or no it be so."[136] The true Christian does not slide blindly into believing whatever is in the air. Rather, he has examined religions and so knows his to be the true or at least the truer one.

Boyle seems to have conceived his early religious experiences as constituting a unit. Certainly they form one in his autobiography. And when this record is examined as a unit, it reveals a pattern. Perhaps these early experiences went into creating it. In any case, Boyle, wittingly or not, imposes it upon them in the telling. He suffers doubt. This does not cause him to reject religion but sends him on his spiritual quest. His doubting, then, becomes an integral part of his piety. More than this, it at least partially defines the nature of this piety. For the doubting is what makes him demand so much of himself in the way of belief and practice. It is not enough for him to merely subscribe to the tenets of his religion. This would never quell his doubt. His belief must instead be for the purest of reasons, the excellency of religion itself. He must then prove that this is his motive by making his life a constant testament of his faith, by acting out whatever he thinks his high conception of religion entails. And the more piously he lives, the less reason he has of heeding or dreading his doubts because he thus demonstrates to himself the virtue and hence the excellency of his faith.

If this analysis is correct, it clarifies several points. It helps explain why Boyle could make, as he claims to have done, such a difficult promise at his conversion and then, in justification of his doing so, say "that though his fear was (and he blushed it was so) the occasion of his resolution of amendment, yet at least he might not owe his more deliberate consecration of himself to piety to any less noble motive, than that of its own excellence."[137] The analysis does not shed much light on why young Robert consistently denied "the importunities" of "his boiling youth." But it does help explain why he rebuked one "mad young" fellow who thought "what a fine thing it were, if men could sin securely all their life

time, by being sure of leisure to repent upon their death-beds,"
and why Boyle could say, instead, "that piety was to be embraced,
not so much to gain heaven, as to serve God with."[138]

Finally, this analysis of Boyle's religious sensibility further
suggests why Boyle became a member of Hartlib's circle and so enthusiastically took up the aims of the invisible college: what more
compelling proof could he afford himself of his piety and of the
consequent futility of his fears than that which would come from
serving the public good and thereby forwarding the providential
design? He would extend knowledge of God's creation and the
workings of providence—all for the glory of God and the use and
benefit of man. What better way was there of calming and salving
a conscience besieged by doubt? The reader will see why an
analysis of Boyle's account of his own early religious experiences
had to wait until now. Their significance for his intellectual and
spiritual development begins to come clear in the light of his involvement in the work of the invisible college. Perhaps this interest
first led him also to see something of the signficance of these experiences. This suggestion is strengthened by the fact that Boyle's
account of his religious experiences was written between January
1648 and July 1649—that is, during the period of his active engagement in the affairs of the Hartlib circle.[139] In any case, the autobiography gives the clues to the significance of the religious experiences, whether Boyle saw any of that significance or not. The
connection between Boyle's conversion and his commitment to the
ideals of the Hartlib circle helps us to understand what those ideals
meant to him. They were not just ends in themselves. They were
also bound up with his conversion and hence the expression of the
spiritual and intellectual quest which that conversion had set off in
him.

# Chapter 2

# Ethic

# and Experience

When Boyle went to England in 1644, his future was unclear and the prospects none too bright. His father was dead and the family fortune wasted on the war against the Irish rebels. Civil war in England itself complicated the picture. The first earl had willed certain manors to his son. But who was to say, given the circumstances, how soon he might be able to take possession and, once acquired, how long he might be able to maintain them? In the face of such uncertainty Boyle moved cautiously, applied himself to resolving his predicament, and took advantage of opportunities as they presented themselves. He eventually got possession of Stalbridge and settled down to making it profitable. He would not get hold of his Irish estates until the English defeated the rebels and regained control of the country a few years later.

In this long-drawn process he learned to match his conduct to the times. Thus he could write, in circa 1646, to an unnamed English aristocrat that a man of his rank should use discretion in choosing his companions. The wrong sort of company "engages us to . . . riot and expensiveness." Such excess

is now signally unreasonable, being not only extremely unsuitable to the sad condition of our times, but peculiarly obstructive to those, who make applications to the state for relief or compensation of losses; since the same expences that

43

beget want, pass for arguments of plenty, in the opinion of
those, whose belief our want is as great a requisite to the removal of it, as the justness of that belief were a misfortune. . . .[1]

If distressed members of the old elite would learn to moderate their
tastes, they would make an impression that would the sooner get
them the desired relief.

Boyle did not adapt himself to the new situation on the grounds
of pure expediency, however. To his mind, men would, as they
moderated their desires, grow more virtuous. He referred the
whole enterprise to the workings of providence: even the hardships of civil war and social dislocation pointed a moral and conduced to make men better. The quiet pursuit of his own interests
did not exhaust the demands of Boyle's piety. Hence, as has also
been suggested, he involved himself in the work of the invisible
college. This interest gave him new scope for his pious sensibility.
He could now seek the public good as well as his own, employ the
same habits in both enterprises, and in both forward the same providential design. As long as a man sought the public good, he ad-
vanced his own. Hartlib's ideas and projects offered Boyle an outlet
for his own religious promptings.

Boyle's piety, which emerged out of his experiences, was primarily of two sorts—certain early psychic crises and the business of
negotiating survival and a livelihood in a deeply divided society.
Once formed, this piety demanded of him an unusual degree of
self-discipline. Only such strength of will could grant him sufficient
detachment from ordinary desires to allow him to pursue his designs and so to satisfy his conscience. Not only did this piety shape
Boyle's own conduct and self-image. It also molded his opinion of
other men and his interpretation of what was happening in the
world around him. He fancied that his own endeavors benefited
the public as well as himself. This was his standard of righteous
action. But England during the civil wars presented him with the
ugly spectacle of men pursuing their self-interest without regard
for what seemed to him to constitute the public good. His sense of
the discrepancy between his standard and the common practice

must have been all the keener when he witnessed the contrast between what he demanded of himself by way of fulfilling the standard and the seeming license, amounting to rapacity, of many others.

In a manuscript dating from the mid-1640s, he names in descending order of their guilt those who failed to measure up. First are the "Atheists." It is not always easy to know what a seventeenth-century figure means by the word, but here Boyle seems to be referring to those few who actually denied the existence of God or at least the Christian God. Second on the list are "Macchiavillians," men who are not bound by any moral rules in the pursuit of their own economic and political gain.[2] These men are impious because such morality as they deny is a part of the obligation one accepts, if he is to be a Christian. Third are "Profane Persons. Such as are not Atheists in their Opinions but in their Lives: & use to scoffe at Religion & call those Puritans, & nice, squeamish Fooles that profess it."[3] "Macchiavillians" of course might also be "Profane Persons." But here Boyle seems to be referring specifically to those who give themselves over to the pleasures of the world without thought to the duties. They are typical cavaliers, members of the old elite, whom Boyle sees as having in the end to pay for their heedlessness.

Besides these three types of irreligious men, there are two more. First are the hypocrites who—at least as guilty as "Profane Persons"—use religion to "deceive the Religious & others more neatly & unsuspectedly; who as our Savior says, Mt. v. 3.14 Devour Widdows houses, & for a Pretence make long Prayer; & to whom Religion serves for a Stalking horse, to deceive the Simple with." Hypocrisy can take another form. "Others there are," Boyle continues, "that do it for By-Respects, as hope of advancement or advantage from som Godly Kinsman . . . or Religious great one: & these People ar Virtuous Mercenerys, that serve but for their Pay."[4] Second, there are many who perform their Christian duty "Out of meere Hope or Feare of Reward or Punishment in this Life or the Next" rather than from any love of virtue itself. As Boyle says, "the World is commonly beholding to the Magistrate for these Peoples Virtue, & their honesty (however in this corrupted

Age so magnifyed for it's rarity) is rather Innocence then Virtue; &
themselves rather good Subjects then Good Men."[5] Boyle would
scarcely include these last among the real offenders against religion, especially as "in this corrupted Age" there were so many
others who posed so much more serious threats that even the
"honesty" of those who were obedient merely from fear was
"magnifyed for it's rarity."

Boyle's circumstances in the 1640s demanded an effective response if he was to make his way in the world. His piety dictated
the type of response; it had to be one that did not compromise his
faith, that he could, in fact, justify in terms of his faith. He had to
feel that he was pursuing his own interests not as "Macchiavillians"
and "Profane Persons" did, but rather in such a way as to be
advancing the public good.

It is scarcely surprising then that one of Boyle's chief intellectual
concerns (if not his primary one), from the time he returned from
Geneva, was to define the moral life—and to formulate how to
overcome the obstacles in the way of its achievement. A long manuscript treatise, "The Aretology or Ethicall Elements of Robert
Boyle," in the Library of the Royal Society of London bears witness
to his serious interest in this matter.[6] The evidence shows that
Boyle wrote his "Aretology" over a period of at least a year. The
title page of the manuscript shows that he began the composition
at Stalbridge in 1645. He was still working on the treatise on March
30, 1646, as he wrote from Stalbridge to Lady Ranelagh in a letter
of this date, saying "My *Ethics* go very slowly on. . . ."[7] On October 22, 1646, he wrote, this time from London to Marcombes,
"The *Ethics* hath been a study, wherein I have of late been very
conversant, and desirous to call them from the brain down into the
breast, and from the school to the house. . . ."[8] Perhaps Boyle had
finished the manuscript by then. He makes further mention of his
opinions respecting ethics in a letter to Hartlib a few months later[9]
and in a letter to another friend, John Mallet, almost four years
after that.[10] Boyle's interest in ethics was a deep and continuing
one, and of the utmost importance for an understanding of his
evolving world-view. This work will now turn to a consideration of
his "Aretology," the closest he ever came to a systematic statement
of his ethical position.

## Virtue and Descent

Boyle was born into an aristocratic world of power and privilege. Boyle's father, to be sure, had climbed to the top by dint of struggle and sacrifice. Some of his work ethic may indeed have rubbed off on young Robert. If so, the fact would help to explain why Boyle did not ultimately identify with the mores of the bulk of the aristocracy. This is no more than a hunch and in any case would not account for the depth of Boyle's alienation from the aristocratic way of life. But the fact remains that the aristocracy was the world in which Boyle moved. Knowing only this, one might reasonably suppose that he worked harder in order to enjoy more of the fruits of this world. Certainly this is what his father's career might have suggested to him. And it would be less reasonable to suppose that if he worked harder than other members of his caste, he would reject the values, as well as the leisure, implicit in the aristocratic way of life. Yet reject them he did—and this is the problem. Before going on to a full treatment of this rejection and its psychic and intellectual consequences, we will first consider the main outlines of the aristocratic ethic, as he understood it.

The primary characteristic of this ethic was "the close-knit alliance of honor and virtue. . . ."[11] Gentlemen proved their moral worth by conforming their behavior to the specifications of a code of honor. This standard of conduct was binding upon all men who were by birth or wished to become gentlemen.[12] The ultimate determinant of the satisfaction of this standard was also public: the judgment of one's peers. So neither the terms of the code nor the fulfillment of its requirements were a matter of private conscience.

Ideally, conscience should have been totally socialized. There should have been no discrepancy between public and private dictates. One's conscience was responsible for bringing one's conduct back into line whenever a discrepancy appeared. It was not for conscience to question the code itself. Under the aristocratic ethic, moreover, one did not take lonely pride in the fact of his virtue. This would have been small comfort for such a strict observance to a public standard. More significantly, any virtue worthy of the admiration of one's peers was public, not private.[13] Conversely, the prospect of such honor or admiration was the incentive productive of such virtue.[14] In other words, there was little if any room for private virtues in the aristocratic code, as it was regularly formulated, if in fact such virtues could be said to exist at all insofar as this ethic was concerned.[15] One who met the demands of the code won the approval of his peers. Public recognition of virtue provided the honor so highly prized by subscribers to the ethic; it brought earthly happiness to the possessors.

This was the ethic in which Boyle was raised.[16] Evidence suggests that it was the basis of his first systematic attempt to set out his ethical views. Among his papers at the Royal Society of London survives the beginnings of a treatise called "The Gentleman." It is an unfinished ethical handbook in the tradition of the widespread manuals of the sixteenth and seventeenth centuries— among the most famous are Conte Baldesar Castiglione's *Il Cortegiano* (1528; first English translation, 1561), Sir Thomas Elyot's *The Boke Named the Governour* (1531), and Henry Peacham's *The Compleat Gentleman* (1622). Boyle's contribution to this Renaissance literary genre is just a little over six manuscript pages. Although fragmentary, it reveals that at the time of its writing Boyle still adhered to the ethic of his childhood. The question is: when was it written? There is no date on the work itself. The handwriting is the same as that of "The Aretology" and other early pieces. It would make no sense, moreover, for Boyle to have written this particular piece after "The Aretology" because the ideas in the latter work were the basis of his mature moral philosophy and they are clearly in conflict with the sentiments expressed in "The Gentleman." In the absence of any other evidence as to its date, it can be ascribed with some safety to the days before Boyle reversed his opinions in "The Aretology."

How do the views set out in "The Gentleman" conform to the main lines of ethical theory in the Renaissance? Boyle begins by paying the customary lip service to the notion that "the true Seat of Nobility is much more properly establish't in the Mind then in the Blood. . . ."[17] "Yet," he goes on to say, "the very First Attribute . . . I shall require in the gentleman I am to discourse of, must be, that he be Born one."[18] Here he was stating an important assumption lying behind the aristocratic ethic: with a few rare exceptions, it applied only to those who had the necessary qualifications, principally the breeding and wealth, to practice the code—i.e., to those who were born gentlemen.[19] To attempt with any hope of success to live up to the mark usually presupposed at least a sufficiency of worldly good fortune.

Boyle spends the remainder of "The Gentleman" spelling out this assumption. It is not just that custom confines gentle status to those who are gentry by birth. Nor is it merely "that Great Persons are beleev'd, together with the Lives they give their Posterity, to transmit to them very effective Seeds or Sparks of that Greatnesse of Courage & Desseins that was eminent in themselves. . . ." There are in addition "more Certin & more solid Advantages."[20] A gentle pedigree gives a man the edge over those born without it. His peers are predisposed to like and accept him, his inferiors to respect and obey him, and his betters to confide in and promote him.[21] A born gentleman is in the best position for obtaining office and preferment or what Boyle calls "considerable . . . Employments."[22] His peers use their connections to advertise his merit to those who "are able . . . both to Employ & to Reward it."[23] The recommendations of his friends are almost bound to pay off: "generally Princes are found more willing . . . to conferre great Places upon Person[s] of high Birth sooner . . . then on others; not onely because their Engagements to the Publick are stronger, & (they) themselves more in their Eye: but because . . . those Persons are less . . . grudgingly . . . obey'd; in whom Nature seems to have conspir'd with Fortune in Desseining to commands."[24] A gentle birth is most important as a means of advancement, an expedient to greater temporal success.

In his emphasis on the expediency of descent, Boyle departs, more than most writers of primers for would-be courtiers and gentlemen, from the main lines of this Renaissance tradition of ethical theory. As we shall see, this element of expediency is to play a large, curious, and important part in Boyle's revisions of this tradition worked out in "The Aretology." But in that work temporal success is no longer obtained through the expedient of descent. Another, presumably better, device has been found, and the issue of expediency is swept under the carpet.

For the moment we must deal with why Boyle broke off his attachment to the old ethic and went on to adopt a new one. The

basis of the old ethic, the assumption of an almost necessary causal
connection between descent and virtue, offers a clue. Boyle came
into the world with the requisite advantages prescribed by the old
ethic. As he says in his autobiography, written a year or two after
his "Aretology," "He was born . . . in . . . 1626-7 . . . at a
country-house of his father's, called *Lismore*, then one of the noblest seats and greatest ornaments of the province of *Munster*, in
which it stood. . . ."[25] But, as has been shown, the Irish rebellion
and English civil wars wiped away most of whatever native advantages he might have enjoyed. The sentence just quoted goes on to
say, "but [Lismore is] now so ruined by the sad fate of war, that it
serves only for an instance and a lecture of the instability of that
happiness, that is built upon the uncertain possession of such fleeting goods, as itself was."[26] The suggestion is that aristocratic birth
is no reliable ground to build happiness upon and, hence, the aristocratic code, as traditionally conceived, no fit ethic by which to
live. Boyle's own displacement as a result of events in England and
Ireland acted as a catalyst, triggering and sustaining his rejection of
an inherited ethic.

One might then ask: why was Boyle so exceptional in his rejection of this ethic if many others were also experiencing social dislocation? Perhaps no human experience can be exactly duplicated.
Boyle's experience may have been more sustained or more severe
than most. One thing is certain: what was unique in Boyle was a
strong religious faith that seems to have fed upon challenges beginning in childhood and which could meet and resolve this new
one. Other unknown factors may also have contributed to Boyle's
rejection of the aristocratic ethic. There is evidence aplenty, however, for the role Boyle's piety played, and, in the absence of any
other presently available evidence, it may be assumed that this religious factor, as it acted upon and was nourished by his experience of social and economic dislocation, can claim a major share of
the credit.

The defining characteristic of Boyle's religious sensibility was the
impulse—or perhaps compulsion—beginning, as far as one can tell,
in childhood, to prove the credibility of his faith by demonstrating
to himself the moral superiority or excellency of the life in which

he took his faith to be issuing. His piety thus drove him to make his life a model of Christian virtue. So he could be led to say:

> Besides, that one of the Principall Ends that God propos'd himself in the Creation, being his owne Glory; & man being no way more able to glorify his Maker, then by a Virtuous Life & holy Conversation, it must necessarily follo, that this Exercice of Virtue is one of the Principal Ends of man's Creation.[27]

His conscientious piety set him off, one would think, from others in the aristocratic circles in which he moved. He was witness to the sort of comment his behavior evoked within these circles. Their values led them to regard Boyle's conduct as sanctimonious. But his belief was too strong to be daunted by such disparagements. In fact, any attack upon his piety seems to have made him all the more willing to endure. As he says, "any affront or loss sustained upon that score [of virtue] turns to a blessing, by producing in us, towards religion, the usual property of sufferers for a cause, more zeal and passion for the party men have been sufferers for." Besides, the weight of argument, he claimed, was on his side. First, in order to practice Christian virtue, one must begin by admitting and repenting one's sins. No idea could be less vain. Second, Boyle asks, "And will you quench the spirit, and refrain from being virtuous, lest men should think you know yourself to be so?" If one is to be virtuous, as religion prescribes, there is no choice but to be knowledgeable of one's virtue, "virtue being a habitude elective, and election prerequiring knowledge."[28] In any case, God would not play tricks and "make it our duty to seek, what it were our sin to find." Third, Boyle suggests how much more compelling his piety was for him than the opinions of his detractors. "Certainly it is better to be accused of vanity, than guilty of relapses; and if some reputation must be lost, it is fitter that you should be dishonoured by other men's faults, than God by yours." Boyle returns here to the merits of suffering. God "is good enough to recompense his servants, not only for being good, but for their not being thought so for his sake; and to make one day their dishonour (not only the soil, but) the purchase of their glory."[29] Suffering enhances the cause by enhancing the sufferer in God's eyes.

Seemingly, Boyle could not be shamed into conforming to the mores of his caste. In fact, the application of social pressure produced just the reverse effect: it made him truer to his faith than ever. So there was no way of shaking him loose from his religion. It was more than a competing alternative to the aristocratic ethic. Between the two there was nothing to choose. Religion alone had divine sanction. Anything to the contrary would perforce have been the work of the devil.

Thus Boyle's faith gave powerful impetus to his rejection of his childhood ethic. Together with his experience of social dislocation, it turned his mind in new directions and helped him arrive, in the end, at an ethic of his own. In the record Boyle leaves for the years following his return from the Continent, faith and experience merge into a single pattern of development. They work upon and reinforce each other to the point where it is quite impossible to know what to attribute to the one and what to the other or how to measure their relative contribution to the change Boyle's thought and sensibility underwent. What would have happened had one or the other factor—either faith or social dislocation—not been a part of his total experience is a matter for speculation. The most one can say is that if one or the other had been absent, the change would probably not have been as decisive, dramatic, and profound in its implications.

According to that current of thought in which Boyle was raised, descent is a benign influence conducive to the happiness of gentlemen, to whom alone the ethic applied.[30] Gentle birth is typically generous to this elite, affording them both the wealth and the leisure that will in turn allow them to satisfy the requirements of the code to which they subscribe and so obtain the honor in which their happiness lies. Fortune, however, had dealt harshly with Robert Boyle, and so his experience did not confirm the theory. Circumstances had cost his family much of their wealth and put an end to his quiet and relatively carefree days on the Continent. As a result he had been thrown back upon his own resources and was forced to salvage whatever he could of his losses. He managed well enough in the end. He could even take a certain pride in what he had accomplished—the more so for having done it by himself. But he could no longer conceive birth and station to be benign, as earlier he and his father before him had done. What happiness he enjoyed after the civil wars began was at fortune's expense. He came to see gentle status not as man's ally but as his potential enemy. Boyle conquered fortune and procured happiness, so he thought, to the extent that he cultivated virtue. His strong faith came to his service by furnishing him a means of overcoming his circumstances. This was the point at which belief and experience merged in Boyle, thus giving rise to his distinctive piety and forming the substance of his new ethic.

The ethic of Boyle's childhood, like his adopted one, made happiness a function of virtue. But the older ethic also posited the possibility of a perfect virtue and hence a perfect happiness—and Boyle in his adopted view could not. Traditional ethics, as Boyle read them, saw no conflict between virtue and descent. In fact, birth contributed to the production of virtue, so that nothing stood in the way of a perfect happiness. But Boyle's experience caused him to think otherwise. Gentle rank might be inimical to virtue and hence to happiness. Virtue, of course, could resist and partially overcome fortune's sway. But the tension between the two was constant and there could be no final resolution. Hence, there could be no perfect happiness.

As a result of Boyle's novel view of birth, happiness could no longer derive from any of the traditional goods associated with a gentle descent. These goods were fleeting at best. So the goods of body, health, and beauty,[31] and of riches[32] could not give happiness. Neither could the "Honor & Renowne" in which so many men—"The Politician & Sojer"[33]—in Boyle's own time sought their felicity. He took particular pains to explode the argument for "Honor & Renowne" as the basis of happiness:

1. Honor is often gotten by Ill men, & that too for Evil Axions. 2. It depends upon other men's Judgements: being a Good without either Lock or Key: & so, 3. may be got without our Merit & lost without our Fault: So that many Bad men

have it, when many Good men go without it. 4. It betters nether the Body, the Mind, nor the Fortune. 5. If it be bad, it is not to be esteem'd: & if Good, it is but the Shaddo of Virtue, which by Consequent is the worthyer of the 2. 6. Lastly, it can do a man no good at all after Deth; for in hev'n it is Needles; & Hell, Bootless.[34]

In opposing virtue to birth, Boyle is not saying that the latter can never be good to man. Some gentlemen obviously do enjoy good fortune for a time. But in whatever form good fortune comes, it is always of highly uncertain duration. Boyle does say, however, that gentlemen can minimize this uncertainty by cultivating virtue. Thus, for instance, would gentlemen be surer of winning "tru Honor." For its two "Propertys" are "that [it] is given, 1. By Good & Judicious men. 2. For great Deserts as the reward of Virtue."[35] Boyle goes on to say that what passes for honor among the self-seeking men in his own reckless age is not honor at all, for it is not the reward of virtue but the fawning of hangers-on and the adulation of the multitude. In Boyle's own words:

> Hence we may perceive how little Honor there is in that which has usurp't its title: since it consists cheefly in the Praises of the Vulgar, whose Prayse is none: & is often given to Ill Axions; which so they be Great; if they wud seem Good, tis no matter whether they be so or no. . . .[36]

In a sense, then, Boyle is the real traditionalist, true to the ethic of his childhood in spirit if not in form. For while upholding the ideal that happiness should be the reward of virtue, an ideal strictly faithful to the spirit and content of the inherited ethic, he is exposing the current practice of this ethic in an attempt to bring it into line with the older ideal. According to Boyle, men commonly keep the letter and violate the spirit. They seek the rewards of virtue, like honor, without earning them. Worse, some men are hypocrites—they ascend to positions of power and win public acclaim by the most unscrupulous means, all the while pretending to act out of the purest motives and thus seem only to be receiving their due.

If in all this Boyle is behaving like a traditionalist, in order to do so he has had to shift the emphasis in his moral philosophy. To save the spirit, he has had to sacrifice the form. Boyle proves at least to his own satisfaction that in order for men to obtain happiness under the circumstances in which they find themselves, they will have to defy fortune—even the supposedly good fortune of gentle birth. This defiance of fortune requires on man's part the strongest possible adherence to virtue. Virtue is the only road to happiness; it is happiness itself. This fact in turn makes the so-called goods of fortune mere "Adjuncts of Felicity."[37] "Now the Question is," Boyle writes, "whether a man may be happy with the sole goods of the Mind, without the Possession of those of the Body or Fortune." His answer is one measure of his psychic and intellectual transformation:

> To which I answer, that those outward Goods make not to the Essence of Felicity but are necessary to it's Eminence: that is, they ar not absolutely requisite to the Beeing of a happy-man: but they conduce extreamely to his Wel-being. For the Being of Felicity consists in the Habitude of Virtue: expressing it self by frequent Axions: but certinly the Operations of that Habitude cannot be so wel exercised without those accessary helps. . . .[38]

Nothing could better suggest that Boyle combines within himself the roles of radical and traditionalist, innovator and conservative—a curious and complex phenomenon that has come to be associated with modern revolutions.

We have shown why and how Boyle rejected the conventional ethic of his caste. Let us now pause to consider his relation, as he himself saw it, to the great traditions of moral speculation in the West. By doing so, we shall arrive at a better understanding of the view he adopted to replace the ethic that for him no longer worked.

Boyle steeped himself in ethical theories before setting out to write his own. He is critical of most—of Plato,[39] Aristotle,[40] and "The Peripateticks" or "Schoolemen."[41] But in the course of criticizing the aristocratic ethic, which relied principally upon Aris-

totle and his commentators for its theoretical foundations, Boyle
singles out one moral philosophy for at least qualified praise:

> & Laertius in his Life, intentions a certin Epistle of his to one
> Menecaeus, wherein expounding himself, he seems to place
> Felicity, not in the Pleasure of the Man & Senses; but in that
> of a helthful body, & the calmnes of a Mind untrubled with
> Passions. Which Opinion, tho it be not altogether tru (that
> Pleasure being but a consequent of Happiness & not happi-
> ness it self) yet dos far more savor of a Philosophy than the
> other view, placing happiness in health, strength and beauty
> alone and so entrusting it to fickle fortune.[42]

Here Boyle is quite obviously referring to Diogenes Laertius and
his *Lives of Eminent Philosophers*. In the passage quoted above, Boyle
gives the impression that included in the "Life" is "a certain Epistle" from "Laertius" himself "to one Menecaeus." But when one
turns to the *Lives* itself and finds the "Epistle" in question, one
learns that, though it is indeed written to one Menoeceus, it is not
from Diogenes Laertius. Its true author was Epicurus![43] Either
Boyle is not being careful enough to tell the reader who the author
is, or he is being more than careful to conceal the real author's
name. "The Aretology" is a manuscript treatise and as such shows
signs of being no more than an unrevised draft.[44] But the alternative explanation—that Boyle is hiding his appreciative interest in
Epicurus—gains ground when one recalls that Epicurean doctrines
were contradictory to the fundamentals of Christian theology—
belief in a created universe, a providential God, and the independent existence and immortality of the soul. As such, Epicurus
posed a threat to both church and state, since it was generally
thought that if men did not believe in an afterlife where they
would receive their just deserts, they would be more prone to vice
and rebellion.

But this is not to imply that Boyle would gain nothing from reading Epicurus. In fact, the evidence suggests otherwise—that
Epicurus did speak to Boyle and that he listened. In "The Aretology" Boyle makes a tacit distinction between "Epicurean" in its

conventional usage and the thought of Epicurus himself. It should also be noted that just as Epicurus' ethical theory is a self-professed attempt to insulate man against an indifferent universe so is Boyle's ethic an attempt to arm man against a hostile fortune. It would seem highly probable that Boyle is reading Epicurus in the lig... of his own experience and finding him helpful as he formulates his own new ethic. Otherwise, why would he bother to read, praise, and obviously ponder so heretical a pagan? By at least 1645 or 1646, Boyle had read Diogenes Laertius' *Lives* and so had been put into touch with the philosophy of Epicurus.[45] Since Boyle, several years later, would adopt and develop a corpuscular view of matter whose ultimate source in antiquity is Epicurus, it is well to remember that Diogenes Laertius treats not only of Epicurus' morals but also of his physical theories and that the two were inextricably connected in both Epicurus' mind and Diogenes' account. What is significant in this regard is the fact that Boyle went to Epicurus first, as far as one can tell, not primarily for his atomic theory but out of an ethical concern. Boyle's deep interest in atomic theory came later. This work will argue that there is an intimate relation between that ethical concern and this later interest.

## Virtue and Circumstances

Boyle's reappraisal of the relation between virtue and birth is only half the story; in opposing one to the other—virtue to inheritance—his conception of virtue also changes. It acquires a new character and content. Let us turn then to this second aspect of the transformation in ethical theory in Boyle's early writings on the subject.

To Boyle's mind the times cry out for an extreme remedy. How else are what he sees as the insidiously persuasive claims of fortune to be arrested and virtue thus defended as the only ground of true happiness? Fortune can come in one of two forms—as prosperity or adversity. Either form is pregnant with pitfalls. Boyle himself knew hardship. The danger lies in giving up without a struggle. Boyle offers a solution: "That since tis the Will only that

gives any thing a sweet or bitter relish (as to the Soule) if we can
incline our Wills to the Desire of that which other men think harsh
why shud those Difficultys be a Terror to us. . . .''[46]

It is not enough for man to steel his will against adversity in
order to endure it. He must actually bring his will "to the Desire of
that which other men think harsh. . . ." Boyle says that many gentlemen already do as much—sometimes even for idle reasons:

> See a pressing Instance of it in our Greatmen, that wil often-
> times leave Plenty & Prosperity at home, & crosse the Seas to
> seek out Dangers & Opposition, which they will cheerfully &
> with delight go on upon for the Purchase of an Empty Title,
> or the honor to be talk'd of. Tennis, which our Gallants make
> a Recreation is much more Toylesom than what many others
> make their Work; & yet those deliht in the one & these detest
> the other; because we do this out of necessity, & the other out
> of choice.[47]

So the task of disciplining one's will to make necessity one's
choice, Boyle concludes, is not that difficult. The results, moreover,
can be as rewarding as they are amazing. Had not Boyle's own experience, since his return from the Continent, been vivid testimony
of the fact that apparent misfortune could work to one's advantage,
once one learned to fit desires to circumstances? Certainly Boyle believed that such was the case.

Prosperity, like adversity, might entangle man in its snares. As
one prospers, one cannot avoid temptations. "To go out of the
reach of Temtations is to go out of the World."[48] This being the
case, Boyle proposes that men overcome temptations through
self-denial. He suggests that there is even a certain savor in such
victory: "a Temptation like Samson's Lyon, tho difficult to be kild
is ful of hony/sweets/ when ded."[49] Boyle does not elaborate further. One can only suppose that he meant that there is a certain an-
ticipatory delight in denying the gratification of a desire in prospect
of a future return all the greater for the denial. We shall come back
to a fuller treatment of this question shortly.

Boyle thus advises that whether a man's condition be one of
prosperity or hardship, he should attempt to abstract himself from

its immediate effects and look to the future. In adversity, to be sure, man is to embrace his difficulties. But here too he must first enure and numb himself to them in order to go on enduring them and thus in the end to make them work to his advantage. This process of abstraction from the impingements of fortune or one's immediate circumstances curtails a man's fear and so frees his energies for overcoming hardship. In prosperity a parallel process allows a man to resist and finally deny the blandishments of fortune and so maximize his chances of continued and perhaps even greater good fortune. Should his fortunes alter for the worse, as they sometimes will despite his efforts, this process of abstraction allows him to suffer the loss with a minimum of disquiet and so maximize his chances of recovery.

Man then is to strive to achieve a certain inner calm or imperturbability of spirit. The goal Boyle is characterizing, however, does not constitute retreat from the world but engagement with it on terms better fitting circumstance than did the conventional ones. Of circumstance Boyle writes, "our Inferior & Ignobler World, is the Stage whereon Inconstancy (perpetually) acts her part in 1000 varius Postures. . . ."[50] Against this "Inconstancy" Boyle seeks a stay. His religion here serves him well. He writes: "Nothing more unalterable then God's decrees, or more un-vary'd than the Motions of the Spheares. The Good Angels ar confirmed in Good; & the wisest men most constant in their Resolves; & in Sum the Perfectest things least subject to change. . . ."[51] He finds his model of constancy in God and God's providence and, as the passage implies, his stay in the belief that men can emulate the perfection and constancy inherent in things divine and providential. Thus will men gain the strength and wisdom to cope with this "Inferior & Ignobler World." As an afterthought Boyle remarks: "Look but how long the wrangling Lawyer or greedy Merchant ar in the Prosecution of their Suits & Traffic: & shud we be less constant in the Pursuit of Felicity than they in that of an Inferior Good?"[52] Boyle's aim is imperturbability. But this in turn is but a means to felicity in a world in which "the wrangling Lawyer" and "greedy Merchant" also go abroad. The object of Boyle's project is not a retreat from the world. There is an emphasis upon the disciplining of the will, thus allowing man to abstract himself and to live undistracted by circumstances. But this discipline is merely preparatory. What it does is to fit a man to be a more effective combatant and hence, in the long run, to benefit from these very circumstances.

"The Peripateticks" claimed that virtue flourished where fortune was kind—that is, among the elite. Conversely, virtue withered whenever fortune took a turn for the worse. As has been shown, this is the view that Boyle had inherited and subsequently rejected. He writes: "I think it fit to admonish the Reader, that it is not causely [causelessly?] doubted, whether outward crosses & impediments have so much Power to diminish & Eclipse the Axions of Virtue as the Peripateticks do generally give them."[53] Boyle could call this ethic into question because he did not share one of the assumptions of its exponents—that men are kept virtuous in order to receive the praises of their peers. If "outward crosses & impediments" inhibited or prevented a gentleman from proving his virtue and winning such praises, then one of the chief inducements to its practice would fall away. But Boyle insists that virtue does not depend upon its public recognition and acclaim: "It seems a popular Error to Imagine the Worth of Virtue to be lessen'd, only by being les known, & wanting that outward splendor that renders them notorius."[54] Is it possible that the last word here is carefully chosen? It is "notorius," not "honorable," as it would perhaps have been if Boyle had held to his inherited view. His experience had taught him to distrust "outward splendor." It might not herald virtue so much as mask unworthy deeds, and this discrepancy between theory and practice was often a measure of hypocrisy and deceit. Whenever this discrepancy does not exist, then, it is true, he says, "that divers externall axions of Virtue may be hindered by the want of these outward helps. . . ." But when it does exist—as is the case, so he thinks, in his own day—then "outward splendor" itself, seen in the older ethic as an inducement to virtue, will act instead as an impediment. So at such times only "the Inward Acts of the same Vertus" that according to the inherited wisdom receive their just public reward—only these "are Privileg'd from the Power of those Impediments."[55]

Boyle was, in any event, less interested in the "externall axions of Virtue" than he was in "the Inward Acts of the same Vertus."

These latter, as has been shown, allowed man to persevere whatever the conditions, and in fact to triumph over circumstances by letting them work in the end to his advantage. Far from withering "the Inward Acts" of virtue, adverse circumstances could, on the contrary, actually even strengthen such "Acts." As Boyle says,

> And lastly, it oftentimes fals out that those very wants & Crosses, that hinder us in the outward Operations of some Vertus; occasion the Practice of Nobler Axions: besides the confirming us in the love of those Vertus we cannot Exercise: as when a man by being taken Prisoner looseth the liberty of fihting; yet he learns, Patience, Humility; & inwardly may exercise his Courage in a hiher degree then before, by conquering his owne Reluctations, & overcoming his outward adversitys.[56]

This new ethic with its focus upon "Inward Acts" rather than "externall axions" and "outward splendor," upon the deliverances of one's own will rather than a public standard, altered Boyle's conception of what constituted honorable conduct, honor being central to the inherited ethic. A short manuscript treatise, "Of Valour"—which is separate from "The Aretology" but which, apparently, is contemporary with it—bears witness to this alteration. According to Boyle there are two kinds of valor—"Gowned [civil] & Military . . . : whereof the Latter moderates our Passions in the Dangers & myserys of Warre, & the Former dos it in those that we arr subject to in Times of Peace."[57] "The Moralists," Boyle claims, "cheefly insist upon Military Valor."[58] So he will too. But this declaration of intent belies what in fact he goes on to say.

His real interest is not the "Military" but in the "Gowned." At first he says that the two kinds call for at least equal courage. It is,

> no lesse tru Valor with Constancy to venture & Sustaine the Losse of Goods, Liberty, Wife & Children for the sake of Virtue, nor perhaps with an undaunted Spirit to Struggle with a fit of the Gout or welcom Deth in a bed with a compos'd Spirit & Setled Resolution, then to meet Deth in the Field,

> where there is hopes of Scaping it by Victory or Flight; &
> where thousands of Common Soldiers for 6 pence a Day
> hazard an equall Danger.[59]

Since, he continues, men regard as cowards those who "express an
excessive Feare" of dangers other than the military,

> why shud we not ascribe Courage to them that moderate
> those Feares. For Terribilia being . . . the Object of Valor;
> what matters it whether they come in the Shape of a Mutiny
> of men or in that of the humors, & whither they assault
> us. . . .[60]

Besides, he adds, "were there no other Valor than the Military,
Peace, which all men beleeve a Blessing, wud to gallant men prove
a Curse, by affording them no Practice for their Virtue. . . ."[61] This
passage suggests that some would have denied the parity of the
"Military" and the "Gowned" that Boyle posited—would in fact
have stressed the "Military" to the virtual exclusion of the
"Gowned." Despite this rather prevalent attitude, Boyle did not
stop at asserting an equality between them. In the end he even argued that the "Gowned" was primary and the "Military" merely
derivative: "Virtue is not ty'd to Fields or Breaches; tis the successful Combat with our Passions that is true Valor; that with our
Enemys is so but as it is Symtome & the Effect of the other (in the
minde)."[62] For Boyle, that essential valor generative of honor does
not consist primarily in brave performances in battle but in the
willpower to ride out difficulties, whether military or not. Valor is
not a matter of "externall axions" but of "Inward Acts" and as
such is not a strictly martial virtue.

The emphasis of the inherited wisdom upon the doing of "externall axions" to satisfy a public standard has led in many cases, so
Boyle believes, to an excessive

> feare of unmerited Dishonor . . . , & engaged men into very
> unwarrantable Actions; as we see in those great Princes of
> former Ages, who to avoid the being made a Spectacle to the
> Roman People, in following the Victors Triumphan Chair,

murder'd themselves: foolishly permitting the Conqueror to Triumph over their Resolutions rather then their Bodys.[63]

Boyle is dipping into history for an example of something similar to what he sees men doing in his own day. Those subscribing to the inherited ethic—gentlemen and aristocrats—go to any lengths to avoid doing anything that their peers might construe as shameful. Certainly Boyle was referring to acts of desperation, whether actual suicides or not, when he wrote:

And sure he is but a Novice in the Knoledge of men that ignores the sad Effects of the Excessive Apprehension of unprocur'd Infamy: whilst many Sensible Spirits, not considering that true Infamy is the Ofspring of our Ill Actions not other men's bad Opinions; to avoid a Shame that they do not deserve, do those things that deserve a greater shame than they wud avoid; like that mad Seaman who to avoid the (being wet with the) dashing of a Wave, leapt into the Sea. An excessive Feare of Dishonor it self is Dishonorable.[64]

Boyle applied Ockham's razor to the mental operation issuing in this kind of folly: "True Infamy," he said, is the "Ofspring of our Ill Actions not other men's bad Opinions. . . ." He was here opposing to the aristocratic standard of conduct, sanctioned by the inherited code, his Christian standard, sanctioned by both his faith and his experience. His ethic served him well in the current difficulties—much better, it would appear, than the traditional ethic was serving others. Experience seemed to justify his assertion of the superiority of "Inward Acts" over "externall axions." This assertion in turn altered his conception of that essential aristocratic virtue, honor. As he said, "An excessive Feare of Dishonor it self is Dishonorable."

Fighting to make his way in the world against the blows dealt him by civil war, Boyle was not long in seeing that fortune, even the fact of his gentle birth, was his antagonist, not his ally as the conventional ethic of his caste maintained. Drawing strength from his religion, he set about opposing his will to circumstances in such a way as to turn them in the end to his advantage. All of this he encapsulated in his ethic. The focus was no longer on a public standard but on the will of the individual.[65] The real test of fulfillment was not public but private—no longer the praise of one's peers but one's endurance and ability to surmount difficulties. The dictates of self-interest were more compelling than were the terms of the traditional code. In his own view, however, Boyle did not sell out to circumstances and thus stoop to sheer expediency. This would have been to capitulate to "the Macchiavillians" against whom he inveighed. They lived solely for themselves and served only their own interests exclusive of those of society in general. If they had had their way, they would eventually have brought all men down into their orgy of greed. In such a state there could have been no religion—no proper relation between man and God—and hence no proper relations between men.

To make sure that this would never happen, that in fact precisely the opposite would take place, Boyle's ethic set out to teach men how to live in harmony with providence. According to the ethic, if man opposed his will to circumstances in the appropriate fashion, providence would eventually work to his advantage. Everything in Boyle's own experience, he thought, confirmed his view. So if Boyle's ethic represents an adjustment to circumstances, on the one hand, it also represents a reaction to the "Macchiavillian" sellout to circumstances, on the other. If Boyle's own survival depended upon his adjustment to circumstances, the survival of his religion and his society in any acceptable form depended upon a collective adjustment to these same circumstances—and in precisely the manner he practiced and prescribed.

Boyle held that happiness was the result of virtue and that virtue was essentially independent of external circumstance. But he did not see the ambiguity of his position. The overriding ambiguity was that while he asked men to internalize the moral life, they were to do so in order to cope with and eventually overcome external circumstance. While conscience was to be their guide, success was to be measured in terms of how well they fared in the world. If men lived as he hoped they would, providence in the fullness of time would bestow upon them a durable, material reward. Boyle's plea for an internalization of man's ethical pursuit had two aims. In stating these, one exposes the ambiguity of Boyle's position.

First, the moral life that he asked men to cultivate at once offered an alternative to the "Macchiavillian" approach to circumstances and insulated men against the actions and the consequences of the actions of any who adopted this approach. As an alternative to "the Macchiavillians," Boyle's ethic was Christian in its object. The opposition between the ethic and its alternative is clearly between something religious and something irreligious.

Second, Boyle's ethic supplied the means not only of avoiding the "Macchiavillian" alternative but also of achieving a material reward more certain than the one that the "Macchiavillian" alternative would have promised. Boyle writes,

> ev'n Virtue as Wel as Fortune has her Trumpets & her Crownes, which somtimes she bestows upon her Favorites. And indeed it is generally observed, that Greatness built upon Vice, like a Top-heavy Tree, where the Branches ar too big for the . . . [trunk?] dos easily becom a Windfall: whereas that Greatness whose Foundation is Virtue; as it is perhaps longer in building, so it is by far more difficult to be pulled down. Besides that a Crown got without Wickedness, may be lost without Misery: Whereas those that trample upon their Honesty to rayse their Fortunes, seldome meet with fals, but they break their Necks. [66]

Boyle also squares this second object of his ethic with his religious faith: when men internalize virtue in the manner he prescribes, they bring their lives into harmony with the operations of providence, and temporal success is all but a by-product of lives lived in such a way.

That this providential ordering of events to the benefit of the virtuous was as much a motive to Boyle's ethical enterprise as the threat of "the Macchiavillians" gains further support from "The Aretology." Boyle at first states his position thus: happiness is a matter of virtue—the internalized moral life—and has practically nothing to do with external circumstances. But he later says in the same essay:

> That all seeking for honor or advantage by Virtue seems not absolutely condemnable: for since we allow most things in the

World more Ends/uses/ then One, I kno not why we shud
give Virtue leave only to Content us & not also make us great
or honorable.[67]

The internalized moral life is an end in itself, the root of contentment, and as such, so Boyle claims, is impervious to changes of
fortune. But he is saying here that virtue, as well as being its own
reward, can also be a means to the improvement of one's temporal
condition. Viewed in this light, external circumstance is no longer
an impediment to the moral life. It has now become an incentive.
Boyle's original theory to the contrary, the opportunity for "honor
or advantage" may be an inducement to virtue. If one drove the
logic of the argument to its ultimate conclusion, virtue would become merely expedient to the achievement of worldly success. This
in turn would raise the question of the sincerity of the Christian
piety reinforcing the ethic. Boyle, of course, never pushed the argument so far. He could not have done so and still remained true
to his faith. His faith, in fact, is probably what kept him from following the logic to its end.

But whether Boyle saw the irreligious implication of his ethic or
not, he sensed the ambiguity and felt the resultant tension between
virtue as felicity itself and virtue as a mere expedient to temporal
gain. His response to what he felt was to try to reconcile the two
extremes and so to explain away the ambiguity. In his attempt he
brings the weight of philosophy to bear: "The Filosofers tel us that
Subordinate Ends destroy not one another. And sure since it is unlawful to acquire Riches & honor by forbidden / . . . / meanes, it
will not be unlawful to pursue / . . . / them by those that ar vertu-
ous. . . ."[68] Scripture, he claims, also holds out the prospect of
a reward to virtue: "Besides that the Scripture in many places bayt-
ing Virtue with hev'n & Prosperity dos not obscurely intimate, that
it is lawful for us to desire / . . . / What it is Just with God to Promise."[69] A man, Boyle argues, does not always have to have virtue
uppermost in his mind:

Neither dos it seem that tho in the General a man be rihtly
Principled in the Ends of his Axions, yet in every particular
Acts he is bound to look at Virtue or Happiness as the Princi-

pal End of that Acts: as the Soldier is not oblig'd to think upon the Peace of the Kingdome he fihts for, in every particular thrust he makes, or blow he wards. . . .[70]

None of these attempts, however, resolves or even addresses itself squarely to the difficulty of how virtue can be at once its own reward and expedient to worldly success. So the tension remained for Boyle and for his followers through the remainder of the century and into modern times.

Two factors eased the tension in Boyle's mind. First, his own experience demonstrated how well the ethic served when put into practice. Because the ethic had worked to his advantage, he could attribute to it a providential sanction. Second, it was transparently preferable to the alternative, which was to take the route of "the Macchiavillians." So, despite the tension created by the ambiguity, in the end Boyle could say that true virtue:

> seems to consist . . . in a due Subordination / . . . / of Ends. . . . Tho in Virtuous Actions we may have Ends besides Virtue; yet we must have none beyond it. Fir if we value any thing above Virtue, & that thing chance to come into Competition with Virtue, we must necessarily desert the one to adhere to the other. No no, Virtue like oyle in Water, is never truly but when it swims upon the top: she disdains to dwel any where, where she is not queene, & wil never truly tye her self to him, that courts her for her Dowry, not for her Selfe. Honor & Reward shud be the Attendands/ consequences/ not the Ends of Virtuous Actions; they shud be the Fruits /prizes/ of the Victory, not the Motives to the Warr.[71]

Such a statement, of course, does no more than obscure the ambiguity.

In view of this ambiguity what can now be taken as Boyle's position respecting the moral life? He seems to be saying that when conditions are adverse, man should internalize the moral life and put faith in providence to overcome the external threat. But when conditions are more favorable, man can look to external incentives to replace or complement his own strength of will as motives to virtue. One's response to external circumstances entirely depends upon whether these appear as impediments or inducements—not only to virtue but to temporal well-being. If they are impediments, one internalizes; but if they are inducements, one acts positively upon them.

Essentially, what has changed is Boyle's conception of the connection between virtue and fortune. According to the old ethic, gentle lineage was a means to virtue by way of providing a setting—ancestry, wealth, leisure, and company—conducive to the cultivation of virtue. According to Boyle's ethic, however, fortune is a means to virtue by way of providing a goal and inducement. This change in the conception of fortune, furthermore, rests upon a more basic change in the larger setting. In the old setting birth was a prerequisite to virtue. But in the new, good fortune in the form of birth or lineage no longer exists at the start; rather it is to be strived for, and so in this sense is an important incentive to virtue. What has occurred in Boyle's mind then is a turning away from the notion of good fortune or birth for the sake of virtue toward that of virtue for the sake of fortune in the sense of worldly success. This would be an altogether accurate description were it not for the fact that under the conditions in which the traditional ethic was obtained there had probably always been a large discrepancy between theory and practice. Honor must frequently have gone to those who ideally did not deserve it, who may in fact have achieved it by cunning pretense to virtue. Boyle was witness to the widening of this discrepancy under the impact of the civil wars. What he was actually doing in his ethical thought, whether he realized it in these terms or not, was bringing theory into more realistic connection with the situation—his own in particular—than had hitherto been the case.

Boyle kept the category of the heroic. But in his hands heroes became God's agents, and Christ was made their model—"Christ with all Vertus in a heroicall Degree."[72] Heroes after the manner of Christ, then, lived according to God's design, doing his bidding and defying fortune or circumstances by which the devil tried to thwart his design. "Whomsoever it pleases God," Boyle writes,

> to worke som great Reformation in Sciences or Arts, or som
> notable change in Kingdoms or Common-welths; or generally,

any extraordinary Alteration in the state of humane things; he dos for the most part excite Heroick Spirits, which he makes his Instruments to effect it.[73]

Aristocrats still have the edge in the pursuit of heroic virtue and true happiness, "by reason of their Domestick Examples, Undistractedness for want of Necessarys, & other Furtherances. . . ."[74] As Boyle says in another place:

> outward Goods make not to the Essence of Felicity but are necessary to it's Eminence: that is, they ar not absolutely requisite for the Beeing of a happy-man: but they conduce extreamely to his Wel-being. For the Being of Felicity consists in the Habitude of Virtue: expressing it self by frequent Axions: but certinly the Operations of that Habitude cannot be so wel exercised without those accessary helps. . . .[75]

So, "Noble Familys, . . . may (generally) entitle themselves to a greater number of Hero's then others can."[76] But, according to Boyle's revision of the tradition, they no longer have a monopoly of virtue. "Yet have they not made it so much their Property, but that men of meane & Ignoble houses may have a just title to it; if they can make Desert their Plea."[77] Men who do not have the advantage of an aristocratic birth can also rise by dint of their own effort to acts of heroism.

So in a restricted sense there is a leveling or democratizing tendency in Boyle's ethic. When the moral life is internalized and no longer depends upon descent, when men must in fact defy all outward circumstances including gentle lineage, then more people are given the chance to cultivate virtue than were under the old ethical dispensation.

An aristocrat enjoyed certain advantages in the pursuit of virtue and happiness. But, in the long run, wealth and leisure could also work to his disadvantage. He might come in time to take such a life for granted. This would be equivalent to slipping back into the outworn assumption that there was a natural and permanent alliance between virtue and descent, that good fortune assured virtue and happiness. Should the fortunes of such a man change, he would be left without useful skills and so without employment.

Many gentlemen must have found themselves in this predicament during the course of the civil wars. This may account for Boyle's advice:

> every Person that is likely to have any vacant houres from serious Employments; shud lern some indifferent Skill, in Limming, Turning, Watchmaking, Gardening, or Som Manuall Vocation or other. I know this will be spurn'd at by our Gallants as a Proposition fit to be made rather to blue Aprons then to Skarlet Cloakes. But Sure it is not so much below a Gentleman to do Somthing, as it is below both a Man & a Christian to be Idle.[78]

As the last sentence in this passage indicates, however, Boyle was not just warning the aristocracy and gentry to protect themselves against a whimsical fortune. He was also instructing them in their Christian duty—not just to themselves but also to God and their fellow men. He writes:

> 2. Diligence in a lawfull Calling is either Necessary or usefull for a comfortable Provision of Erthly Necessarys & Conveniencys; God's Blessing upon this Diligence being his usual way to enrich his Servants with temporal blessings; & the Apostle tels us that if we provide not for our Familys we ar worse then Infidels. 3 Tim. 5, 8. 3. He is but an useless wastful Drone, & unworthy of the Benefits of Humane Society; whose endeavors in som honest particular Calling, do not som way or other Cooperate (& contribute) to the Good of the Common-welth. 4. An honest Calling is an Academy of Virtue; & gives Occasion both to acquire those Good qualitys that we want & Exercice & improve those that we possess.[79]

Boyle maintains that should men not practice the morality he set forth, they will put the very "Fabrick of the Commonwealth" in jeopardy. In that event, he writes, "the Assemblys of men, will be turned into Herds & Droves of reasonable Beasts."[80] A noble birth and station do not exempt one from the duty of diligence, "there being no reason that because a man is Steward of a great family, he shud cast off all care of Administration. . . ." On the contrary, "to whom most is given of him shal be most required. . . ."[81] Boyle inveighed against the indolence and irresponsibility he witnessed in the lives of the English ruling classes. "Amongst the Romans," he writes, "every man was to weare in the Streets the Badg of that Profession that he liv'd by: (If that law were transplanted hither, I'm afeared our Streets wud hardly be overcrowded:). . . ."[82] The English elite suffered by comparison not only to the ancient Romans but also the modern Italians:

> I remember that while I lived in Italy, I observed that the Greatest Nobility there did exercice Merchandize by their Servants & Factors; & wud laf at ours [nobility] for letting vast summs of mony ly rusting in their Coffers; whilst by keeping Ships at Sea (or a hundred other ways) they miht lay it out to the great benefit both of themselves & the Commonwelth. . . .[83]

But these comparisons did not stop Boyle from his self-appointed task of persuading and cajoling the English aristocracy to come to terms with the world in the manner that his reformulation of the traditional ethic prescribed. It is clear from what has been quoted that he hoped they would adapt themselves to new conditions in such a way as to serve the interests of all while they served their own. They would thus avoid the "Macchiavillian" alternative while escaping the pitfalls of aristocratic sloth.

The aristocracy had traditionally sought honor and glory and made them the chief signs of virtue. Its membership typically considered much concern with the mundane and practical aspects of existence to be unworthy of a true gentleman. And, to such minds, any occupation involving a manual skill was menial in the extreme. These were the prejudices of a close-knit, privileged caste operating within a still feudalized and relatively static social milieu. But Boyle's experience taught him that the aristocratic ethic, as traditionally conceived, did not fit the circumstances and so did not point the way to man's achieving his own express aims of virtue and happiness or in some cases—Boyle's own, for instance—did not even afford the means of survival.

At the same time that circumstances dimmed the luster of the old ethic, they raised a specter of their own: If in fact the aristocratic code was so sadly deficient, men would have no choice but to bow to circumstances; and if this were the case, would it not lead to the unmitigated pursuit of self-interest and so to the creeping spread of all the worst sins of "the Macchiavillians"? But Boyle had a single answer both for this fear and for the bankruptcy of the old ethic. Men would cultivate virtue and procure happiness not by consenting to circumstances and playing along with fortune as "the Macchiavillians" did but by defying both, thereby participating with providence in bringing in an eventually favorable result. Boyle's answer to the aristocratic code on the one hand, and to Machiavelli on the other, was a curious and rather unstable compound of Christ, Hartlib, and Epicurus. With this Boyle hoped to woo the aristocracy—to win them away from archaic loyalties on the one hand and corrupt, new attachments on the other.

This new accommodation to reality that Boyle was asking the aristocracy to make even implied a new attitude toward time to which he is witness: "In the husbanding & Management of Time, Aristotles Rules of Mediocrity seem (almost) unnecessary. . . ." This is so because there is only "one Extreame to be shun'd /avoyded/ which is that of Prodigality /Excesse" or the waste of time. The other extreme, "Avarice of Time, is either Commendable or Impossible." Therefore, he concludes: "Tis onely the Improvement of Time, that can secure our Memorys from the Injurys of Time; disarms /blunts/ him of his All-destroying Scythe, & knocks out his Iron teeth."[84] Boyle takes his final swipe at aristocratic sloth in the light of how the changed circumstances demand that man spend his time on earth and of what the price is of his failure to oblige. "They that make Idleness the Companion /Darling/ of their Lives; must Expect Oblivion, /Obscureness, . . ./ to Digge their Graves."[85] Only the men who are diligent in their duty, as Boyle conceives it, will live in the memory of their families, their peers, and the state.

Boyle's views with respect to the making of moral men bear certain theoretical, political implications of a rather diffuse and general nature. "Heroical Men," he says, "ar more frequently observ'd . . . in Common-welths then in Monarchys . . . ."[86] This is not because there are any fewer potential heroes in monarchies. It is rather for two other reasons. First, "in Republickes the way to honor & preferment lys more open to desert, which is a quickning Spur & a great incitement to Noble Spirits. . . ."[87] And second,

> the lesser Inequality of Men's Conditions in Commonwelths, renders these Heroick Spirits more conspicuus; which in Monarchys wud be swallowd by the Glory of the King or Princes, to whom for the most part ar attributed the most Glorius Acts of their Subjects. Whence it was observed, that after the Roman Liberty had once bowed it's neck to the Yoake of the Emperors, there was in Rome, both fewer Heros, & those too less taken Notice of.[88]

Boyle subscribes to a commonwealth as the ideal form of political society. He does not directly say why, but his remarks suggest an answer. In a monarchy, as distinct from a commonwealth, the traditional ethic obtains, and heroic virtue is thus thought to be confined to "the King or Princes." So "Heroick Spirits," whose virtue owes nothing to a noble station but is rather the result of their own determination, find it difficult in such a state to make themselves known and their virtue felt. In a commonwealth this is not the case. Boyle puts his faith in the commonwealth because he sees that in such a polity his ethic would have more chance of success than it does under an hereditary monarchy. The leveling tendency inherent in the ethic would work better the more leveled things were to start with, and commonwealths were patently superior to monarchies in this respect.

Boyle, being a Christian, believed that man was subject to a "Three-fold Condition." Every man was born into the state of creation, and if God so chose, could pass into the state of redemption, and at the last into the state of heavenly glorification. Boyle saw man as capable of a corresponding "Three-fold Felicity." For man in the first state, he writes, "Felicity is partly Theoreticall namely, Wisdom & Contemplation; & partly Practical; which is the Exercice of Moral Virtue; facilitated by the Accessary Goods of Nature & Fortune."[89] In the second state, man's "Happiness consists in the

Communion with God as his appeased Father in Jesus Christ: & in
the leading a Life worthy the Child of such a Parent."[90] And in the
third state,

> his Happiness consists in that Union with God. . . . Wherein
> the Soule's Ey, the Intellect, sees God: not, (as in this Life,)
> by Reflexion: but; as the Ey sees the Liht, (by admission of it
> into it selfe) by the Dwelling & Habitation of God in us.[91]

In "The Aretology" Boyle is chiefly concerned with felicity in the
state of creation. In another place he calls such happiness "Civil
Felicity."[92] As has just been suggested, it consists in two
degrees—active and contemplative or practical and speculative.
Each degree is conducive to the cultivation of the other. Contemplation helps engender active felicity by leading man to see that
virtue is the only road to all happiness. As Boyle says, "Neither wil
the Wil be induc't to embrace a Quality so distastefull to the Ape-
tite, til the Understanding have judged it extreamely desirable."[93]
Likewise, Boyle writes, that although

> the Contemplative seems the higher & mor sublim De-
> gree: . . . the Practicke seems to have more of Civil Felicity in
> it; as more in our Power, more Profitable; & so conducing to
> the other, that it is almost impossible [for anyone] to con-
> template wel, who has not first, by Active Virtue; subdu'd &
> rang'd his inordinate Passions, & lawles desires; as a man can
> never see the Images of things cleerly in troubled Water.[94]

The preferable life then is neither wholly active nor wholly contemplative but "a Compound of Both. . . ."[95]

The active or practical degree of civil happiness occupied the
lowest rung on Boyle's ladder of felicity. Man could obtain civil
felicity in both active and contemplative degrees in the manner laid
out in his "Aretology." But felicity accompanying redemption and
glorification depended, as did these states of being themselves,
upon "infused Grace from above."[96] Boyle makes this distinction
when he distinguishes between "moral virtues" and "inspired
graces" in a work roughly contemporary with "The Aretology," his
*Free Discourse against Customary Swearing.*[97] Therein he writes:

Moral virtues may perhaps be resembled to great men's clothes, which supply those that see them, with some conjectures of the quality of those, that wear them: but inspired graces (such as repentance is) are like their liveries, whose gaudiness evinces not the footman's deserts, but his lord's splendidness; and in men's esteems entitles the lacquey to nothing but a good master. Those better qualities blood may convey, or industry acquire, like honours conferred by princes, suppose the party deserving; but heavenly donatives are like alms, which ever presume need; and whereby they are more liberally bestowed, stronglier conclude the greatness of the party's wants than merits.[98]

On the one hand, Boyle is making man's redemption and sanctification dependent upon the will of God. In doing this, he is reacting to "the Filosophers & Schoolemen" who

by their Overmagnifying Moral Virtue; have given Occasion to most men, to make an Idol of it; & set it up as the Supreame Degree of man's Felicity: which is an Opinion as Derogatory to God's Honor, as it makes for it; to place our Sovereign Good in him who is the Sovereign Good Himselfe.[99]

But on the other hand, Boyle is ascribing to man the power to chart his own strictly mundane course.

The contemplative life in Boyle's scheme afforded one degree of civil felicity. He assumed that knowledge and moral excellence were directly proportional. This assumption, he admitted, was not without its exceptions. He writes: "It is not only possible but Frequent, to see a man have a great deale of the Liht of Truth in his Understanding, without the least Degree of the heat of Virtue in his Affections. . . ."[100] He then offers an explanation of why this is so:

this arrives, not through the Fault of the Learning, but by the fault of the Man, who being vitiously disposed himself, makes use of a thing, in it's owne Nature Good, to a Bad End. An Inconvenience incident to the most excellent things: since the Worst (& most Pernitius) Abuse, is that of the best things.[101]

Knowledge conduced to virtue only as man also "subdu'd & rang'd
his inordinate Passions, & lawles desires. . . ." This subduing and
ranging was tantamount to nothing less than the internalization of
virtue examined in this chapter and was the process whereby men
attained to the active or practical degree of civil felicity. So this active degree was primary and indispensable to the achievement of
the contemplative degree. The contemplative, on the other hand,
was not indispensable to the practical but rather, as has been said,
conducive to its development.

This is not all that Boyle has to say respecting the contribution of
knowledge to happiness and the moral life. Knowledge is not happiness itself. It cannot be because as Boyle says—following
Ecclesiastes 1:18—"in much Wisdom is much Greef: & he that in-
creaseth Knoledge encreaseth Sorrow." Boyle then undertakes to
explain: "It cannot but Greeve a Knoing man, to see the Irregulari-
tys that Lawless Power to [others?] Acts agenst Justice & Reason: &
to see it self despised, without being able either to help it self, or
Remedy these Disorders."[102] The "Lawless Power" by which the
world thus is victimized can be none other than that of "the Macchiavillians." So knowing this does not make one happy but sor-
rowful. The predicament, however, is not as desperate as it
sounds. Knowing the worst, man can take steps to avoid it. By
learning that reckless greed does not issue in happiness, he can
find out that the opposite of greed, which is virtue, does.[103] Was it
not Boyle's own experience that taught him this? When the aristocratic ethic failed him, he had to find another ethic that would not
fail. And did he not suffer—and therefore grieve and sorrow—in
the process?

But the knowledge productive of virtue and hence of happiness
did not have to emerge out of experience. It could also come from
formal learning. "That Knowledge (even in those Contemplative
Sciences, as the Physics, Metafisics, & Mathematickes) does greatly
conduce to the Practice of Vertu."[104] How was this possible? How
could knowledge of such things, seemingly so unrelated to morals,
teach virtue? Boyle gives an extended answer to the question. First,
all study of God's creation "withdraws & diverts our thouhts oftentimes from . . . sensuall Objects, & so delivers us from many occasions of Sinning (& especially from Idlenes.)"[105] Second,

metaphysics "instructs us in many things, whose Knoledge is to the Ethickes, if not Necessary, at lest Usefull: as the Doctrine of Principles, Causes, & Ends; that Of the Soule with it's Facultys & Immortality, & the like."[106] These two reasons stated, Boyle moves to a third and the root of his arguments. "In the Contemplation both of Naturall & Supernaturall things, we meet with many Incentives to Virtue, & Dissuasives from Vice."[107] God and his creation in their perfection should call forth virtuous endeavor on man's part.

> How can a man that has the least spark of Goodnes in him, consider the Infinitely good & infinitely Perfect Nature of God, without being enflam'd with a Desire of being like him: How can he consider that no les Boundles then undeserved Bounty of the Great Creator, without feeling in himself the Baits & motions of Gratitude.[108]

The ambitions of "the Macchiavillians" seem paltry in comparison to God's purpose in the universe. Such men would do well to learn a humility proportional to this sublime purpose because only in humble submission can one ever hope to enjoy any truly substantial reward.[109] Man must live in harmony with providence before he can receive its benefits. He puts his life in proper order when he subscribes to the ethic Boyle lays down. One way of achieving the desired humility is through the study of physics and metaphysics. Such disciplines can instill due reverence for their objects, from which spring virtue and, with virtue, happiness. The creatures that God has made to inhabit the created order can teach this lesson even more directly.

> And how . . . can he [man] consider the Ruf Draughts & Images of Virtue in the Very Brutes; without a Noble Scorn that he shud make himself inferiour to them by his Actions, that God made so much superior to them by his Birth; & that while all the Creatures unanimously conspire, to attaine in their particular Conditions, the End of their Creation; man alone, shud strive to frustrate his by his Actions, & be the onely jarring Voice to spoile the Harmonious Concert of so

numerous a Set of wel-tun'd Creatures; making use of his
Reason, to becom the more unreasonable.[110]

The creatures dutifully play the parts that God and providence as-
sign them and so contribute to the harmony of the world while advancing, as far as is consistent with the good of the whole, their
own well-being. Men are the only exceptions to the rule among
God's creatures. "The Macchiavillians," on the one hand, and the
indolent gentry on the other, are especially guilty. The gentleman
devotes himself to ruinous self-indulgence. The "Macchiavillian"
for his part seeks his own interests without regard to the consequences for himself or anyone else. He takes his chances with
changeable fortune and in the end is made to pay. Neither gentleman nor "Macchiavillian" cares a whit for the public good; their
pursuits in fact work to its detriment. Such men would profit from
the study of nature. They would see in the creatures the ingenuous
display of the exemplary virtue that is so sadly wanting in all men
and especially among themselves. They might then take steps to
reform their lives in the light of nature and of the models they
have witnessed there. They would thenceforth live as the creatures
do and teach them to—that is, in such a way as to advance the
interests of all as they advance their own. This, as has been
shown, is also the end of Boyle's ethic—only now in this instance
man's "inordinate Passions, & lawles desires" can be "subdu'd &
rang'd" through inquiry into the created order.

The study of nature, then, is not an end in itself; to Boyle's mind
it contributes to man's moral and civic enterprise. All knowledge
ultimately becomes ethical knowledge and the pursuit of knowledge becomes an ethical pursuit. Boyle does not give any hints
about where he picked up this notion of the relation between
natural and moral philosophy. We have already seen, however,
that at the time "The Aretology" was written this assumption was
important to other aspects of his thinking, namely, the habit of
"pursued Thoughts" and occasional reflection. We have also seen
that these techniques probably derived from Comenius via the invisible college. Boyle's belief that the study of nature is a source for
moral wisdom, therefore, may also have come from Comenius and
the Hartlib circle. Certainly this belief in the harmony between

truths of nature and a true morality is in keeping with Comenian pansophy.

There are other similarities between "The Aretology" and the ideas of the Hartlib circle that support the claim of a connection between them. Plattes' *Macaria* gives the formula for an anti-Machiavellian politics just as Boyle's ethic is the formula for an anti-Machiavellian morality. The politics of Macaria and Boyle's ethic would both serve the same end, the public good, and in each case the mechanisms for arriving at that goal are very similar. Royal policy in Macaria would rest upon a calculation of what would best serve the material interests of the political nation. The public good hangs on the success of that calculation. Likewise, Boyle's ethic offers a way whereby man can serve the common good as he serves himself. The sanction in both cases, moreover, is the same. The subjects of Macaria have instituted and practiced true religion, and this is repaid by a providential harmonizing of the public good with the pursuit of private interests. Such for the author and the publisher of *Macaria* was tantamount to the fulfilling of the reformation. For Boyle too the role of providence is crucial. The virtuous not only achieve their own ends in time but also benefit the public. Providence makes things turn out this way, protecting the virtuous from the ungodly and threading the efforts of the godly into the fabric of the commonwealth. Read in this light, "The Aretology" may be seen as a contribution to the literature of reformation associated with the Hartlib circle.

We know that Boyle was interested in a settlement or reformation of the English church along the lines set out by Plattes and Dury. We also know that much of his scientific work—for example, his "Invitation to a Communication of Receipts"—was related to the aims of the invisible college, which again were essentially those of *Macaria*[111] and so too looked toward the accomplishment of "the reformation."[112] The process of reformation in science, as considered in the "Invitation" written about the same time as "The Aretology," was the same as for politics in Macaria or morality in Boyle's ethics: providence worked to the benefit of the private individual, in this case the chemist, and the commonwealth alike.

Sharing with the Hartlib circle both the goal of reformation and a certain understanding of how providence would act to take men

there, Boyle may have written "The Aretology" in part as a guide
to and explanation of how men should conduct themselves in
order to make the most of providential actings. A part of the general reformation would be the moral reformation within each man.
Perhaps Boyle saw that his ethic would fit men for service to the
public good and the building of Macaria. Certainly the ethic is consistent with the program outlined in *Macaria* and the aims of the
invisible college.

But of course, as we have seen, the ethic was more than this: it
was also in large measure a product of his experience. In other
words, it answered both of the imperatives in terms of which he
lived during the civil wars—the demands of his economic predicament and those of his religion, the need to secure his fortune and
the drive to fulfill the obligations his conversion had laid upon
him, which to him, as a result of his involvement after 1645 in the
Hartlib circle, meant service to the public good.

On April 8, 1647, Boyle wrote to Hartlib about a sheaf of verse,
"the Divine Emblems," by another protégé of Hartlib's, John Hall
of Durham and Grays Inn. Boyle had not read the poems under
consideration, but this did not keep him from saying somewhat
archly:

> And for the Divine Emblems, that he [Hall] makes us hope
> for, I must reserve my sense of them for their perusal, since
> the opinions I embrace, both about the nature and the teach-
> ing of virtue will doubtless appear as paradoxical to others, as
> they seem probable to me.[113]

He probably saw that to anyone who subscribed to any version of
the traditional code, his own ethic would indeed present a cluster
of seeming paradoxes. By making virtue independent of birth and
at the same time the root of all happiness, Boyle had performed an
intellectual volte-face that no doubt thoroughly befuddled his more
conventional contemporaries. From the tone of the last passage
quoted, one senses Boyle almost hoping that his revision would
have such an effect. But his ethic did not spring simply from the
desire of a young gentleman who wished to startle and amaze in

order thus to show off his wit and intellect. His ethic sprang from something much deeper. His own conversion and subsequent experience led him to the transformation he worked upon the inherited wisdom. Once he made the changes, the new theory explained the facts as he had witnessed, suffered, and understood them. So he could be in earnest where others might see nothing but paradoxes.

In fact, theory and experience fitted so well in Boyle and to such agreeable effect that there is at least one occasion on which he seems to have forgotten the changes he has made in the theory in order to make the fit. This occasion is at the beginning of his autobiography where it deals with his childhood. He was a younger son and saw this as consonant to his purpose. The fact that he was not the "eldest," he writes, "was a happiness, that our *Philaretus* would mention with great expression of gratitude. . . ." He reasoned thus:

> to a person, whose humour indisposes him to the distracting hurry of the world, the being born heir to a great family is but a glittering kind of slavery, whilst obliging him to a public entangled course of life, to support the credit of his family, and tying him from satisfying his dearest inclinations, it often forces him to build the advantages of his house upon the ruins of his own contentment.

As he was not born an eldest son, neither was he born in his mind too low to accomplish his ends. "For . . . , a lower birth (than his) would have too much exposed him to the inconveniences of a mean descent, which are too notorious to need specifying. . . ." So he was happy to be a younger son. His station was an advantage to him in the pursuit of his studies.

> A man of mean extraction is seldom admitted to the privacy and secrets of great ones promiscuously, and scarce dares pretend to it, for fear of being censured saucy, or an intruder; and titular greatness is ever an impediment to the knowledge of many retired truths, that cannot be attained without famil-

iarity with meaner persons, and such other condescentions, as fond opinion, in great men, disapproves and makes disgraceful.[114]

It helped, then, if one wished to serve the public good by advancing knowledge, to be neither too low-born nor too high. Boyle claimed that because he was of middle rank, a younger son, he had the easiest access to the greatest number of knowledgeable people. He also held that his own condition "neither was high enough to prove a temptation to laziness, nor low enough to discourage him from aspiring." He would get just the right proportion of carrot to stick. But if the logic of this thesis is correct, Boyle's sociotheological account of himself puts the cart before the horse. The fact that he was not the "eldest," he writes, so suited "his inclinations, and designs, that, had he been permitted an election, his choice would scarce have altered God's assignment."[115] This makes it seem that "his own inclinations, and designs" were there to start with and that "God's assignment" merely confirmed them. But, as we know, this was not the case. "God's assignment" was more than a matter of his having come into the world a younger son. It also consisted of the obligations his conversion laid upon him and the challenge of the dislocation he suffered during the civil wars. In time he learned to fit his desires to the terms of this situation. Indeed he learned so well—the fit was so true—that to his mind "God's assignment" almost exactly matched "his own inclinations, and designs," even though it was in fact the other way around.

# Chapter 3

---

# Revelation
# and the Revolution

---

Boyle's response to events in the mid-1640s took the form of "The Aretology." This was to be one of the mainstays of his thinking as he faced events down to the Restoration. This chapter shows how, in coming to terms with issues in England in the late 1640s and 1650s, he elaborated on the ideas enunciated in "The Aretology" and went on to work out his full-fledged and distinctive natural religion and philosophy.

## Boyle and the Radical Sects

On August 6, 1648, Boyle finished a treatise entitled *Some Motives and Incentives to the Love of God, Pathetically discoursed of, in a letter to a friend,* and often called simply *Seraphic Love.* The "friend" is called Lindamor in the text. Boyle uses this pseudonym elsewhere to refer to his brother Roger, Lord Broghill.[1] But here it seems to apply to someone else, as Boyle tells us that the "friend" died before the discourse was published (while Roger was very much alive).[2] Regardless of the identity of Lindamor, Boyle has written the piece as a corrective to what he regards as his friend's preoccupation with carnal love to the neglect of God. Boyle writes in what may be taken as a summary of his argument against carnal love, "The letting out our love to mutable objects doth but enlarge our hearts, and make them the wider marks for fortune, and capable of being wounded in more places. . . ." The unintended irony and hence the pathos could hardly be thicker. But as the next part of the sentence suggests, these sentiments cannot be dismissed as priggish and nothing more. Boyle continues,

> for although love may, as well make us participate the joys, as resent the infelicities of the parties loved, yet even the least unhappy persons do in so fickle and so tempestuous a sea, as we all find this world, meet with so many more either cross-winds, or stormy gusts, than prosperous gales. . . .[3]

Carnal love has its "joys" he says, but its sorrows are greater because it involves a man intimately in the life of his beloved, thus making him subject to the hand of fortune as it works not only in his life, but in hers as well. So in such a world as Boyle has experienced and conceives his to be where, as has been shown, fortune is more hostile than benign, carnal love conduces to more pain than pleasure.

Just as his analysis was the same in 1648 as two or three years earlier, so was his proposed solution. The only remedy to the stings of fortune that carnal love, like all other worldly things, would bring, was resort to and love of God. Whatever happens is God's will. Thus whatever happens to a man who loves God is not merely bearable but perfectly acceptable because in loving God one's "chiefest desire" is to see the Maker's will fulfilled. But what needs to be made explicit is that Boyle's version of the love of God is curiously self-interested. He writes,

> When you have resigned, or rather consigned, your expropriated will (if I may so call it) to God, and thereby (as it were) entrusted him to will for you; all his disposals of, and his dispensations towards you, are in effect the acts of your own will, with the advantage of their being directed and specified by him: an advantage, that does at once assure you both of their rectitude and success.[4]

A man resigns his will to God not in despair of life but in the confidence that God's "disposals" on his behalf will produce "an advantage" assuring him "both of their rectitude and success." One flies to God not to escape the world but to enhance one's temporal prospects. This is not to say that Boyle's piety was insincere. He loved God, to be sure, but his love was exquisitely calculated. During the second civil war, then, he harked back to the ethic he had worked out to meet the challenge of the first. Only this time the tension between virtue for virtue's sake and virtue as expedient to worldly success does not seem to have occurred to him.

In exposing the dangers of carnal love Boyle is admonishing those who in a hostile world would live frivolously and so invite ruin. In this light Boyle's remarks can be read as an extension of his argument in "The Aretology" against foolish indolence, especially on the part of those of gentle status. But carnal lovers are not the only ones who come in for attack in this treatise on the love of God.

We have already noticed that when Boyle considered the question of church settlement in 1646 he recognized the danger presented by increasing sectarianism. In 1648 when *Seraphic Love* was written the sects were more active than they had been two years before. Sectaries in the New Model army became more assertive the longer Parliament debated disbanding the troops without pay. And as parliamentary control of the armies broke down and the New Model became an independent political force, sectaries throughout the country grew more vocal and identified with the soldiers' cause. Sectaries in and out of its ranks looked to the New Model as God's instrument for carrying on the work of reformation begun in the first year of the Long Parliament that would end in the rule of the saints, the sectaries themselves. At the very least many sectaries advocated abolition of tithes and reform of the law. If they should win, the national church would be dismantled, property in the form of tithes and legal fees lost, and political power transferred to men representing lower elements in the society than the traditional rulers.[5] The effect of this prospect on Boyle's thought was dramatic and important. Boyle at this very time was in process of securing his fortune and developing the habits and mental set to aid him in doing so. And now all that he was working for and believed in was being jeopardized by increasing sectarianism. As a result in *Seraphic Love* Boyle strikes at the roots of sectarian belief.

Many sectaries preached that man is so depraved when he comes into the world that he can do nothing to merit being saved. Redemption for those predestined to election has to come entirely from God. When a man is saved his corrupt will is extinguished or made perfect; from then on it is not he who acts but God who acts in him.[6] This divine acting, however, was not the same for the sects as it was for Boyle, who also held that when men truly love God, they resign their wills to him. This doctrine in the hands of the sectaries could be used to challenge all established authority; the subversive possibilities therein were not lost on Boyle, and so he set about not merely differentiating his own view from theirs but, more significant than that, employing his to challenge and oppose theirs.

Let us examine his argument: "the expressions of our love to God ought to be regulated, not by our blind and wild fancies, but by his revealed will (as Christ says, *if you love me, keep my commandments.*)"[7] And what are those commandments? They are to pursue one's "own secular relations" and to aid "distressed Christians," charity and self-help which together keep a man too busy to indulge in the sectary's mystical effusions and transports. Not until "their divesture of mortality dispenses them" can the saints be rid of the obligation to work for themselves and others and become totally absorbed in loving God.[8] Here is a crucial difference between Boyle and his opponents among the sectaries. For them the rewards of election come in this life. Whatever they do is right because they lose the capacity to sin from the moment they are saved.[9] This was their license for social revolution. For Boyle, of course, such views were but "blind and wild fancies." Men cannot undertake social revolution because the virtues upon which it would have to be grounded to succeed do not obtain in this life; the perfecting of the saints is deferred to the next life.

The perfecting, moreover, comes as a reward for work done here below. This represents a subtle but important departure from Boyle's position as stated in "The Aretology." There he stressed man's dependence upon "infused Grace from above" for salvation. But now, putting the vexed question of predestination aside,[10] he claims that God "allows man that highest satisfaction . . . of cooperating to his own [eternal] felicity."[11] Man's performance in this life helps to determine his condition in the next; work, pursued according to providential design, is rewarded on earth and in heaven.

By 1648 Boyle had modified the position he held two or three years before and adopted a theology of works. The momentum for doing so seems to have sprung again from his dialogue with the sects. They had grown more and more active in the intervening years, and their belief in absolute predestination, that salvation is all in God's hands, posed yet another threat to the social order. Boyle makes it clear that this is at the root of his fear by opposing their view on social grounds rather than on theological ones: the doctrine of predestination releases men from the useful social discipline that springs from a belief in salvation as something merited from God, not merely decreed by him.[12]

For Boyle the only proper temporal expression of the love of God is work: "just men here on earth must express their love to their master by (that busy distracting, and remoter way of service) trading with his talent trusted to them. . . ."[13] In this way only can we both "love God with all our hearts" and "our neighbour as ourselves" and so satisfy the conditions of seraphic love. Thus we avoid what "too many professors are now wont to do," which is to "dash in pieces the two tables of the law against one another. . . ."[14] The implication is that the sectaries, by loving God to the exclusion of their earthly obligations, set man against man to the detriment of religion and social order. To love God as Boyle suggests, on the other hand, makes for social harmony by enabling men to love one another. We already know that primary among "motives and incentives to the love of God" is Boyle's assumption, derived from his experience and enshrined in his ethic, that godly labor yields rewards to the individual in the long run. If he now says that such labor amounts to loving *our neighbour as ourselves,* he means this only in the sense that he thinks the private pursuit of personal rewards via trust in providence conduces to the public good. His ethic promotes love among men in no deeper sense nor could it. In this regard his experience, as we saw in the previous chapters, and now by 1648 his dialogue with the sects were defining: in a word to love is to work. Here all is revealed—the degree of his commitment to his own prudential calculus, his fear of the sectaries' far more expansive notions, the distance between the two, and, above all, the emotional price he paid for launching out on the conquest of fortune by adopting the moral posture he did.

## Boyle, the Insurgents, and the New State

There were other occasions for Boyle's application of the ethic than his thoughts on love—divine and carnal—afforded. One of the most interesting episodes in Boyle's young life occurred in 1649. After the first earl's death, his son, Roger, lord Broghill, did not disavow the king but continued to fight the Irish rebels at the direction and with the support of Parliament.[15] Sometime between October 1648 and the regicide he "deserted" the parliamentary commissioners in Ireland and "retired into England to a small estate he had left him by his father, at Marston in Somerset-shire. . . ."[16] The events of late 1648, culminating in the regicide, had driven him into the royalist camp, and so while he was at Marston, he worked to get into France in order to serve Charles I's son, the heir apparent. He sought a license allowing him to travel abroad and let it be known publicly that he had to "go to Spa for his gout." But his real and secret intention was "to beat up reinforcements on the Continent to renew the Munster war in the name of Charles the Second."[17] In this scheme Roger involved his younger brother, Robert, who was staying with him at Marston. On March 26, 1649, Robert drafted a letter there "that he addressed to an unidentified lady soliciting her aid to secure from the French ambassador (Pierre de Bellièvre 1611-1683) a pass for his brother Roger. . . ."[18] Whether the letter was sent is not known. The draft in part reads:

> Your Goodnesse has so well acquainted me with the Great-nesse of itselfe, that it assures me that it makes You consider as a Service the Opportunity of doing a curtesy. This Confidence, Madam, gives me that of beseeching You to be pleas'd to procure from the French Embassador (who I know cannot refuse so just a Desire to so powerfull an Intercessor) a Passe for Lindamor[19] & a Leashe of Servants to travell into France &

To & fro there; as long as they neither Do nor Carry any thing that may forfeit the Protection they shall live under. I will not so much suspect a Goodnesse I have had such happy proofes of; as to represent to Y.[our] L.[adyship] that you may possibly do somebody no unacceptable Service, to helpe into France a Person, who elsewhere might (perchance) crosse (or at least retard the Progresse of Desseins) & who is now dispos'd to this Retirement by Considerations that it is farre more easy for Y. L. to guesse then safe for me to write.[20]

Roger made an effort in his own behalf to procure a pass. He wrote to the father of his brother-in-law, "the earl of Warwick, who had an interest in the prevailing party," requesting a license. To Warwick, Broghill did not write as Robert did in his draft and say he, Roger, wished to go into France. Rather Broghill masked his intention.[21] But for all his secrecy Oliver Cromwell discovered and apprehended him. He was not punished straightaway, however. Broghill had fought hard and well against the Irish rebels. Now Cromwell had the responsibility of "subduing . . . the Irish. . . ." So

he had obtained leave from the council, to make an offer to lord Broghill, that if he would serve in the wars against the Irish, he should have a general officer's command, and should have no oaths nor engagements laid upon him, nor should be obliged to fight against any but the Irish. . . . Cromwell told him, he must resolve presently, for there was no time to deliberate, because the council, from whom he came, were resolved to send his lordship to the Tower, as soon as ever Cromwell should return to them, in case this offer was not readily accepted.[22]

The above account is mostly that of Thomas Morrice, Broghill's early biographer. How much credence it is to be given is not certain. But if Morrice is to be trusted, one thing is clear: Broghill had little or no choice. He could remain irreconcilably royalist and languish in the Tower. Or he could accommodate himself outwardly to the new regime and be left free to keep his own counsel and to work privately for the king. In the end it was a question of which alternative would better serve his advantage and that of his party. The answer was plain.

> Lord Broghill, seeing no subterfuges could any longer be made use of, and finding his liberty and life were in danger, whereby he might be rendered utterly incapable of serving his majesty, and not knowing but, by accepting this offer, he might afterwards be serviceable to the royal party, he resolved to accept it, upon the conditions, which Cromwell mentioned. . . .[23]

In this family crisis Boyle invoked the aid of his ethic. On March 25, 1649—the day before Robert drafted his letter to a friend of the French ambassador on his brother's behalf—Robert wrote the first and only entry on a page headed, "A Miscellaneous Collection. Begun March the 25th 1648/9." The entry reads,

> We cannot without regret mention or call to mind the losse of our Estates, & yet we can remember without Sorrow, the Losse (in Adam) of our first State of Innocency.
> Over-sollicitous persons are worse natur'd to themselves then the very Divell, for he would by no meanes be tormented before his Time.[24]

In the above passage Boyle's reference to "the losse of our Estates" is unclear. He may have meant by it the possible forfeiture, as a result of his brother Roger's recent desertion and impending plans, of his family's—and therefore his own—claims to lands in Ireland. Or he may have had in mind the more general consequences for the propertied classes of the events of the previous year. In view of the context in which he made the remarks the former interpretation would seem the more probable. But if this phrase is unclear, the point of the whole passage is not. Consistent with his own ethic as set out in "The Aretology," he is saying that in the face of a crisis, like the one that his own family was then experiencing, men should not lose their nerve but rather bide their time and let things take their course. Preoccupation with the difficulty can only make matters worse. According to Boyle's ethic, providence virtually guaranteed that events would conduce to the advantage of the virtuous. So if men would but gird themselves round with virtue, they would weather any temporal reverses and perhaps even come out ahead in the end as a result of the temporary setback. It was in the spirit of this ethic that Boyle recorded the comment of March 25, 1649. He had formulated the ethic in response to an earlier situation and was now putting it to use in the midst of this new adversity.

Cromwell intercepted Lord Broghill before he could leave England and made him choose between the commonwealth and the king—or more particularly between a fresh command in Ireland and the Tower. Broghill did as his interests dictated and went back to Ireland. There lay his family's patrimony. So he would reclaim what was theirs, should the rebels be beaten and the kingdom restored to England. At first glance Broghill's decision seems to have been a betrayal of the Stuart cause, and doubtless it was to some extent. But there was more to it than this. The decision was not, to be sure, a sign of unswerving devotion to the crown. But Broghill did not make it purely to advance his own interests. As has been shown, he made it on condition that he would not have to swear any oaths or sign any engagements of loyalty to the commonwealth.[25] His only responsibility was to serve in the wars in Ireland. He saw, furthermore, that he could do better by the Stuart crown while fighting and serving himself, his family, and England in Ireland than he could locked away in the fastness of the Tower. Here then is the crucial distinction. Broghill did not make his decision out of desire for self-aggrandizement. Indeed, he was induced to make it by circumstances. It was the result of a reckoning. All things considered, he thought he made the wiser choice. He did not wish to make it; had circumstances been more favorable, he would have joined the royalists in exile.

In 1649 Cromwell set about in earnest to root out rebellion in Ireland. Within the next few years he proceeded, with the help of Lord Broghill, to accomplish the task. As the country was pacified, the English returned the lands to those families, like the Boyles, who had been dispossessed by the native rebels. In his will the earl of Cork had divided up the Irish patrimony among his sons. When

it was safe to do so, Robert crossed over into Ireland, took possession of his portion and stayed on to put his house in order. He
was in Ireland for a year from June 1652, excepting "two months in
August and September, when he was in London and Stalbridge."[26]
Then he made a second trip, lasting from "October 1653 till the
first week in July 1654 at least. . . ."[27] Of his strictly personal and
business affairs in Ireland little is known.

We are somewhat luckier for the years before his Irish visits—that
period between Broghill's attempted defection to the royalists and
the reconquest of Ireland—when the family's Irish patrimony was
in doubt and Boyle was plunged again into considerable uncertainty. Partly this was economic in foundation, as we saw when he
wrote in March 1649 at the nadir of the family's fortunes of what
looked to be "the losse of our Estates."[28] But the patrimony itself
was not the only issue. There was also religion, which, as we saw
in *Seraphic Love,* was linked to the question of wealth and power.

The period between 1648 and 1655 was one of enormous radical,
sectarian activity.[29] The revolution grew more extreme in 1648-49,
with the purging of Parliament, the regicide, and the abolition of
the House of Lords. The army became the supreme arbiter in the
state. The sword rather than laws and constitutional processes
ruled the day.[30] Many radicals and sectaries in and out of the army
took these changes to be God's work, preparing the way for the
building of Jerusalem.[31] Those who were not sympathetic to this
phase of the revolution saw it as the leading edge of anarchy and
barbarism.[32] Boyle was one of these. Specifically, he shared the
view that the army and the sectaries, having already destroyed the
established civil authority, would next strike at Christianity. There
was some point to this view because many radicals advocated dis-
establishment of the church and implementation of the idea that
congregations should be nothing more than gatherings of like-
minded believers without ties to any outside authority.[33] This
threatened organized religion as conventionally understood, and to
some—Boyle among them—it was tantamount to no real Christianity at all. It is sometimes impossible to know exactly which sectarian ideas and activities Boyle feared, but we do know that for him
the very survival of true religion and Christian society was at stake

in England in 1648-49. And we know this via one of the most im-
probable and hence least explored sources for the study of his
life—the only romance Boyle ever published, *The Martyrdom of
Theodora,* written at precisely this period.[34]

In brief, *Theodora* is about a Christian saint who eventually gives
up her life rather than forswear the faith and worship the pagan
gods of official religion in the Roman empire.[35] As such it is a
thinly disguised allegory about the threats to true religion presented by the alliance between the New Model and the sects at the
moment of its composition.[36] Boyle also intended it in some sense
as a pattern of action in face of the distressing religious situation for
the circle of friends among whom it circulated in manuscript after it
was written. On January 25, 1650, he writes: "As Herbs ev'n after
they are gather'd do still retaine their Medicinall Virtues; so may
Th:[eodora] yet after her Death cure our distemper'd Minds by hir
Example; & prove an Antidote against those Passions & Temptations, she so generously resisted in hir life-time."[37]

Theodora's martyrdom is meant to inspire others to keep the
faith in less extreme and dramatic ways by not succumbing to the
sectaries. In a word, Boyle is preaching passive resistance where
God's laws are in conflict with man's. Boyle states his precise position in these terms: "if we cannot yield an active obedience to the
commands of the civil sovereign, we do not refuse him the utmost
we can consent to, which is passive obedience: and when our consciences permit us not to do those, to us, unlawful things, that he
commands, they enjoin us to suffer unresistedly, whatever penalties he pleases to impose."[38] *Theodora* was not published until 1687,
which is further evidence for interpreting it as politico-religious allegory because it must then have been intended and read as an attack on the Catholic policies of James II. More evidence for the allegorical significance of the work is the following undated remark
found among Boyle's papers: "Whatever Papers be found of mine
relateing to Theodora, I desire may be burnt without fail."[39] Such
probably were Boyle's fears in 1648-49.

The next important evidence we have for Boyle's attitude toward
the sects comes in March and November of 1651 and indicates a
significant change in his thinking. He says now that while the sects
still pose a threat to true religion, its very survival is no longer at

issue. Indeed he suggests that the challenge itself is beneficial: the sectaries' errors incline the godly to discover and spread the truth, and the light of that truth stands out more sharply when set against the darkness of those errors.[40] He has returned to his position of the mid-1640s when the sects did not present to him the threat they later did and when he could thus argue that multiplicity in religious opinion was not bad because it might serve to test and reveal truth and so vanquish error.

Another sign of this shift in Boyle's thinking comes in his attitude toward government. In *Theodora* government is seen as a hostile force which is due no more at best than passive obedience. But sometime between the regicide and the Restoration Boyle wrote a dialogue on government where his view has altered. The precise date of its composition is unknown. But it too expresses the more confident mood for which there is no solid evidence, as we have just seen, before the spring of 1651. Whereas the dialogue, so far as the evidence allows, may have been written at any point between the regicide and the Restoration,[41] it probably does not date from 1649 or early 1650, which is the period to which the defensive mood expressed in *Theodora* applies. Exactly how then does Boyle's attitude toward government in the dialogue differ from his view in *Theodora?* The answer lies in his different views of the relationship between government and sectaries in the two works. In *Theodora* the government is depicted as an enemy of true religion; the implication is, given the work's allegorical nature and the date of its composition, that the government, or more particularly the army, because it represents the radical sects, would undermine Christian society. In the political dialogue, on the other hand, Boyle makes the sects out to be the enemies of government—and of religion, at least by implication. Let us examine the argument.

There are two chief enemies of established authority—the "Macchiavillians" and "the vulgar," a term, which in the context of the dialogue, means the sectaries or the lower orders susceptible to sectarian demagogy. The workings of providence eventually remove the threat of the first sort.[42] But the second, it seems, were not to be so easily undone. Boyle agreed with "the vulgar" that the right to or possession of power does not necessarily confer the ability to use it with wisdom. But he also believed that it is better to trust the one or the few who hold power than for every man to claim, as "the vulgar" themselves do, that he alone can exercise it to best effect.[43] Boyle thought that this was so because he assumed that each man acts as a "free agent" and as such, unless otherwise instructed, pursues his own interests whether consistent with those of the whole or not. Thus, when "the vulgar" take issue with the government, they do so for utterly selfish reasons. Limited in their vision by the blinders of untutored self-interest, they rush on unable to tell whether their aims serve the public good or not—and naked self-interest being what it is, they probably do not.[44] The government having been thus challenged or subverted, if men discover—and they probably will—that their interests have not been served, the situation will continue to deteriorate. Those who feel their interests threatened by this initial challenge or subversion will undertake to challenge or subvert, and so on to chaos.[45]

Not content to rest his case merely upon the grounds of his analysis of what would happen if "the vulgar" prevailed, Boyle gave the government the sanction of religion by suggesting that when men obey, they become eligible to receive "divers peculiar blessings, that God oftentimes vouchsafes to our obedience to his viceregents, and his institutions."[46] Here, as in "The Aretology," the motive of conduct is the opportunity of reward. This, however, is not the same for Boyle as the self-interest of the sectaries. Theirs is reckless, offends providence, and is punished. But the pious and hence certain way of realizing one's interests is, Boyle suggests, by an effort of calculated obedience.

Here is the difference between the dialogue that "treats of Angling improved to spiritual uses" and *Theodora*. In the latter there is no possibility of a calculated obedience. Rather men are obedient only to the extent that when their sovereign's commands violate God's law and they refuse to obey him, their consciences "enjoin" them "to suffer unresistedly, whatever penalties he pleases to impose." In Boyle's political dialogue, on the other hand, the question of the sovereign's violating a higher law has been quietly dropped, along with the concept of passive obedience. Indeed the notion that obedience brings "peculiar blessings" implies that government, all government, works in harmony with divine providence and that obedience ought to be less passive and more positive. The clue to explaining this reversal in Boyle's thinking is provided by what he says in the dialogue about the sectaries and their "vulgar" followers. They are now the enemies of government where in *Theodora* they were identified with it. Boyle's dialogue should thus be read as a rationale for his acquiescing in the government established during the interregnum, when it was written. There may be better governments, and evidence indicates he thought there were,[47] but this one was certainly better than the alternative—that is, giving in to the sects, which would lead to no government at all. He does not preach devotion to the republic but merely acquiescence in it as the lesser evil. He argues not for active support, but for calculated obedience—and with good reason.

As it turned out Boyle's worst fears, expressed allegorically in *Theodora*, were misplaced; the sects did not gain permanent control of the government. Rather their activities were held in check, their programs for the most part went unimplemented, and in the course of the interregnum government grew more and more conservative.[48] Boyle could not have known this when he wrote *Theodora*. Nor could he have foreseen that the government would not only do nothing to damage his interests but would do everything to promote them. The republican army, which he most feared, reconquered Ireland, and the republican government subsequently resettled their Irish estates upon the Boyle family. These were indeed "peculiar blessings" granted in return for Roger's decision to serve under Cromwell in Ireland and Robert's decision to obey the new republican authorities. Boyle's ethic met the test and was confirmed by experience once more: providential rewards followed from the efforts of both brothers at calculated obedience, and *The Martyrdom of Theodora* was shelved until 1687, when it was brought out and dusted off in response to the only other crisis of the century comparable to 1648-49.[49]

## Learning and Revolution

Boyle did not take the government of the republic for ideal. It deserved the subject's obedience. But there were various internal

threats from the sects, "Macchiavillians" and others, whose removal would promote civil and ecclesiastical order. There was also
the problem of the Jews. In the late 1640s and early 1650s men
were beginning to discuss their readmission into England.[50] Some
sectaries felt a certain affinity for the Jews, considering them to be,
like themselves, a part of the elect nation. Readmission would be a
step closer to the ingathering of the saints preparatory to the fulfillment of the millenarian prophecies on which many sectaries
pinned their hopes.[51] Boyle may have been aware of what the
readmission of the Jews meant to the sects. In any case he feared
that if the Jews were free to practice their faith in England

> it may seduce many of those numerous Unprincipled (and
> consequently) Unstable Soules, who having never been sol-
> idly or settledly grounded in the Truth, are equally obnoxious
> to all sorts of Errors: specially in a Time & Country, where
> that Profane Thing call'd Learning is so discountenanc'd, at
> the same time when those Adversarys are admitted; who
> without it will hardly be confuted.[52]

To the sects, learning was "Profane" because it was uninspired,
a product of human effort not directly dependent upon infusions
from above.[53] Boyle's attitude toward learning, however, prompted
him to say, "I do with some confidence expect a Revolution,
whereby Divinity will be much a Looser, & Reall Philosophy
flourish, perhaps beyond men's Hopes."[54] Whereas England in the
interregnum was far from perfect, at least the advancement of
learning was such in 1651 as to lead Boyle to look forward to an
intellectual "Revolution." More than that, learning offered a tool
for the reform of the commonwealth; the impending "Revolution"
in the realm of ideas could promote religious, political, and moral
reformation.[55] Boyle's interests, secured by the outcome of the civil
wars in England and Ireland, and his outlook shaped by the
Hartlib circle, committed him not to the republic as it stood but to
its further reformation. And his studies, both biblical and scientific,
furnished him with the means.

## The Revolution and Natural Wisdom

On August 31, 1649, Boyle wrote to Lady Ranelagh:

> I will not now presume to entertain you with those moral
> speculations, with which my chemical practices have enter-
> tained me; but if this last sickness had not diverted me, I had
> before this presented you with a discourse . . . of the theolog-
> ical use of natural philosophy, endeavouring to make the con-
> templation of the creatures contributory to the instruction of
> the prince & to the glory of the author of them. . . .[56]

The study of nature offers insight by turns into morals, politics,
and divinity. This assumption was at work earlier in Boyle's
thought—in what he said about "pursued Thoughts," in his early
habit of "occasional reflection," and in "The Aretology." For the
source of Boyle's belief in the existence of instructive relations between different orders of being, moreover, one need scarcely look
further than to his reading of the Bible. To Boyle the Scriptures
demonstrated how God used events, natural and political, to teach
men their duty and presage the future.[57] This seventeenth-century
commonplace was an underpinning of his thought. Augmenting
his scriptural sense of the relations between things was his contemporary interest in astrology,[58] the Cabala,[59] and indeed, as his
remarks to Katherine reveal, alchemy itself.[60] From these also
flowed the sense that human destiny is bound up with the order of
nature and that the latter properly approached will reveal something of the former. Boyle's belief in the existence of these relation-
ships is one thing; his understanding of their nature, of the unify-
ing factor or connecting principle, is quite another, and the subject
to which we now turn.

Among the Boyle papers is a manuscript[61] entitled "Of the Study
of the Booke of Nature. For the first Section of my Treatise of Occasional Reflections."[62] Though it is undated, we can piece together a few scraps of evidence to suggest roughly when it was
written. By Janury 25, 1650, Boyle had at least begun and may
have finished among other "Treatises" one called "Occasionall Reflections."[63] Is this "my Treatise of Occasional Reflections" for

which "Of the Study of the Booke of Nature" was to be "the first Section"? Such would appear to be the case, and if so, then Boyle may have only just finished "Occasionall Reflections" by January 25, 1650, because there is a reference in "Of the Study of the Booke of Nature" to a work not published until 1649 or 1650, *The Divine Pymander* translated by John Everard.[64] The last piece of evidence suggesting that "Of the Study . . ." was written in 1649 or shortly thereafter stems from a comparison with Part I of *Some Considerations Touching the Usefulness of Experimental Natural Philosophy*, a large portion of which was written between 1649 and 1654 or 1655.[65] Man of the ideas and references, even particular passages, in the two works are the same.[66] Indeed the whole tone and intent are very similar.

"Of the Study of the Booke of Nature" seems to be an early attempt to elaborate that vision of the harmony between various spheres of reality which he communicated to his sister so cryptically in that letter of August 31, 1649. He makes it clear that the kind of study of nature he is referring to is not the sort that provides more knowledge of physical reality:

> I shall now onely treate of the World, in reference to Reflexions Civil or Divine. . . . Ev'n in these Relations the Study of it is in Learned Persons, neerly ally'd to a Duty, & to all Persons, an Advantage.[67]

Boyle's interest is in what nature tells men about religion and civil affairs. "Nor does the Contemplation of the World only Convince us that God made it; but that he Governs it, not alone bearing Witnesse to his Essence but to his Providence."[68] He then quotes Scripture to support this opinion.

> To skip the Many Passages the Scripture abounds with to countenance this Truth; do not Young Ravens that cry (Ps. 147.9. see Job. 38.41.) wake David's Devotions, & the Sun of David does he not make the Ravens bring food to nurrish the Apostle Fayth, as once they did to feed the Prophet's Body; & make God's feeding of them an Argument of his Care of us: & dos not our Savior crowne Providence with a Garland of Lillys, whilst he employs them to convince his over-anxious

Disciples, of one of the most distrusted peeces of Providence.[69]

Put simply, Boyle is saying that God rewards men's trust, a belief that was a part of the legacy of traditional Christian piety. And in the next paragraph, he adds:

And from this [Providence] there is yet a further Benefitt, Derivable: for as God is infinitely Wise; so his greate Substitute Nature (which is nothing but the active Power & Law by him plac't in the World, & all the Ingredients of it) moves to hir Ends with the compleatest Prudence imaginable. . . .[70]

Boyle does not specify what this "compleatest Prudence imaginable" is. At most his words imply that it is a supernatural means of producing harmony throughout the created order. This interpretation gains support from what he says next. He holds out the possibility of man's emulating nature's "Prudence"—presumably with the same harmonious result:

& had we but the Witt & Curiosity to consider skilfully the Sagacity with which she [nature] foresees stratagems, whereby she declines things offensive [&] . . . steales to the Accomplishment of hir Desseins: & could we but dexterously apply these Observations, to the Conduct of our selves & our Transactions, both in our Private Conditions & Publike Capacitys; we might learne thence as much a solider as innocenter Prudence then from the Bookes of Macchiavell or Tacitus: & have both the honor & Satisfaction; of governing our selves by the same safe Methods, & the same greate Maximes, by which God governs the World. But this sagacity being a Doctrine that supposes a forward Degree of Knowledge, & requires as well as Deserves a long & Circumstantiall Explanation, I shall reserve it, till I be readyer in it, & others riper for it.[71]

Men do not have to restrict themselves to a study of the nonhuman world to acquire such knowledge—observation of man would yield the same. An undated passage in another manuscript, which on the basis of style and handwriting as well as content seems to come from approximately the same period, states:

> There be hid in the Bosome of all humane actions, certain se-
> cret Axioms & Principles of Wisdom, the skill of whose extract-
> ing were possibly worth that of making the so coveted Elixir.
> And there are certain Hints . . . which to discerning Eyes (as
> Plants do to Physitians by their Signatures reveale their Prop-
> ertys;) discloze much of what they conceale. [72]

So far Boyle has been maddeningly cryptic. What are these "secret Axioms & Principles of Wisdom"? The clue may lie in the following passage, which though also undated, again from style, handwrit-ing, and content, appears to come roughly from this period:

> The lives of Ancient Heros much lesse instruct ours, then a
> just contemplation of our owne because of the Disparity both
> betwixt Times & Persons: which dos create so greate Differ-
> ence in Civil Affaires, that the same Action which formerly
> was cry'd up for Gallantry or Prudence, now often passes
> under a quite contrary notion. [73]

In the margin beside this passage Boyle significantly adds, "& how many grosse mistakes the Ignorance of the True Motives & Cir-cumstances dos occasion, in the tru Estimate of actions he must'not be a Machiavel that ignores." Circumstances, Boyle is saying, have altered. Because of this change, the old model for exemplary con-duct no longer holds. "The same Action which formerly was cry'd up for Gallantry or Prudence, now often passes under a quite con-trary notion." What was once gallant or prudent may now be con-sidered precipitate or foolhardy. Taken together with the marginal note, the passage suggests that men must become more calculat-ing. They cannot afford to be too daring. In any given instance they must weigh the prospect of loss against that of gain—the risk against the opportunity—and then take the course that will best serve their interests.

The old aristocratic code, as has been shown, no longer fitted the circumstances. A man's place was not set now by birth and privilege alone, and there were no fixed rewards for specific deeds. A man had to rely upon himself—his own strength and cunning— if he were to survive and prosper in the new order. As Boyle says, "& how many grosse mistakes the Ignorance of the True Motives & Circumstances dos occasion, in the tru Estimate of actions he must not be a Machiavel that ignores." Is Boyle saying then that every man must be "a Machiavel" in the pejorative sense? No, he is not, and this is just the point. The transformation to which Boyle in these quoted passages is witness was the result of the civil wars and regicide. For Boyle the outcome of these events in each case had proved favorable.

In the middle 1640s he had acquired his inheritance in England. The second civil war and regicide, to be sure, had put his family's Irish holdings in jeopardy. But his brother Roger had calculated his and his family's interests, as Robert said men should, and made the correct decision. Roger had gone back to Ireland at the head of an army, even if under Cromwell's general command, rather than going to the Tower. The price of such liberty was high—partial accommodation to a government run by regicides—but with liberty went the prospect of military victory in Ireland, rewarded by the family's repossesion of their Irish patrimony. During the next few years the prospect became a reality, as the rebels were defeated and the family at last obtained their vast Irish estates. As early as December 20, 1649, Boyle by letter from London was asking Broghill, now governor of Munster and immersed in the reduction of the rebels, to keep an eye on the management of "my fortune in your province. . . ."[74]

Robert had not been the victim but in every case the eventual beneficiary of circumstances. He did not exploit them as "the Macchiavillians" did. Indeed, he did not have to, since they consistently turned in his favor almost as a matter of course. So there was no reason for him to think that every man must be "a Machiavel"; quite the contrary, generalizing from his own experience. To his mind, man need only make decisions based on a reckoning of long-range interests, and in time providence would resolve circumstances in his favor. Birth and privilege are no longer equal to the times—in fact they can lead to ruin. Against fortune, prudential calculation is the only sufficient guarantee and is sanctioned as such by the outcome or providential dispensation. In the mid-1640s, while writing "The Aretology," Boyle made a virtue of "necessity." But after the events of 1649, necessity itself had become virtuous.

His cryptic comments respecting "Prudence"—divine and human—become clear now that they can be set and seen within their larger biographical and cultural context. Boyle carried his generalization from experience, the providentialist assumption, so far that he read the pattern not only into human affairs but also into the ordering of the universe. "As God is infinitely Wise; so his greate Substitute Nature (which is nothing but the active Power & Law by him plac't in the World, & all the Ingredients of it) moves to hir Ends with the compleatest Prudence imaginable. . . ." He claimed that, as a result, men could learn the pattern from a study of the creatures and apply it to the conduct of their own affairs. But as has been shown, the source of this pattern lay deep within Boyle's own experience and within his psychic response to and reflection upon this experience. He did not derive the pattern from nature. On the contrary, he imposed it upon, and read it into, the created order as a result of the compelling impression that his particular experience had made upon him.

Boyle's vision should now be clear. One can see how his "chemical practices" could and probably did "entertain" him with "moral speculations" and how he saw "the contemplation of the creatures" as being "contributory to the instruction of the prince and to the glory of the author of them": from the proper study of nature man would learn the prudence that would allow him to enjoy the blessings of providence. His adventures of 1649, of which there is record, and perhaps similar experiences in neighboring years, of which there is no record, prompted him to come to the conclusions about the essential nature of all reality that his remarks of 1649 or thereabouts show that he did. In the absence of other pertinent evidence it seems legitimate to establish a highly plausible connection between Boyle's known experiences of 1649 and these conclusions. Even if this connection should prove unfounded, one would

still have to explain how Boyle arrived at these conclusions, and
the only plausible explanation would require the postulation of experiences like those of 1649 of which there is record.

Boyle's "Of the Study of the Booke of Nature" was not the only
occasion he took to suggest the nonscientific uses of natural
philosophy and to illuminate his understanding of the harmony between truths and the interrelation of different spheres of reality.
Much more important in this regard than the manuscript jottings
we have just considered is "Part I" of *Some Considerations Touching
the Usefulness of Experimental Natural Philosophy.* Written between
1649 and 1654 or 1655, these five essays are perhaps as close as
Boyle ever came to the "discourse . . . of the theological use of
natural philosophy" mentioned in his letter to Katherine in the late
summer of 1649. Many of the themes mentioned in "Of the
Study . . ." are elaborated on in "Part I" of the *Considerations,* and
since the two pieces probably were written during the same period,
we shall refer to the one or both as where relevant.

In "Part I" of *Considerations* Boyle set out to refute those who
claimed that study of the created order leads to preoccupation with
second causes to the neglect or exclusion from consideration of the
first, the Creator himself.[75] On the authority of the Bible, Plutarch,
Cicero, Macrobius, Seneca, Philo,[76] Galen[77] and Clement of
Alexandria,[78] Boyle asserted that nature is a temple and man the
priest. All creatures embody evidence of God's glory. But man
alone enjoys reason enough to witness this evidence and "return
thanks and praises to his Maker," which he does "not only for
himself, but for the whole creation."[79] God thus accomplishes one
of the two ends of the creation, the manifestation of his glory. So
the study of nature, far from being irreligious, is man's primary
duty to God and "the homage we pay for the privilege of
reason."[80] Through such study man also benefits. Not only does
nature supply his wants and appetites, it teaches him virtue and
piety. The benefit of man is God's other aim in the creation; so He
accomplishes both of his ends at once.[81] Viewing the universe as a
temple and man as the priest settles the question of God's purpose
in the creation. Some, in the seventeenth century, said that it was
to manifest his own glory and nothing else; others said that it was

also for the benefit of man.[82] Boyle subscribed to this latter view but argued via the analogy of temple and priest that the two theological positions are not mutually exclusive. Quite the contrary, both imputed purposes are met in the one act of man's contemplation of nature, the two sides in the theological debate are reconciled, and natural philosophy is again understood to serve the faith instead of subverting it.[83]

Boyle's answer to this debate is by no means his main object in adopting his position. Before we can understand his larger intentions, however, we must briefly consider the reservoir of ideas from which they are drawn. In exploiting the analogy of temple and priest he is putting to his own purposes the so-called hermetic tradition.

The basis of this intellectual current was a corpus of forged texts written between 100 and 300 A.D.,[84] but presented to the world as the works of Hermes Trismegistus, an Egyptian priest of remotest antiquity to whom all knowledge and the power or uses of knowledge were revealed.[85] The tradition was revived in the late fifteenth and early sixteenth centuries by the Florentine Platonists Marsilio Ficino and Giovanni Pico, and continued to play a major role in European thought at least until the early eighteenth century.[86] Isaac Casaubon had dated the hermetic texts in 1614 and so demonstrated that Hermetism rested on a myth.[87] But the tradition did not die so easily. Many thinkers, including Boyle, did not know or accept Casaubon's work.[88] Perhaps this is because the promise Hermetism held out was so compelling: if men could but recover the lost wisdom of Hermes all would be revealed and with that knowledge the world could be restored to something like its original purity and harmony. In this regard Hermetism helped to shape the thought of Andreae and Comenius, who in turn were seminal to the Hartlib circle, Boyle included.[89] He knew the tradition through various sources. Besides the ancients already cited, he read Pico and Mornay (who was one of the most important Protestant Hermetists of the sixteenth century)[90] for their Hermetism.[91] And on both he lavished praise.

What use did Boyle make of the tradition for the ideas about man's place in the creation? He picked up and elaborated on the hermetic doctrine that man was created both to contemplate and to

govern God's creatures, the rest of creation being incapable of
doing either.[92] This doctrine exalts man's place in the scheme of
creation,[93] and this high estimate of man's powers, or at least potential powers, comported with Boyle's view that man can serve
himself while serving God. How does Boyle's argument run? Man
is created to celebrate God's power and wisdom as manifested in
the creation. But in order to ensure that man will not neglect this
celebration

> God has furnish't Man with . . . a Multiplicity of Desires; &
> whereas other Creatures are content with those few obvious
> & easily attainable Necessarys that Nature has almost every
> where provided for them; In man alone every sense has
> numerous greedy Appetites, for the most part for superfluitys
> & Daintys; that for the satisfaction of all these various Desires,
> he might be oblig'd with an inquisitive Industry & range,
> anatomize & ransacke Nature & by that concern'd survey
> come to a more exquisite Knowledge of the Workes of it; &
> consequently to a profounder Admiration of the Omniscient
> Author.[94]

The more one studies nature the more pious one becomes, and the
more pious the readier to celebrate God's glory: according to "Mercurius Trismegistus," "There can be no Religion more true or Just
then to know the things that are; & to acknowledge thanks for all
things to him that made them; which thing [Boyle adds] I shall not
cease continually to do."[95]

Via Hermetism Boyle accomplishes two things. First, he assimi-
lates the study of second causes to the worship of God, the first
cause—natural philosophy to religion. Second, and more significant, he uses Hermetism to reconcile material self-interest to piety:
through the study of nature man worships God while gratifying
his "numerous greedy Appetites, for the most part for superfluitys
& Daintys." Piety and acquisitiveness are met in natural
philosophy, and the baser is transmuted into the nobler in a kind
of spiritual alchemy. Of course the engine of the whole process is
not spirit but appetite. This is Boyle's twist on Hermetism rendered
to serve his peculiar ideological and psychic requirements. But the

twist is hidden—even perhaps from Boyle—in the luxuriance and seeming loftiness of hermetic doctrine. Hermetically and superficially, greed has been sublimated into godliness. That, however, is doublethink. Actually godliness has been made to run on gain. The hermetic tradition may have been passed on to Boyle in part via Andreae, Comenius, and the Hartlib circle, but the particular uses to which Boyle put hermetic doctrine were as much a response to his own experience as they were the result of his participation in a more general intellectual movement.

In Boyle's hands the hermetic doctrine of God's two purposes in creation performed yet another ideological function. To the extent that man plays his part in fulfilling these purposes, Boyle argued, he will answer the four real enemies of true religion—indolent gentry, "Macchiavillians," sectaries, and philosophical heretics. Boyle thus stood the case of the detractors of natural philosophy on its head. Not only is the study of nature not irreligious; it is itself the best defense against irreligion. Wherein does this study consist and how would it overcome the fourfold threat to true religion?

First, there was the problem of the indolent gentry that Boyle dealt with in "The Aretology." Now he claimed them to be "lulled asleep by custom and sensuality."[96] "Custom" had restricted their "Acts of Devotion to the Begging of Blessings from God, and returning them to Him in the Person of one's Neighbor"[97]—that is, traditional piety and charity. This was acceptable as far as it went. But God's mercy is not his only perfection. There are also his wisdom and power, "for whose Manifesting he was pleased to construct this vast Fabricke."[98] These attributes had "exacted both Men and Angell's Adoration, before they needed" his mercy. To Boyle "it appears something selfish and to imply an injurious Disparity betwixt Perfections, all equall because all Infinite, to let God's Mercy . . . engrosse our Thoughts," to the neglect of his other attributes.[99] Men should thus also worship God through the contemplation of his creatures. Boyle went on to suggest that gentlemen should devote a portion of the Sabbath to such contemplation, supporting his case by an appeal to Mosaical authority.[100]

Besides the impediment of "custom," there was that of "sensuality." Left to themselves, men take the line of least resistance. Because of their superior faculties they can delight in observing the created order without the slightest exertion. "The bare beholding of this admirable structure, is capable of pleasing men. . . ."[101] Anything more requires application. At this point "sensuality" takes over in many, and they refuse to make the effort. Boyle replied, "if we (contenting ourselves with the superficial account given us of things by their obvious appearances and qualities) are beholden for that we know, to our nature, not our industry, we faultily lose both one of the noblest imployments, and one of the highest satisfactions of our rational faculty."[102]

In the study of the creatures Boyle found an alternative to indolence. Second, he provided the same alternative to the pursuits of "the Macchiavillians." As he had affirmed in his "Aretology," their preoccupation was with the acquisition of fame and power regardless of the consequences. Boyle now claimed that if they were successful, it was due not to their knowledge but to their birth and fortune. Such success could give them neither honor nor contentment—not honor because their positions rested less upon anything they themselves had designed and accomplished than upon circumstances beyond their control; not contentment because circumstances change and foil the successful—knowing this, they could not possibly enjoy any peace of mind. In essence they could take satisfaction neither in what had already happened nor in what was going to happen. True honor and contentment come, Boyle suggested, not from the pursuit of fame and power but from the study and knowledge of the creatures,[103] because natural philosophy teaches men the ways of God and how to live accordingly. "We might learne thence as much a solider as innocenter Prudence then from the Bookes of Machiavell. . . ."[104] So Boyle's answer to the threat of "the Macchiavillians" was the same as his advice to the indolent: to apply oneself to the investigation of the world, to the performance of one's priestly function, the role to which God has assigned man, in the temple of nature. The reward will follow—a life proportioned to divine providence and a deep and permanent happiness as distinct from the one, hollow and tenuous, that fortune holds out.

Third, there was the problem of the sectaries, again, who believed that learning is not to be trusted because it is the work of corrupt man. For Boyle, of course, learning was the engine of reformation. The sects claimed that learning, besides being tainted, is unnecessary. God speaks directly to his saints and thus reveals to them the truths of things.[105] Thus, men can dispense with human learning and let divine illumination be their guide. Such a view makes each man's private vision the measure of wisdom. The political and social implications of this view disturbed Boyle in *Seraphic Love* and in his defense of the republic against "the vulgar," already examined. In the early 1650s when he wrote the essays in hand, these implications were anything but academic. On the basis of their claims to divine inspiration many sectaries, some in high places, preached an imminent millennium amounting to one form of radical revolution or another.[106] This situation posed a threat to the existing order. So Boyle's judgment and interests, realized under and protected by that order, led him again to oppose its sectarian challengers. He said to them as to the indolent and "the Macchiavillians" that knowledge is the product of industry, of the sustained exertion of intelligence, of the application of reason to the observation of the creatures. Visions, he suggested, generate an excitement in their subject detrimental to his understanding.[107]

Here again Boyle enlisted the hermetic tradition in support of his position.[108] Only Hermes Trismegistus had possessed the full hermetic wisdom. All subsequent philosophies were supposed to have been derivative of this source and as such to have been nothing better than pale copies and partial glimpses of the whole truth.[109] Boyle assumed in his use of the tradition that the early Hebrews possessed something like the complete hermetic wisdom.[110] The ancient Egyptians, according to Josephus, learned true "astronomy and philosophy" from Abraham. Later, Aristotle, according to other "Jewish authors," borrowed from Solomon's "matchless records of nature." Since then much of Aristotle's natural philosophy had been lost. Boyle offered an explanation. The missing Aristotle is what he took from Solomon and as such represents the true philosophy of nature revealed by God to the leaders of his chosen people. He may have caused such wisdom to be lost as a part of his conscious design. Boyle wrote:

Providence perhaps deprived the world . . . , upon such a score, as it did the Jews of the body of Moses, lest men

should idolise it, or as some Rabbies are pleased to inform us,
lest vicious men should venture upon all kinds of intemper-
ance, out of confidence of finding out by help of those excellent writings the cure of all the distempers their dissoluteness
should produce.[111]

Neither visions nor revelations from on high, therefore, would
bring knowledge befitting a true Christian: visions impair understanding, and divine revelation, though affording complete comprehension, would for that reason tempt men to lives of sin.

Boyle's way, on the other hand, the way of reason and industry,
is not open to attack upon either of these grounds—quite the contrary. First, the man who conditions himself to Boyle's way will be
less given to excitement than the visionary and so less susceptible
of any impairment of his understanding. Second, the sustained
application of intelligence to a searching inquiry into nature will itself make a man virtuous. Negatively the very labor of the search
will keep a man from vice. Positively the inquiry will reveal more
and more evidence of God in the creatures and so cannot help but
have a morally and spiritually beneficial effect. A man will thus
grow so piously conditioned that when he makes discoveries, such
as cures, he will regard them not as inducements to vice where-
with to patch up "the distempers" that future "dissoluteness should
produce" but instead as gifts of God or at most rewards of virtue.

It is curious that Boyle used the hermetic tradition to support his
position, because certain sectaries did the same.[112] The hermetic
tradition obviously was capable of various, even contrary interpretations. In the case of the sectaries it fitted their view that God
gives his saints the benefit of immediate revelations. If so, then
what would keep them from regaining the wisdom of Hermes not
by hard labor and "Profane" learning, but by divine inspiration?
Nothing, as long as one accepted their premise, which Boyle and
other social conservatives[113] did not. In this regard Boyle may have
appropriated the tradition to his own purposes partly in an effort
to steal the sectaries' hermetic thunder. There is some evidence for
such a view.

One of Boyle's chief sources for the tradition was *The Divine Py-*

*mander,* translated by John Everard[114] and published in London
in 1649 or 1650, the same time that Boyle began writing his own
hermetic natural philosophy. Everard's view, moreover, of the relative merits of learning and divine inspiration as means to truth was
precisely that of the sectaries which Boyle was attacking,[115] Everard
himself having been "haled before High Commission in 1639 for
familism, antinomianism and anabaptism and fined a thousand
pounds."[116] Boyle cites Everard's translation in his own hermetic
writings undertaken shortly after it came out.[117] But these citations
are not to denounce Everard's "sectarian" or inspirational Hermetism. Indeed the fact that Everard's views are associated with
the sects is never mentioned. Either Boyle did not know that
Everard's views were sectarian (after all, *The Divine Pymander* was
only a translation and not a statement of Everard's own religious
opinions), or else he chose to put the Hermetism of *Pymander* to a
quite different purpose from the one Everard intended—to support
his own theology of works rather than Everard's theology of
inspiration—and to do so and not tell his reader. The latter interpretation seems likely because it is difficult if not impossible to
believe that Boyle knew *The Divine Pymander* without knowing
about its translator who had been for more than a decade a prominent, indeed infamous, London preacher.[118]

A sectary might have argued that Boyle's way to knowledge
makes a man rely for understanding upon himself alone and that
therefore his own way was more godly, because he depended, instead, upon divine illumination. Boyle's position, however, precluded such an argument: just as natural philosophy can deepen
piety, so God can reward such piety in a man by furthering his
understanding of nature. God's contribution, to be sure, does not
come in the form of a sudden and total revelation of nature's
secrets—as this might produce undesirable consequences. Boyle
wrote, for instance, "I dare not affirm, with some of the Helmontians and Paracelsians, that God discloses to men the great mystery
of chemistry by good angels, or by nocturnal visions. . . ."[119] Boyle
said "some," not all, "Helmontians and Paracelsians" because he,
too, used the work of Paracelsus and J. B. van Helmont in his own
chemical studies.[120] Who then were the ones from whom Boyle
was dissociating himself? They would seem to have bee ɪ the sec-

taries again whose view that knowledge is a matter of visions and divine revelations derived from, among other sources, the works of Paracelsus and van Helmont.[121]

Evidence suggests that in taking this position Boyle was answering Thomas Vaughan, a contemporary Hermetist who believed that through divine illumination men can arrive at a complete comprehension of the universe.[122] Vaughan himself was not a sectary.[123] But his views were similar to those of some sects, and Henry More, for instance, attacked Vaughan's works in order "to admonish others of their fanaticalness and folly."[124] So God does not furnish synoptic visions of the nature of all reality but does contribute in less direct and immediate ways, by protecting men's experiments from "unlucky accidents" and by providing shortcuts and "pregnant hints" leading to fruitful conclusions, to a proper inquiry into nature.[125] These divine services do not so much supplant as foster Boyle's way of proceeding in the study of nature via reason and industry. How can God do otherwise, when reason and industry, not visions and revelations, are what make and keep men virtuous?

Boyle answered sectaries, "Macchiavillians," and indolent gentry alike by calling for the sober pursuit of natural philosophy. Only by applying intelligence and industry to the study of nature can men at once gratify their material desires and fulfill their duty to God. His answer to the three forementioned enemies of learning and piety was that the proper study of nature consists in employing correct procedures. His answer, in short, lies in methodological considerations. This constitutes another part of the ideological background to Boyle's insistence on experiment as the key to science and to his devotion to working out an "experimental philosophy."

The fourth threat was that of philosophical heretics who might be either Aristotelian or Epicurean. Boyle's answer to them does not lie in the argument for proper method which he used against the other three. Rather, against this threat he argues for a certain theory of nature. The signal consideration is no longer method but content. He undertook to develop this argument in "Essay IV. Containing a requisite Digression concerning those, that exclude the Deity from inter-meddling with Matter." This essay represents his first unequivocal affirmation of the ideas that were to be the basis of his scientific work. They consisted of a particulate theory of matter that was treated as an hypothesis to be tested by experiment.[126] The strictly technical and intellectual origins and aspects of these ideas, Boyle's so-called corpuscular philosophy, have been dealt with elsewhere.[127] But the full story of his adoption of these ideas has not been told because it has not been seen how they comported with his contemporary religious and ideological position. How then did Boyle's corpuscular philosophy not only explain the phenomena but do so in such a way as at least at the outset to serve an ideological function? An answer to this question emerges from "Essay IV" where Boyle treated contemporary Aristotelians and Epicureans, who claimed "to be able to explicate the first *beginning of things* and the world's phenomena, without taking in, or acknowledging any divine Author of it."[128]

Those who followed Aristotle in this regard said "that if a man put one end of a long reed into a vessel full of water, and suck at the other end, . . . the suction drawing the air out of the cavity of the reed, the water must necessarily succeed in the place deserted by the air, to prevent a vacuity abhorred by nature."[129] This explanation, Boyle said,

> supposes that there is a kind of *anima mundi*, furnished with various passions, which watchfully provides for the safety of the universe; or that a brute and inanimate creature, as water, not only has a power to move its heavy body upwards, contrary (to speak in their language) to the tendency of its particular nature, but knows both that unless it succeed the attracted air, there will follow a vacuum; and that this water is withal so generous, as by ascending, to act contrary to its particular inclination for the general good of the universe, like a noble patriot, that sacrifices his private interests to the publick ones of his country.[130]

But to claim that irrational creatures are capable of such reason and virtue is, Boyle said, to put them on a par with man.[131] Worse than this, since such creatures are not possessed of rational and

hence immortal souls and yet can do everything that man is supposed to be able to do by reason of his immortal soul, the implication is that he does not have one either.[132] So Boyle objected to
this Aristotelian position in the last analysis because it leads logically to a denial of the immortality of the human soul as conventionally understood.

No doubt his objection was whetted by the fact that such a denial based upon arguments like those of the Aristotelians was current among religious and political radicals during the 1640s and
1650s,[133] the obvious examples being Milton and Richard Overton,
the Leveller leader.[134] Neither Milton nor Overton was an atheist.
But less radical thinkers saw a threat of atheism or at least of disorder in the mortalist's position. If men came to believe that the
soul is mortal, conventional religion would lose one of its strongest
sanctions. What differences does it make what one does in this life,
if the individual soul does not survive intact into the next, there to
receive its just deserts? This attitude would leave the door open to
every form of vice and rebellion. Of course Boyle would oppose
such a view that would undermine his ethic of rewards and
punishments and so give "Macchiavillians" and sectaries a free
hand.

Respecting the latter, he may have had the Digger Gerrard
Winstanley's views, or views like his, specifically in mind.
Winstanley was a materialistic pantheist who held that God insofar
as man can know him is immanent in the universe and that divine
reason pervades all creation. This closely resembles, if it is not
identical with, the view Boyle is attacking that the world runs on a
rational animism innate in every creature. If Boyle was thinking of
Winstanley, then he had more than the threat of mortalism,
atheism, and disorder on his mind, because Winstanley's
materialism was of a piece with his Digger radicalism, which was
of the extremest sort.[135]

Boyle's corpuscular philosophy offered an alternative, avoiding
any mortalistic implications, to Aristotelian explanations. The rising
of fluid in a tube when one end is sucked and the other immersed
in the liquid is due not to "nature's detestation of a vacuity" but to
strictly material factors—"the pressure of the air (against the liquors
and the sucker's chest) and their respective measures of gravity
and lightness compared to that pressure. . . ."[136] This and similar

explanations of other phenomena led Boyle, in the same essay, to adopt his corpuscular theory of matter:

> methinks we may, without absurdity, conceive, that God, . . . having resolved before the creation, to make such a world as this of ours, did divide (at least if he did not create it incoherent) that matter, which he had provided, into an innumerable multitude of very variously figured corpuscles, and both connected these particles into such textures or particular bodies, and placed them in such situations, and put them into such motions, that by the assistance of his ordinary preserving concourse, the phaenomena, which he intended should appear in the universe, must as orderly follow, and be exhibited by the bodies necessarily acting according to those impressions or laws, though they understand them not at all, as if each of those creatures had a design of self-preservation, and were furnished with knowledge and industry to prosecute it; and as if there were diffused through the universe an intelligent being, watchful over the publick good of it, and careful to administer all things wisely for the good of the particular parts of it, but so far forth as is consistent with the good of the whole. . . .[137]

The creatures behave "as if each . . . had a design of self-preservation, and were furnished with knowledge and industry to prosecute it. . . ." But it is really God who makes them do so, and the immortality of the human soul is thus preserved.

By making God the origin of motion in "(most of) the . . . phaenomena of nature" excluding man, Boyle also answered "the modern admirers of Epicurus." Although he adopted their atomic conception of matter, he refused to accept their view, which excluded God from the creation and government of the world, that motion is inherent in the atoms.[138]

The proper study of nature, according to Boyle, would diminish if not eliminate all threats. But more positively, what sort of order would this study produce, while counteracting the enemy? Boyle suggested that the creatures teach men the same lesson as the Bible, because

not content to have provided him [man] all, that was requisite
either to support or accommodate him here, he [God] hath
been pleased to contrive the world so, that . . . it may afford
him not only necessaries and delights, but instructions too.
For each page in the great volume of nature is full of real
hieroglyphicks, where (by an inverted way of expression)
things stand for words, and their qualities for letters.[139]

In fact a knowledge of God's works is often necessary to a proper
understanding of his word, "the Scripture being so full of allusions
to and comparisons borrowed from the properties of the creatures,
that there are many texts not clearly intelligible without some
knowledge of them. . . ."[140] The most important instance to
Boyle's mind of the function of the creatures in this regard is the
light they shed for man upon divine providence and human prudence. Indeed, the Scriptures tell man to go to nature for instruction in both of these crucial matters:

> Christ commands his disciples to *learn of serpents and pigeons*
> prudence and inoffensiveness. The same divine teacher en-
> joins his apostles to consider the lillies, or (as some would
> have it) the *tulips of the field,* and to learn thence that difficult
> virtue of a distrustless reliance upon God.[141]

What is most interesting and significant is the lesson Boyle
learned from "serpents and pigeons," when he supposedly did go
to nature and observe them. The serpent is wise, the dove "harmless" or innocent. The serpent's wisdom consists in "a serpentine
wariness in declining dangers"; the dove's innocence, in "not alone
an inoffensiveness toward others . . . but also as harmless a way of
escaping the dangers they are actually ingaged in, as that of doves,
who being pursued by birds of prey, endeavour to save themselves
not by fight, but only by flight."[142] The serpent's wisdom, in other
words, equals the dove's harmlessness. Where the dove's
harmlessness is wise, the serpent's cunning is innocent. Both creatures act out of an instinct for self-preservation, when it comes to
"declining dangers." The dove especially manifests to man the
value of rational calculation. Against fierce "birds of prey" the gen-

tle dove is not a match. So in such a case the creature endeavours to save itself "not by fight, but only by flight." The dove and serpent then are images or types of prudence. As such, Boyle said, "our great Master" recommends them "to his disciples."[143]

Boyle might well have made the example of "serpents and pigeons" the most important light that nature sheds upon Scripture. The biblical lesson that might be learned from the dove and the serpent is that men need only make rational calculations on the basis of what they take to be their long-run interests, act accordingly, and trust in providence to do the rest.

The other virtue that nature can teach preparatory to the establishment of a Christian commonwealth is "a provident industry"[144]—something which "The Aretology" had also prescribed. Certain creatures display a diligence that man would do well to imitate.[145] The proper study of the creatures also, as we have seen, demands industrious application. Such efforts in these directions as man chooses to expend will indeed be highly "provident." The upshot of Boyle's ethic is a "provident" meliorism: a man who pursues his aims with industry and prudence and entrusts the outcome to providence can be certain of ultimate success.

In the case of an industrious inquiry into nature, there is a threefold reward. First, there is an increase in useful knowledge.[146] Second, there is an improvement in man's moral and spiritual condition because such an inquiry enhances piety by revealing to man evidence of God and ways to bring human affairs into harmony with the natural and providential order of things. Third, Boyle suggested that the proper study of nature bridges religious and political divisions among men. It knows no boundaries and draws support, as Boyle showed in his treatment of the hermetic tradition, from all religions.[147] And because "it is the first act of religion, and equally obliging in all religions," performance of this obligation should take precedence over that of any other. Too often, however, the reverse is the case,

> Which makes me somewhat angry with them, who so busy themselves in the duties and imployments of their second and superinduced relations, that they will never find the leisure to discharge that primitive and natural obligation, who are more

concerned as citizens of any place, than of the world; and
both worship God so barely as Catholick or Protestants,
Anabaptists or Socinians, and live so wholly as lords or coun-
sellors, Londoners or Parisians, that they will never find the
leisure, or consider not, that it concerns them to worship and
live as men . . .[148]

The suggestion is that what men have in common in the way of
this primary obligation to acknowledge God's glory through the
proper study of nature is much more conducive to their happiness
both here and hereafter than the things that divide them—perhaps
because such study is what overcomes these divisions. The assumption in the Comenian and Andreaen pansophies to which
Boyle was heir was that the discovery of the true knowledge of nature would lead to the fulfilment of the reformation and the establishment of peace, prosperity, and good government. Boyle subscribed to such a view in his "Aretology." But here he is making
the connection between his natural philosophy and irenism more
specific. The prudence nature teaches, the practical uses she yields,
and the discipline she requires if men are to master her secrets—all
of these should induce men to settle their religious and political
differences, to pool their talents in the study of nature, and to worship God through such study that would amount to a common
faith, a natural religion devoid of dissension.

### The Revolution and Scriptural Wisdom

Besides *Some Considerations Touching the Usefulness of Experimental
Natural Philosophy,* Boyle wrote during the same period, in 1651
and 1652, *Some Considerations Touching the Style of the Holy Scriptures.*[149] The views he develops in this latter work are consistent
with those of the former. In "Part I" of the *Usefulness* Boyle argues
the premise implicit in Christian Hermetism of the harmony of biblical and natural truth and accepts the view of Sir Francis Bacon[150]
as developed in *The Advancement of Learning* that theology and
natural philosophy are complementary. Boyle went on to say that
both God's word and his works, when properly studied, reveal the

same truths.[151] Indeed, Boyle shows in the example of the doves and serpents how nature can elucidate Scripture. It should not surprise us, therefore, that the Scripture-based religion Boyle argues for in the *Style* turns out to be the same as the nature-based philosophical religion of "Part I" of the *Considerations*.

True religion rests on "the doctrine of the gospel, together with the light of nature, (which it excludes not, but rather supposes) . . . ."[152] The one confirms the other and vice versa.[153] A signal instance of this harmony of truths lies in the very design of nature and Scripture. In their complexity and beauty they both reveal that they could be the work of no lesser agency than the divine wisdom.[154] The study of nature and Scripture alike teaches industry, patience, and humility. Only by the exercise of such virtues can men come to understand the intricacy of God's word and work.[155] There is no room in either kind of study for the lazy or the glib. Scripture and nature have this too in common: they both produce an irenical effect. We have seen Boyle argue for an irenism implicit in the proper study of nature. In the *Style* he says the same for scriptural study. By concentrating on an appreciation of the holy texts themselves, men can be led to put out of their minds the doctrinal issues that divide them and to find the ground for a common faith.[156]

Another benefit that Scripture, like nature, furnishes to men is instruction in the art of government. The Bible offers the only reliable political advice because its authors, being divinely inspired, could penetrate the secret counsels of state where ordinary commentators cannot.[157] Good government, on the whole, is informed by scriptural religion. It humbles the mighty before the governor of the universe,[158] and it furnishes to them the instructive model of God's perfect government.[159] Boyle may have been thinking here that Scripture teaches the same prudence that, as he has said elsewhere during this period, nature does, though he does not make this connection explicit.[160] But this small point does not gainsay our argument. We have established that nature and Scripture teach most of the same virtues. Not only is there a harmony between biblical and philosophical truths but these truths, whether derived from God's word or his work, are instructive: they provide

the grounding for moral, political, and religious reformation as well
as personal salvation.

Boyle had several things to say about the specific nature of this
reformation. It would not come through human effort, but rather
by divine fiat. Man's part was to prepare and live expectantly for it;
God's was to perform it.[161] The ensuing earthly order would be
one in which morality, government, and religion would be per-
fected; that is, the virtues exemplified in nature and Scripture
would be universally known and practiced. All men would be
sober, prudent, industrious Christians;[162] those for whom it was
possible would be assiduous students of nature and Scripture;[163]
learning would flourish and its fruits abound.[164] Rulers would take
their lessons from nature and Scripture and would be at once
humble and effective, wise and innocent, doves and serpents.[165] In
religion the irenic ideal would be accomplished.[166] The study of
God's word and work would bring men together in a common undertaking; the lessons learned there would unite them further and
their preoccupation with such pursuits would lead them to forget
their differences or at least to submerge them in favor of the better
things that united them. The new order would deal with Boyle's
now familiar enemies. The gentry and "the grandees" or "Macchiavillians" would be reformed: they would become the devoted
students of religion and natural philosophy, a revived hermetic
priesthood.[167] Sectaries, antiscripturists,[168] and atheists would be
punished severely; the intimation is that they would be weeded
out by the hand of God.[169] In all it would be a sober Jerusalem,
reflecting the morality Boyle had worked out over the previous six
or seven years.

The change, he believed, was imminent. The evidence in the
*Style,* where he reveals the most about the nature of the new order,
is slight on the question of when the change will occur. He may
not have wished to commit himself to a date in anything that
might be made public. The closest he comes in the *Style* is to refer
to "less licentious and more discerning times, (which may be,
perhaps, approaching) . . . ."[170] But this is hardly a firm prediction
of the future. Elsewhere, however, he is more positive. We have
already noticed in his letters to John Mallet of late 1651 and early
1652, which is precisely the time that the bulk of the *Style* was writ-

ten, that he is expectant of an imminent "Revolution, whereby Divinity will be much a Looser, & Reall Philosophy flourish, perhaps beyond men's Hopes."[171] This notion of a "Revolution" seems remarkably close to the idea, developed in the *Style,* of a new order established by God whose main feature would be the sober and sobering pursuit of true philosophy and religion.

Boyle was not alone in his hopes for some such imminent "Revolution"; he shared them with Mallet[172] and intended to discuss them with him the next time he saw him.[173] They shared especially an enthusiasm for biblical study. Boyle persuaded his friend to devote himself to "that heavenly Employment."[174] And in March 1652 Boyle promised "to digest and transcribe my thoughts concerning the Scripture" and send them to Mallet in response to his "Commands."[175] Among these "thoughts" may have been the *Style,* which was finished around this time. Strengthening this possibility is the fact that Boyle claims to have written "these papers, with others (that I yet suppress)" at the desire of one Theophilus.[176] He is not further identified, except that he is said to have been the friend of both Robert and Roger.[177] The evidence suggests, however, that Theophilus is Mallet. If such is the case, then Mallet knew the *Style.* It follows that the hypothetical identification of the imminent "Revolution" of which Boyle writes to Mallet with the reformation adumbrated in the *Style* can be more solidly grounded. Hence, it can be argued that Boyle believed the establishment of the new order itself to be imminent.

There is a letter which almost clinches the case and at the same time adds another dimension. Boyle and his sister Katherine shared belief in an imminent apocalypse, when, as she wrote him, "all this old frame of heaven and earth must pass and a new one be set up in its place. . . ." In the same letter she wrote of new "signs" of the coming transformation and revealed that Robert himself believed at the time that it would happen some seven years hence.[178] Although the year of the letter is not recorded, evidence indicates that it was written in the early 1650s, while Boyle was in Ireland,[179] which would make it contemporary with the *Style* and his correspondence with Mallet on the coming "Revolution." This revolution, it now appears in the light of Katherine's letter, would seem to consist in an apocalypse and ensuing millennium. If so, one thing is certain from what we know: Boyle's version of a widely anticipated new heaven and earth was quite different from that of the sectaries whom he was attacking.

This is not to say, however, that others besides Mallet and Boyle's sister did not share similar views. Broghill saw the *Style* in manuscript in 1653 or 1654 and gave Robert permission to dedicate it to him should it ever be published.[180] This would indicate that he accepted its content. What Robert had to say about Christian unity would almost certainly have struck a sympathetic chord in his brother in 1654 if not before.

In that year, during the first months of the Protectorate, Broghill was one of the leading advocates of ecclesiastical comprehension[181] and an important member of the committee appointed to find a workable formula to that end.[182] Each member of that committee could name a clerical adviser. Broghill first asked Dr. James Usher, archbishop of Armagh before the destruction of prelacy, but Usher refused; he then named Richard Baxter.[183] Baxter's religious opinions must have been close to his patron's own. Broghill went to Baxter's sermons[184] and arranged for him to preach on an ecumenical theme before Oliver Cromwell.[185] Broghill especially approved Baxter's efforts to found religion on the Bible by offering rational arguments to prove the Scriptures to be the word of God. Broghill was so taken with Baxter's work in this direction published in "The Second Part" of *The Saints Everlasting Rest* (1650) that he encouraged him to elaborate on the ideas presented there in another discourse. Baxter complied in *The Unreasonableness of Infidelity*, published in 1655, and dedicated to Broghill.[186]

In this work one can see that Broghill's religious opinions, as expressed by Baxter, coincided with many of Robert's views. Baxter seeks Christian unity via study of the Bible and of nature. God's word and his work convey the same message.[187] But it will not do to read the word and ignore the work as some sectaries do, claiming that Scripture alone speaks with divine authority while natural philosophy relies on corrupt human intelligence.[188] Baxter will not have this; his purpose being Christian unity in England, he has chosen as the appropriate instrument not the abrasive fideism of the sects but the healing irenic doctrine of the harmony or unity of truths. Fideism, moreover, is too close to the sectarian emphasis on divine inspiration or in Baxter's phrase "the sufficiency of the Spirit."[189] For those who cherish this view, study and "humane learning" are superfluous at least, if not pernicious; each man's private judgment becomes the measure of wisdom. This would destroy any hope of church unity.[190] Worse still, it would allow the uneducated to read into Scripture whatever heresies served their fancies and so tend to the undoing of religion and society.[191] Indeed, such persons might go so far as to reject Scripture itself as "but the Letter"[192] and to rely on what they regarded as their own direct pipelines to God.[193]

For Baxter[194] and Boyle,[195] the only adequate defense against these errors lay in maintaining that "the scripture is the word of God."[196] To prove this they argued for two things: the necessity of painstaking biblical scholarship and the harmony of natural and scriptural truths. Scholarship would invalidate the shallow arguments of antiscripturists, and inquiry into nature would confirm biblical accounts, properly understood. All men could then agree on the divine origin of the Bible, and that tenet would become the basis of religious unity in England. As Broghill's parliamentary committee and their clerical advisers were charged with the task of finding a formula for unity,[197] and as he favored Baxter's writings in which he claimed to have found such a formula in the doctrine of the divine origin of Scripture, it seems fair to say that this doctrine probably constituted such a formula for Broghill too. Since Baxter's doctrine was the same as the one Boyle enunciated in the *Style*, it is no wonder then that Broghill permitted his brother to dedicate that work to him. They must have shared many of the views expressed therein. Boyle's thought, like Baxter's, no doubt played a part in shaping the religious opinions of his brother Roger, one of Cromwell's chief advisers who was at the same time in the forefront of official efforts during the Protectorate to find a framework for religious peace first, as we have seen, in England in late 1654 and 1655 and then in Scotland in 1656.[198]

There is one more connection between Roger's ideas and those of his brother. Dr. James Usher, whom Roger first nominated to serve as his adviser on the parliamentary committee for working out a religious settlement in England in 1654-55, figured in the irenic efforts of both brothers. Usher's model of church government seems to have served as a basis of the schemes Roger put forward at the time.[199] It was also the plan Boyle advocated for the settlement of religion at the Restoration[200] and probably long before. As he said in his "Essay on the Scripture,"[201] which was never published *in toto* but from which the *Style* was extracted for publication,[202] Usher "much engaged me to the study of the holy tongues,"[203] a task both men undertook for irenic purposes.[204] Both Roger and Robert knew Usher personally.[205] He had been a close associate of their father, and from the 1630s on he was a friend and patron of Hartlib and Dury. There were probably numerous occasions in the late 1640s and early 1650s until Usher's death in 1656 when he could work his influence on one or the other brother. The three of them may have even have met from time to time in London.

Just as Boyle's views on irenical religion in the *Style* were shared by others, so was his millenarianism. Mallet and Boyle's sister Katherine shared this belief, but there were also others in Katherine's circle with similar views. Perhaps the most interesting one was Henry Oldenburg, who came to England in June 1653 as an official representative of Bremen, the city where he had been born and raised, to the new English government.[206] Evidence suggests that by May 6, 1655, he may have become sufficiently acquainted with Lady Ranelagh to be corresponding with her about fundamental questions of personal religious belief.[207] Certainly by March of the next year he seems to have known her brother as well,[208] and the first extant letter in a long correspondence between Boyle and Oldenburg is dated April 15, 1657.[209] In 1656 and 1657[210] Oldenburg was in correspondence with Lady Ranelagh[211] about the coming new heaven and earth. She saw Cromwell as God's agent in the building of a Protestant union preparatory to the destruction of those traditional embodiments for Protestants of antichrist, empire and papacy,[212] and the establishment of a new world order under God.[213] Oldenburg shared these views. He copied and saved extracts from her letters about these matters and during the same period wrote to Hartlib,[214] Boyle, and others[215] on the same themes. He looked forward to a Protestant union,[216] and the collapse of the Catholic powers which for him too signified the anti-

christ.[217] To Boyle he wrote, "the continued success of the Protector is an evident sign that Heaven has some extraordinary task
for him."[218] The context of the letter makes it clear that the "task"
Oldenburg had in mind for Cromwell was the one Katherine also
set for him. Oldenburg, moreover, was enthusiastic about John
Dury's mission to the Continent.[219] Cromwell sent him beginning
in 1654 to Switzerland, the Rhineland, and the Netherlands to
open negotiations for a European union of Protestant churches.[220]
This was interpreted by Dury[221] and Oldenburg[222] as being one
more step in preparation for the triumph of Protestantism over
Catholicism and the coming of a new world order.

Boyle and his sister were close friends of Dury in the 1650s and
shared such sentiments with him. All four—Boyle, his sister, Dury,
and Oldenburg—held what was a widely current view[223] that England in the 1650s stood poised for the fulfilment of the reformation
in what would amount to a new heaven and earth. But not all who
thought this agreed on the nature of the order that would follow
the destruction of the Beast. Many sectaries conceived of the
apocalypse as constituting one form or another of social upheaval
in which the world would be, to use the phrase of the foremost
historian of the subject, "turned upside down."[224] But for Boyle's
circle the hoped-for transformation did not imply radical social revolution. Indeed, there had already been too much of that to suit
Boyle's taste. Instead, the change would be in the nature of an intellectual, moral, and spiritual reformation, a reform of conduct
and not of institutions, something akin to what Boyle intimated in
the *Style,* his letters to Mallet, and elsewhere.

Certain things had already been accomplished, pointing the way.
For Lady Ranelagh the profusion of sects and doctrines is not a
source of anxiety but cause for hope, as it represents "ye cleerer
breaking forth in this age than formerly of that light of truth,
which shews liberty of conscience to be one of the most unques-
tionable rights belonging to men as men. . . ."[225] The religious
freedom to discuss, publish, inquire, and question was the way to
the discovery of truth. This is reminiscent of Boyle's views in the
1640s and the position he set out in "An Invitation to the Communication of Receipts" written in the late 1640s and published by

Hartlib in 1655. Not for nothing was Lady Ranelagh the friend of
Milton, Hartlib, and Dury, all of whom held similar views.[226] For
her, liberty of conscience is what distinguished true religion from
false, Protestantism from Catholicism. This freedom and the truths
it discovered were more powerful agents even than Cromwell for
the undoing of Catholic Europe and the making of a new world
order.[227] The strength of Protestantism lay in liberty of conscience;
the weakness of the foe hinged on the opposite—tyranny in religion and government.[228] Religious freedom for Lady Ranelagh, of
course, could not be boundless. She believed along with her
brothers Roger and Robert that the ground of true religion was an
acceptance of the Bible as the word of God.[229] Like them, she held
that a religious settlement combining scriptural authority, liberty of
conscience for Protestants, and toleration by government of different forms of ecclesiastical structure and discipline would offer the
best prospects for accomplishing the joint purposes of Protestant
strength, harmony, and truth.[230] Such a settlement for Katherine[231]
and probably for Robert would be preparatory to the new heaven
and earth. It is not clear whether Roger shared their millenarianism.

Boyle, then, was party to an intellectual circle sharing something
approaching a common vision of the future. Boyle's writings dating
from this period come as close as anything else to telling us about
the nature of this vision. The evidence from Boyle and the others
suggests that when they peered into the future what they saw was
a sort of Comenian pansophy. There would be peace, unity, and
good government; the whole enterprise would be informed by the
progressive discovery of scriptural and natural truths. There is additional evidence that the initial inspiration for this vision was pansophical and Comenian. In 1657 and 1658 Boyle was involved in a
scheme with Hartlib, Dury, and Benjamin Worsley, among
others,[232] for acquisition from the state of confiscated Irish land in
order to set up an institution for the advancement of learning along
Baconian and Comenian lines[233] and for pansophical purposes.[234]
Broghill seems also to have favored the scheme.[235] The pansophical
influence was as alive in Boyle's thought in the 1650s as it had
been in the 1640s. In his case, however, that pansophical vision

had come by the early 1650s to acquire a particular meaning. The significance he imputed to the vision derived from his experience of and response to the events of the period.

The new order, as far as he was concerned, would have to answer the threats to religion and truth thrown up by the civil wars and interregnum. We have already seen how his natural philosophy and scriptural theology would attempt to overcome or at least neutralize those challengers, especially sectaries and grandees, "Macchiavillians" and "the vulgar." At the same time that Boyle's reform program sought to deal with the opposition, it also embodied the teachings of his ethic. Ideally, both ends would be accomplished at once: the widespread practice of virtue, as he understood it, would itself dispel the opposition. In particular, knowledge of God's word and work would not come in a flash in the form of an immediate intuition or direct revelation. Rather it would come via lengthy inquiry and collective effort, error gradually giving way before further study.[236] This would require industry, humility, sobriety—virtues high on Boyle's list—and the results so obtained would reinforce those virtues and show up the alternatives—the indolence of the gentry, the arrogance of the grandees, and the enthusiasm of the sects. These ideological factors embodied in Boyle's pansophical vision are essential to understanding the origins of his scientific method.

His "experimental philosophy," that is, his insistence that every scientific idea must be treated as an hypothesis ever subject to further tests and ultimate invalidation, must, of course, have technical and philosophical roots apart from these ideological ones.[237] But these last cannot be ignored without doing an injustice to the richness and complexity of his thought and the factors contributing to its development. Ever since his composition of "An Invitation" experimentalism had presented itself to Boyle as a powerful option because of the dictates of his pansophy. These in turn reinforced the more technical influences leading him, in the 1650s, to evolve his experimental philosophy—perhaps his chief contribution to modern science.[238] Not only does the pansophical aspect of Boyle's thought help to explain the evolution of his scientific ideas, it also sheds light on their significance *for him,* the place they held in the larger fabric of his thinking. If we ignored the pansophy, we might regard Boyle as merely an early and highly sophisticated empiricist *tout court*. But he was, after all, both an empiricist and a millenarian of sorts and found nothing contradictory in being so. Indeed he read the empiricism in the light of his idea of reformation. We must learn to do the same.

## Boyle and the Radical Challenge in the Later Years of the Republic

If Boyle's circle in the later 1650s shared a common pansophical vision, they also shared a common enemy: the sectaries. Besides the evidence we have already presented respecting Boyle's view of the sects, there is another piece, probably dating from the late summer and autumn of 1655.[239] It consists of a collection of notes on sermons preached at that time by leading Fifth Monarchy men, including John Simpson and Cornet Day, at Allhallows, London.[240] The Fifth Monarchists as a movement were spawned out of the radical sects of the late 1640s and early 1650s.[241] They hoped for a millennium constituting a social revolution.[242] To that end they saw themselves as God's agents ready to use any means available, including and especially violence.[243] In common with other "radicals" they believed in "inward inspiration" and so saw little of value in "learning and the universities."[244] On these grounds alone Boyle and his circle would have opposed the Fifth Monarchists. But by 1655 when the sermon notes in hand were taken, there was added reason for opposition, as the notes make clear.

In the early years of the republic the Fifth Monarchists had worked in tandem with Cromwell,[245] especially during the period of the short-lived "Barebone's Parliament" (1653). But upon its dissolution and the creation of the Protectorate, which put power in more conservative hands,[246] this was no longer so. Indeed, the Fifth Monarchists considered Cromwell a usurper, an offender against God, who in return would rain destruction upon him and his state.[247] This, for the Fifth Monarchists, would be tantamount to the apocalypse and the advent of the millennium in which they, God's elect, would rule.[248] They particularly resented Cromwell's foreign policy of 1654-55, by which he made peace with the Dutch and started a war with Spain in the West Indies.[249] The upshot of this policy was that the Dutch got what the English gave up, namely, access to Spanish sources of raw wool and Spanish markets for finished cloth. "The real or potential economic effects" of this reversal counted with the Fifth Monarchists because many of their number and potential number were drawn from cloth-workers.[250] As a result they saw English reverses in the West Indies in 1655 as signs of the approaching apocalypse.[251] To help it along they sought to build an alliance with other disaffected groups against the Protectorate.[252]

The sermons on which the notes in hand were made were probably a part of this effort.[253] We do not know who took the notes or whether Boyle ever saw them. We do know that Boyle attended at least one conventicle of sectaries in this period (probably 1659).[254] They were not Fifth Monarchy men but rather the followers of Sir Henry Vane, the republican leader. Boyle's intention in going to hear him preach seems to have been similar to that which lay behind the notes in hand—to scout out the enemy. As it turned out, Boyle did more than that at this meeting: he rose and corrected Vane's interpretation of an Old Testament prophecy "that the sense of the scriptures might not be depraved."[255] So the presence of these reports on Fifth Monarchist meetings among the Boyle Papers, when taken along with the other evidence we have of Boyle's attitude toward radical religion in the 1650s, suggests that someone in his circle if not himself took the trouble to attend and make careful notes and that Boyle too must have been aware of the danger presented by Simpson and his crew. Their vision of the new heaven and earth was not that of Boyle's group; the two interpretations could not have been further apart. The Fifth Monarchists, moreover, would stop at nothing to see the Protectorate in ruins; Cromwell's defeats were signs of their forthcoming victory. Boyle's circle, on the other hand, tended to see Cromwell as God's agent for good; his successes were signs of the coming of their millennium. And Broghill after all was one of the Protector's chief councillors.

More than this, Broghill was a member of that group in the highest councils of the Protectorate—both of Oliver and his son Richard who succeeded him at his death on September 3, 1658—

who believed that a viable political settlement could be reached in
England only by creating a mixed government of king, Lords, and
Commons, and who to this end advised Oliver Cromwell to take
the title of king.[256] There is evidence that Boyle shared these views
and promoted them in print. Not that he wrote anything for publication expressive of Broghill's position. But in 1659-60 he and his
Oxford associate Thomas Barlow, Bodley's librarian, encouraged
Robert Sanderson, who at the Restoration resumed charge of the
episcopal see of Lincoln until his death in 1663, to revise for publication some *Ten Lectures on the Obligation of Humane Conscience*,
which Sanderson had read in the Divinity School at Oxford in
1647.[257] To this end Boyle gave fifty pounds to the impecunious
former bishop,[258] who in turn dedicated the lectures to him when
they were published.

It was not for nothing that Boyle and Barlow wished in 1659 to
see printed some lectures delivered in 1647. The army forced
Richard Cromwell to resign in April 1659 and restored the Rump
on May 7. But the worst was still to come. In the autumn of 1659,
when Sanderson was revising his lectures for publication,[259] effective working relations between army and Rump had broken down
and the constitutional crisis was deepening into a trade depression
and growing disorder. The Protectorate had collapsed and the
army had become the final arbiter in the state. The army and its
erstwhile creature the Rump represented radical opinion both sectarian and republican. Spokesmen for army and Rump preached
variously the broadening of the franchise, the destruction of any
form of established church, virtually unlimited toleration, and an
imminent millennium whose nature would be further destructive of
settled society.[260]

Such doctrines had been widely current in and out of the New
Model and the Long Parliament in 1647 when Sanderson gave his
lectures,[261] and in them he spoke in particular against theories of
popular sovereignty put forward most notably by the Levellers[262]
and argued instead for the preservation of king, Lords, and Commons. To Sanderson this meant two things, both of which were
contrary to the radical ideas he was attacking. First, once men are
in power, even if they have been elected by the enfranchised, they
are accountable only to God.[263] This notion was meant to counter

the extreme republican view that not only should officials be elected by "the people" but that the people can remove their elected representatives from office when they cease to represent them.[264] Second, laws are made by the joint action of all three agencies—king, Lords, and Commons—and nothing else is legal.[265] Such joint action constituted popular consent in the only sense in which this doctrine can be properly understood.[266] Sanderson says in summary: "I do believe that a better way cannot easily be thought upon by the wit of man, to moderate on the one side the Power of Kings, and to check, and to restrain on the other side the Licence of the People."[267]

What Sanderson wrote in 1647 was still timely twelve years later, and no doubt the revisions he undertook at the request of "some friends"[268] were designed to make it even timelier. Were Boyle and Barlow among those who requested these revisions? Evidence would suggest they were.[269] But it is enough for our purposes that Boyle and Barlow pressed for the book[270] and that Boyle compensated its author for his efforts. This tells us that Boyle shared Sanderson's—and Broghill's—opposition to the radicalism, especially the republicanism, of 1659 and likewise their commitment to making English government work along the lines of a mixed monarchy. Indeed Boyle may have been looking toward the possible restoration of Charles II. There is some evidence in Sanderson's lectures to support this claim. His last word on the nature of the state is on the subject of revolution:

> if there be a just fear that the Common-wealth will be ruinated . . . by . . . seditious Subjects, unless somthing be effected which is not permited by the Laws, . . . it is lawful for the *Subjects* by the *presumed Will* of their Prince . . . to recede from the word and sence of particular Laws to assist the *endangered Country,* and to be serviceable to the *safety* thereof, as to the *supremest Law.* [271]

This seems to have been added in 1659 after the fall of the Protectorate that spring[272] and as such to be a recognition of that fact and of the ensuing danger from "seditious Subjects." If this is so then implicit in the statement is the assumption that steps must be taken to restore right government, that is, a mixed monarchy. But this is not spelled out. Instead he closes by saying "I shall . . . proceed to prosecute the rest, as God shall permit and opportunity shall inable me."[273] But given the unstable situation in late 1659 and the early months of 1660, he says, it is "unsafe to adventure further. . . ."[274] So his lectures were first published in 1660 in Latin without his being able "to prosecute the rest." In the late summer or autumn of 1660, when the Restoration was a *fait accompli,* they were published in English translation.[275] By then there was no reason "to prosecute the rest"; what there was could be read as an apologia for what had already happened.

Boyle and his circle did more than react to the enemy, whether Fifth Monarchist or republican. They offered a positive program and worked for their own conception of the future. We have already seen them devising pansophical schemes for the advancement of learning. This they continued to do throughout the interregnum.[276] In religion the aim was to spread the reformation everywhere at home and abroad.[277] For foreign parts, translations of the Bible and books of sound, religious instruction were necessary, and in the 1650s Boyle began what would be a lifelong sponsorship of such work and its distribution.[278] At home what was needed was a scholarly output to prove the Bible to be the word of God, and thus to silence its detractors. Here too Boyle, his sister, and brother patronized the work of others,[279] and Robert himself began to write treatises to this end. All of these efforts in natural philosophy, biblical scholarship, and apologetics will be dealt with more fully in the next chapter. The point to be made here is that these various projects were seen to be interconnected parts of a single enterprise—the accomplishment of the reformation. The spirit animating every effort, whether scientific investigation or the propagation of the faith, was the same: pansophy; and so was the goal: the advent of a new world order in which all men would live as Boyle's ethic prescribed, and the true hermetic wisdom, the language of providence, would have been restored and put into practice.

# Chapter 4

# "The Reformation of the World" and the Restoration

Boyle embraced the Restoration. But this was not meant as a rejection of everything in the previous twenty years. Quite the contrary, he saw the Restoration as offering a better means than the republican experiments of 1659 of achieving the ideals he had worked out during the civil wars and interregnum—the advancement of learning; the propagation of a Scripture-based, irenic Christianity; and the universal practice of his providentialist ethic—the ideals of Boyle's pansophical reformation. This chapter deals with his attempts to achieve these ideals. Again, as in the previous chapter, the focus is not on the technical and purely intellectual aspects of his science, which have been ably covered by the historians of science, but rather on his social vision, the ideological factors contributing to it, and the role it played in shaping his natural philosophy. This aspect of his thought has received less thorough and sophisticated treatment from historians of science or, for that matter, anybody else.

## Prudential Calculus and Providential Order

At the Restoration one of Boyle's central concerns was the settlement of religion. Even more than usual was this the case because for the moment in 1660 the fall of the Protectorate and the return of the monarchy left the religious question hanging, or so it seemed. Hindsight makes it seem that the defeat of all attempts at toleration and comprehension and the creation and implementation of the so-called Clarendon code were almost inevitable. But this is not the view that many, Boyle included, held at the time. After all, the king himself had declared in April 1660 at Breda for limited toleration as one of the main building blocks of his restoration. In this atmosphere of uncertainty in 1660 Boyle and his Oxford associate Peter Pett[1] hoped for a limited toleration but feared "that the restored clergy might be tempted by their late sufferings to such a vindictive retaliation, as would be contrary to the true measures of Christianity and politics. . . ."[2] To help prevent this, the two of them decided that each would write and publish a piece explaining the advantages of an ecclesiastical settlement based not on "retaliation" but on "liberty of conscience."[3] Pett was to show the political advantages and Boyle the advantages accruing to foreign states where liberty of conscience was already operative. As it turned out Boyle decided that Dury could do this better than he, rewarded him when he had finished, and sent the tract to Pett, "who published it at the end of his own in 1660, (though the booksellers, according to their custom, antedated in the title page 1661) and inscribed both . . . treatises with the last letters only of the writers names,"[4] as one did not express openly views such as they held without risking the suspicious attention of the authorities.[5] Boyle also asked Thomas Barlow, who was Pett's friend too,[6] to contribute a piece dealing with "the theological part of the question."[7] Barlow complied but chose not to publish it for fear "of losing . . . his station in the university . . . and all his hopes of future preferment."[8] It was finally published posthumously in 1692 by the then Sir Peter Pett.

The most revealing of these tracts is the one written by Pett entitled *A Discourse Concerning Liberty of Conscience*. Boyle probably read it before publication, as Pett made this a condition of his writing it.[9] Even if Boyle did not keep his promise in this regard, we may safely assume that Pett's tract expressed Boyle's views because the whole project was conceived and carried out as a collaborative undertaking. What does Pett say and what does this tell us about

Boyle's religious views at the time? In particular, how did he think the church should be settled and why?

Pett's position, and hence Boyle's, is chiefly characterized by a prudentialism in matters of religion. This is expressed in a number of ways in Pett's *Discourse Concerning Liberty of Conscience* and is the basis of his and Boyle's view of church settlement. Religious toleration is mainly a matter for rational calculation. A number of factors enter into the calculus. It is better for nonconformists to be allowed to worship openly than to be persecuted because the latter policy will drive them to secret conspiracy whereas the former will make their activities public and hence capable of being kept in check.[10] This proposition assumes, of course, that there are too many sectaries for them to be stamped out by a policy of persecution. This is one of the main considerations for Pett and Barlow alike.[11] Indeed Barlow goes so far as to say that in the context of the Restoration to adopt a policy of toleration is merely to make a virtue of necessity; that is, there are too many nonconformists for persecution to work, and toleration at least wins the authorities some modest measure of goodwill from them.[12]

Neither Pett[13] nor Barlow believed toleration should be unlimited; indeed they would set more or less the same conditions. On this point Barlow is the more explicit. Not to be tolerated are those who claim allegiance to a higher authority than the state. This would include papists and sectaries who claim to be in touch with the spirit world. He adds that those such as Quakers and Adamites should be excluded because they endanger true religion, the latter by their nudism and the former by their social insubordination.[14] Pett, however, is more prudential with regard to the Quakers. There are so many that their persecution would alarm smaller sects and so they should be tolerated unless it is clearly determined that they constitute a menace.[15] Just as his prudential calculus would make him lax about the Quakers in this particular, it would make him rather more severe on the sects as a whole in another regard: he would force them to work. This would prevent them from wandering and so stop the spread of their dangerous views. Not only must they work, but they should be made to wear themselves out with work. They would then be too weary to study heresy or to read Jacob Boehme,[16] one of the chief progenitors of that rage among sectaries for inner light or immediate illumination.[17]

Finally, Pett saw that the multiplicity of sects was itself an inducement to toleration: there were so many different ones and there was such disunity among them that a policy of toleration would result in their canceling each other out and hence balance or stasis would be achieved. For Pett this situation was in contrast to one in which there were only two religions in a state vying for popular loyalty.[18] Here prudence would not dictate toleration. This *aperçu* into the dynamics of religious pluralism was perhaps the master stroke of Pett's, and Boyle's, prudentialism.

*Liberty of Conscience,* the title of Pett's discourse, dealt not only with the toleration that should be granted to nonconformists but also to the privileges that should be afforded to those who stayed within the church. Pett was devoted to a church settlement that would maximize this latter kind of liberty. In order to understand him we must find out what such liberty meant, what sort of church would best promote it, and why it would do so.

Liberty in this second sense was freedom from the oppressions of religious authorities or, to put it positively, the freedom to pursue one's interests unimpeded by authorities. Pett claimed to speak for gentry, merchants, and a majority of the clergy, because he identified the interests of these groups with the national interest and the Protestant cause. The problem of ecclestiastical settlement was to find a church that would further this interest. In other words, the church should not only serve a spiritual end but should be subordinate and expedient to various mundane interests. Thus, according to Pett, no form of church government is by divine right. Rather that church is right which best serves the nation's good.[19] A settlement cannot be grounded on supernatural authority but only on prudential considerations. The church to Pett's mind, and presumably Boyle's as well, has become another factor in that rational calculus by which the national good is pursued.

What are the interests of merchants, gentry, and clergy which define this good and to which established religion must be made to conduce? The clergy's interest is to participate in the governing of a church which in structure and personnel commands the respect of the laity, especially the gentry. The gentry's interest is in church governors, king and bishops, who do not claim to be so by divine right. Episcopacy by divine right might disenable the king from nominating bishops and entail a system of church courts from which there would be no appeal "to the King in Chancery"[20] by the gentry whom Pett sees as being the group that would suffer most from a separate legal jurisdiction in the hands of the clerical hierarchy. The bishops would be a law unto themselves in religious matters, removed from responsibility to king, lower clergy, and the gentry themselves in and out of Parliament.[21] Pett obviously assumes that a system of checks on the power of bishops works to the advantage of the gentry. For the same reason the king should not be made all powerful in the religious sphere. If either authority, royal or episcopal, were to be so, the gentry would lose their liberty both in and out of Parliament, and the state's chief bulwark against ignorance, superstition, error, and tyranny, would be destroyed.[22] Just as the gentry must be protected by a proper church settlement in their main interest—their political independence and freedom from religious domination—so the merchants must be protected in theirs—trade. Religion must be made to serve commerce and industry as well as clergy and gentry. These three interests are seen to overlap. For instance, what serves the gentry serves the clergy and vice versa, or conversely, what injures trade damages the other two. Taken together, the interests of clergy, gentry, and merchants constitute the national good, so a religious formula must be found that will benefit all three.

What then is the magic word? The answer lies in Usher's model or what was known as moderate episcopacy.[23] This had been bruited about throughout the period 1640-1660 as a workable means of settling the church, particularly after Usher's plan was first published in 1656.[24] Those who favored it did so because it represented a compromise between episcopacy and Presbyterianism and so would stand a better chance than either of gaining the widest possible support. Under the scheme the office of bishop would be preserved but its powers would be pruned away. The bishops would no longer act on their own authority in the most important matters but only with the consent of the presbytery.[25] The episcopal function would be more administrative than decision making.

Although this model was obviously calculated to alienate neither

episcopalians nor presbyterians, this is not the ground on which
Pett pitches his case. Rather he favors it for the service it renders to
the national good, the interconnected interests of merchants, gentry, and clergy. To the lower clergy it gives a greater part in run-
ning the church because in each diocese power is diffused and
shared between bishop and presbytery, which would consist in
large part of parish clergy.[26] There would be an incentive in this
scheme of power sharing for the clergy to become better educated
and to devote themselves more to their tasks: "those men that
could offer the best reasons for things, and shew the greatest
strength of parts, would be most swaying in Ecclesiastical Conven-
tions."[27] And a more effective clergy would build a stronger
church. What worked to the advantage of the vast majority of cler-
gymen would also serve the gentry. They would be more respectful and trusting of the clergy—more respectful because their industry and education would command such respect and more trusting
because power in the church would have been transferred from the
diocesan to the parochial level where the gentry could exercise greater influence.[28]

Moderate episcopacy, moreover, would be justified on the
grounds not of divine right but of the nation's good, and so the
danger latent in the argument from divine right of upsetting the
delicate constitutional balance between bishops, king, and Parliament upon which the proper governing of the church depended
would be averted. Indeed to Pett's mind moderate episcopacy
would strengthen that balance by providing a religion that would
serve the allied interests of gentry, merchants, and lower clergy
while lessening the power of bishops.

Finally, what tied the interests of merchants to church and gentry, and how would these mercantile interests also be served by
moderate episcopacy? The common factor uniting church, gentry,
and merchants was trade. The very "genius" of northern Protestant states like England lay in commercial undertakings and empire.[29] Trading for Pett was virtually synonymous with the national
good. In overseas trade, for instance, lay the chief defense for England and hence for the reformation against Catholic Europe: a
flourishing shipping industry gives command of the sea.[30] In this
connection trade and navigation help to propagate the faith and to

increase useful knowledge, both of which were seen to serve the cause of reformation, the latter by enhancing national power and prosperity and the former by extending the true faith at the expense of the false, whether Catholic or pagan.[31] Trade also puts the populace to useful work and prevents idleness and its fruit which is vice.[32] Not only does this serve the gentry by promoting civil peace and political stability, but the church is served as well because idleness is the seedbed of heresy.[33]

How in particular does a moderate episcopal settlement such as Boyle and Pett advocate encourage mercantile interests and hence the national good? Here there are three points to be made. First, the preaching of those who favor moderate episcopacy is suited to the mercantile genius of the nation. Their sermon style is not elaborate like that of high churchmen, nor is it coarse like that of the sectarian preachers. As a result, it is more persuasive than either. This factor of style is important to the mercantile interest not by itself but when taken together with the message preached: the emphasis is on inculcating in workers morals like industry and honesty conducive to the owners' profit.[34] Second, for moderate episcopalians preaching is more important than ceremonies; this preference also serves mercantile interests, ceremonies being regarded as a waste of both time and money.[35] Liberty of conscience such as moderate episcopacy allows gives yet a third fillip to trade. A policy of toleration would make England a haven for mild dissent, both of those who would otherwise emigrate to freer lands and of those who are persecuted abroad. The nation would thus gain in population, and a growing population would have multiple salutary effects on trade both foreign and domestic. It cheapens wages, raises prices at home, and increases exports while cheapening imports, the precise mechanism for producing these last two effects being left largely unexplained.[36]

These tracts by Pett and Barlow, and sponsored by Boyle, reveal his program for church settlement at the Restoration. But in doing so they also reveal his social vision because they assume that the church serves a higher end not defined exclusively by its spiritual mission of saving souls but rather largely by the mundane interests of gentry, merchants, and clergy which together make up the national good. Pett's tract is almost an abstract of this vision. The rest of this chapter will be devoted to discovering its origins and to showing the several ways in which Boyle translated it into thought and action in the first decade of the Restoration.

Concerning the origins of this vision Pett writes: "The great alteration in the body of the people since these last twenty years, requires that our old ends of promoting the welfare of the Church of *England,* should be attain'd by the conduct of new means."[37] He is of course referring to the period 1640-1660. He does not explain "the great alteration" but concentrates on the "new means" by which the church is to be settled—namely, liberty of conscience. As we have seen this means toleration of dissenters and, more importantly, the establishment of a state church that will not only allow but also enable gentry, merchants, and clergy to pursue their worldly interests. Knowing this, we can glimpse what he means by "the great alteration."

First and most obvious, the civil wars and interregnum spawned a dissenting element too strong, lively, and divergent to be absorbed into a national church. Thus, the only possible remedy is the provision of limited toleration combined with a heavy dose of the discipline of the work ethic. Second, even those who come into the state church will do so only on condition that their material interests are served by the settlement provided. This new motivation presumably is also a part of that "great alteration," though Pett does not explain how this change came about. Whatever he thinks produced it, he is willing to base the restored church upon it and in doing so to come dangerously close to making the church merely expedient to private gain. What saves him is the identity he establishes between the private interests of those groups whom he hopes to see served by the settlement and the nation's good, which itself is identified with the cause of reformation and so can be claimed to transcend the interests of particular individuals or groups.[38] This identification is at the base of Boyle's social vision too, and we are not limited for evidence to support this claim to his sponsorship of Pett's *Discourse*. Boyle wrote enough of his own expressive of this view, indeed much of his social thought before the Restoration is to this point. Both "The Aretology" and "Part I" of *Some Considerations Touching the Usefulness of Experimental Natural Philosophy*, which was not yet published in 1660, stress that private interests, pursued according to the dictates of Boyle's ethic, make for the public good. About 1658[39] Boyle elaborated on this theme chiefly in "Part II" of *The Usefulness*, published in 1671. In the process he anticipated and developed many of the points in Pett's *Liberty of Conscience*.

The second section of "Part II" of *The Usefulness* takes up once more the question of God's purposes in the creation. As we have seen, in the first essays of "Part I" Boyle has reconciled the purpose of God's glory to that of man's benefit. In "Part II" he turns to the means by which man can fulfill the latter purpose; that is, how man can derive benefit from his "Empire . . . over inferior Creatures." His view of the means available to man is consistent with his notion of what constitutes human benefit in the first place. As we have seen, in the early 1650s when Boyle wrote the first five essays of "Part I," he saw man in rather Hobbesian terms as insatiably covetous. But this did not lead Boyle down the path to Hobbes' Leviathan. Boyle's prescription was quite different. Man's greed, instead of making for anarchy and calling for the extreme remedy of Hobbes' sovereign, was a part of God's plan and thus a source of hope. This covetousness sent men into the world for means to satisfy or at least to appease it. Hence came labor and its fruits in trade and manufacture—and best of all the discovery of nature. In all of this God could be glorified through the creatures at the same time that man was being served by them.

When Boyle in "Part II" of *The Usefulness* set about specifying the means by which men could obtain their own benefit, it was within the framework partially established in "Part I" in which benefit was largely defined in terms of the satisfaction of human appetites. In "Part II" Boyle makes it clear that this benefit will come via production and exchange under market conditions. The market situation in which human benefit is chiefly realized is made explicit in "The Preamble" to "Part II."[40] There Boyle distinguishes between "art" and "craft." "Art" is the skill involved in producing goods; "craft" the skill involved in buying and selling them, that is to say, knowledge of market conditions. "And by the latter," Boyle says,

I mean the result of those informations . . . by which the artificer learns to make the utmost profit, that he can, of the productions of his art. And this oeconomical prudence is a thing very distinct from the art itself, and yet is often the most beneficial thing to the artificer, informing him how to choose his materials, and estimate their goodness and worth; in what places, and at what times, the best and cheapest are to be had; where, and when, and to what persons the things may be most profitably vended.[40]

Within this framework the means of fulfilling God's purpose for man and benefiting human life must work. What are these means and what can they do in this context? As set forth in "Part I," they are the knowledge the naturalist gains by careful study of the physical order. Such knowledge works in various ways to stimulate production and exchange, trade and industry. Knowledge is useful to capitalist enterprise; in fact the usefulness of knowledge is defined in essentially capitalist terms. Within these terms then God's purpose can be achieved, man can gain the benefit of his "Empire . . . over inferior Creatures," and "Experimental Philosophy may become useful to human life."[41] What is more, the interaction between knowledge and trade is circular: the naturalist can go to the tradesman for insight into his "art" which may improve the naturalist's knowledge of the physical order, and then he can turn around, "as well by the skill thus obtained, as by the other parts of his knowledge," and "improve trades."[42] The engine in this process is private interest. Men driven on by what Boyle calls "craft" will exploit science for the opportunities it offers for improving their "art" and thus increasing profits,[43] and once more this pursuit of private interest is said to make for the general good.[44] Boyle's own statements dating from about 1658 are at one with the views Pett expressed and Boyle encouraged in 1661.

The potential in this linkage of science and trade caused Boyle to call for a history of trades which would systematize knowledge of manufacturing processes of every kind and make them widely available to benefit merchants and naturalists alike.[45] The project of preparing such a history is not something Boyle dreamed up by himself. Bacon had proposed one such scheme, and in the 1640s and 1650s this was picked up by Worsley, Hartlib, William Petty, and John Evelyn,[46] among others. It may have been in association with the first two that Boyle initially became excited by it.[47] Nor did he simply mouth the opinion of others. "The Aretology" and a little later his autobiography argue for social and intellectual intercourse between gentry and tradesman as a principal means of making gains in useful knowledge. Boyle's suggestion that in order to undertake such commerce gentlemen should overcome caste prejudice no doubt grew out of his own rejection of the aristocratic code and substitution in its place of an ethic of work, individual initiative, and private enterprise. This idea, as Boyle developed it before and after the Restoration in a discourse written about 1658 and published in 1671, is integral to his larger social vision as it had evolved out of his experience of the 1640s and 1650s and as Pett summed it up in his *Liberty of Conscience* in 1661.

Nor was the alliance between merchants and gentlemen, naturalists and tradesmen, in the pursuit of useful and profitable knowledge to be exhausted on what each could teach the other about domestic production. The alliance was also meant to operate overseas wherever Englishmen went or planted themselves. The wealth of England was not limited to "Homebred Riches." "Their number," could be increased "by transferring thither those of others,"[48] and in this enterprise the naturalist would also play a leading part, collaborating this time with colonial agents, governors, natives, and administrators, as well as traders. So the alliance by which private interest is made to conduce to public good is not between science and trade but between science, trade, and empire. Here again Boyle is in perfect agreement with Pett's position in *Liberty of Conscience*.[49] Again, too, Boyle's source for these ideas is the Hartlib circle in the 1640s, and in particular, as Charles Webster has established, Boyle's primary debt in this regard is probably to Worsley.[50]

One more aim Boyle shared with Pett and the Hartlib circle—that empire serve not only the joint purposes of science and trade but religion and reformation as well. Pett had said as much in his tract.[51] And throughout the 1640s and 1650s Hartlib and his associates had worked for the spread of the Protestant reformation and the conversion of non-Christian peoples in colonial areas. Such a project was Elizabethan in origin when it served an ideological function in the protracted struggle with Spain.[52] Among the Hartlib circle it was not only a part of the attack on continental Catholicism; it was also central to the goal of world reformation.[53] Indeed Comenius came to England partially to participate in plans for "the propagation of the Gospel unto the nations of the world, and in particular the sowing thereof so happily made then in New England. . . ."[54] About the mission to the Indians in New England we shall have more to say presently.

In Boyle's mind, as in the minds of many of his contemporaries, the purposes of religion and empire had come to be wedded—and wedded as well to those of science and trade. It was these joint purposes that Boyle saw himself as serving from at least the late 1650s on. Thus he supported attempts not only at a history of trades but also at a search for a universal language that might be common to all literate men and whose structure would reduce to a minimum, if not eliminate, ambiguity and confusion. Various men like Wilkins,[55] Cave Beck,[56] George Dalgarno,[57] and Francis Lodwick[58] were actively engaged in trying to devise such a language in England in the 1650s and 1660s, and there were others, like Hartlib[59] and Boyle,[60] who encouraged their efforts because such a common language would be an invaluable aid in the achievement of the interrelated purposes of science, trade, and the reformation. Wilkins[61] and King Charles II[62] were quite explicit about this.

## Science, Trade, and Empire

In his devotion to these goals Boyle did more than think and write about them. He also had the opportunity to try to translate them into practice. On December 1, 1660, he was commissioned by the king to membership on the Council for Foreign Plantations.[63] Created by the same commission of which Boyle was made a member, the Council along with a coordinate body known as the Council of Trade was to make policy for and oversee the administration of the English colonies in the West Indies and North America. In particular, the Council for Foreign Plantations, according to the instructions attached to the commission, was

To take special care for the strict execution of the late Act
[Navigation Act, 1660] for the encouragement of shipping and
navigation. To consider how the colonies may be best
supplied with servants; that no persons may be forced or en-
ticed away by unlawful or indirect ways; that those willing to
be transported thither may be encouraged; and a course le-
gally settled to send over vagrants and others "who remain
here noxious and unprofitable." To provide learned and orthodox ministers for the plantations, and instructions for reg-
ulating and reforming the debaucheries of planters and servants. To consider how the natives and slaves may be invited
and made capable of baptism in the Christian faith.[64]

The apparent intention behind the creation of the Council then was
to give some order and regularity to colonial settlements, which up
to this point had grown rather haphazardly and not always to best
effect from the point of view of the crown. The council was to
make the colonies as profitable to England as possible by seeing to
it that they were well governed; that they took as settlers those
who were "noxious and unprofitable" at home; and that colonial
traders complied with the Navigation Act, which tied shipping and
production closely to the mother country.

We do not know why or through whom Boyle was appointed.
But there are various possibilities. First, Boyle came to know
Clarendon well and they worked closely on negotiations with
agents from New England after the Restoration.[65] They could have
met through Katherine, an old friend of Clarendon[66] or through
Worsley, whom Hartlib described in a letter dated October 9, 1661,
as having "much the eare of ye Ld Chauncellour, and . . . in reference to ye Plantations . . . Privy to most transactions."[67] Clarendon was a member of the Council and may have seen to it that
Boyle was made one too. Certainly Clarendon shared the hopes of
men like Worsley, Boyle, and Pett for trade and empire, not least
because expansion in these spheres would strengthen England's
military and diplomatic position and at the same time increase the
crown's revenue.[68] Alternatively, Worsley worked with government committees for trade and colonization from 1649 to 1651 and
through such work may have introduced Boyle to merchants like

Maurice Thompson and Martin Noel, who were associated with Worsley in his work with the Admiralty Committee in this period[69] and were to take part in reorganizing commercial policy and trade at the Restoration.[70] Indeed Noel was Boyle's colleague on the Council for Foreign Plantations[71] and one of those most responsible for its formation.[72] By March 4, 1660, moreover, the merchant Thomas Povey, also a member of the Council and one of the chief architects of colonial administration and commercial policy in 1660,[73] who sent to Virginia, asking assistance "to certaine Noble and Ingenious Persons, who by his Majesties encouragement, doe sometimes meete together to enquire into and examine . . . all such things as Art, or Nature have produced. . . ."[74] These "Persons" were that group which two years later would be incorporated as the Royal Society of London. Boyle was one of the leading lights among them. Povey then may have known him in that context and known his interest in promoting the interrelated purposes of science, trade, empire, and religion, and so suggested that he would be a valuable addition to the Council. Certainly Boyle's views and the purposes of the Council were much the same, and the record of his work shows how he must have tried to give those views practical shape.

He was one of the more active members. The three major areas of his concern were (1) the relations between planters and merchants; (2) the provision of settlers to the colonies, especially the West Indies; and (3) the religious question in the overseas empire. Mercantile and planting interests were in conflict over three issues with which Boyle dealt—the problem of the planters' debts to merchants, the question of who could lawfully trade with the colonies, and the price for sugar the planters charged to merchants. In trying to resolve these separate issues, the council adopted a uniform strategy: the interests of traders and planters should be accommodated to each other through compromise. The record indicates that Boyle probably helped formulate this strategy.[75]

On the question of whom the government would permit to trade with the colonies, the English merchants would have excluded continentals, thereby putting themselves in the position of being able to dictate to the planters the prices of both the supplies they purchased and the sugar they sold. To avoid this, the planters wished to open trade up to all comers, English and continental. They argued that such freedom was more advantageous to trade and empire because it offered a stimulus to colonial production. The merchants countered by saying that the three Danish Jews who on one occasion were seeking permission to trade "are a people so subtle in matters of trade . . . that in a short time they will not only ingross trade among themselves, but will be able to divert the benefit thereof to other places; whereas it seems the interest of his Majesty to keep his own trade, that the whole profit may flow in hither. . . ." Boyle and Povey, whom the Council charged with deciding the case, reported that since the arguments on both sides carried "great weight," the Council should not lay down any general rule but that in this case a special license to trade should be granted.[76] Concerning the price of sugar, the Council recommended compromise, a decision in which Boyle was again probably involved.[77] The cost of sugar to traders should be neither exorbitant nor too low, as either extreme would kill the trade. Rather it should be such "as may probably make the Planter comfortably subsist, and the Merchant be encouraged to trade. . . ."[78]

Pett, and Boyle through him, claimed that private interests were the foundation of public good. In practice, however, these interests could conflict and thus be capable of undermining the general welfare. Boyle's solution to this dilemma, which was the same as the Council's, was not to permit free market conditions to prevail nor to favor one party over another but to adjust the separate interests to each other through compromise, thereby minimizing conflict and maximizing the benefit to both public and private interests.

Apart from settling relations between the traders and planters, Boyle's work on the Council involved two other matters: the problem of finding suitable emigrants and the religious question. In both cases the fundamental strategy was to harness private interests to the public good. The Council tried, for instance, to foster a greater degree of liberty of conscience in the colonies than was permitted in England until after the revolution of 1689.[79] This was done in an effort to attract settlers in the way that Pett prescribed. Given Boyle's views on the subject, he was of course in full agreement with the policy of the Council.[80] In dealing with the problem of emigration the Council had another related objective in mind—to identify the right people. This meant a stop to kidnapping. It also meant that "felons condemned to death for small offences, and single persons men, and women found to be Sturdy Beggars" might be suitable candidates "and that ye Justices of ye peace may be impowered at ye generall Sessions, or Assizes to . . . dispose of loose and disorderly people . . . for supply of forraigne Plantations. . . ."[81] One suspects that the provision of liberty of conscience in the colonies was related to the policy of disposing of "loose and disorderly people." Whether this is so or not the immigration policy, like the others, was designed to benefit government at home and planters and traders abroad, public and private interests alike.

The last meeting of the Council of Foreign Plantations that Boyle is recorded to have attended was held on February 1, 1664,[82] but this did not end his deep and active involvement in colonial affairs. On February 7, 1662, Boyle was named governor of "the Company for the propagation of the Gospel in New England and the parts adjacent in America."[83] The royal charter incorporating the Company in which Boyle was so named revived the Society for the Propagation of the Gospel founded on July 27, 1649, under the commonwealth.[84] In this case the king took over what initially had been a puritan project for the conversion of the Indians in New England. The earlier society was started through the joint efforts of men on both sides of the Atlantic. Among New Englanders there were, for instance, Edward Winslow,[85] Thomas Shepard,[86] and above all John Eliot,[87] who learned the Indian language and dialects and attempted to convert the natives. In England Hartlib and Dury[88] figured prominently in the effort to found such a society. Robert Rich, second earl of Warwick and father-in-law of Boyle's sister Mary, patronized Winslow's attempt in England in 1648 to persuade the government to create a society to this purpose.[89] Boyle's initial interest in the project probably came from such sources. For Hartlib and Dury the conversion of the heathen everywhere was a part of their goal of pansophical reformation. To promote this work in New England Comenius had come to London in 1641. The Comenians saw their work in the conversion of non-Christian peoples to the true religion as being a sign that the millennium might be dawning.[90] Boyle shared such sentiments,[91] and his work as governor of the Company should be read as another expression of his millenarianism as it survived into the Restoration.

His appointment must also have had a more politic aspect. At the Restoration the Company was tainted by its commonwealth origins and sectarian associations.[92] Boyle was well placed to restore both its vitality and its respectability. He was a loyal member of the established church. But he was sympathetic to nonconformity and so could work with men like Henry Ashurst and Richard Baxter, who were among the most active promoters of the Company in England at the Restoration, and with men like Eliot and John Winthrop, Jr., who carried on the work of the Company in New England after it was established in 1662.[93] This is probably one reason why Baxter wrote to Boyle as early as October 20, 1660, seeking his "favourable assistance in the worke of propagating the Gospell among poore barbarous infidells. . . ."[94] By the time the Company received its charter in early 1662 Boyle was an active member of the Council for Foreign Plantations, and it probably suited the chancellor for Boyle to be governor of the New England Company as well. After all, one of the functions of the council was to encourage the conversion of the natives in the colonies.

The minutes of Council meetings indicate that it never turned its attention to conversion. There are among the Boyle Papers manuscripts suggesting that Boyle and some of his associates may have thought about a missionary effort in the colonies not limited to New England.[95] But one suspects that if he or others ever broached the council with the idea of a more general propagation in, for example, the West Indies, it was squelched by colleagues who represented the mercantile and planting interests in the colonies and who played a large part in the Council's affairs. The West India interests had reason to share the prevailing view that religion and slavery do not mix. Masters and beneficiaries of a slave-labor system, they would have held that catechizing slaves lessens their value. The expense of religious instruction and the Sabbath rest both represented a financial loss from the master's point of view. Besides, religious instruction might instill notions of equality which could be disruptive. Finally, the consensus "among English settlers of America in the seventeenth century was that only heathen could be enslaved by Christians, and that once the slaves were Christianized, they automatically became free, for it was held that no Christian might hold another in bondage."[96]

In New England the missionary function was served, of course, by a separate corporation, the New England Company. Here, the climate of opinion did not prevent efforts to convert the natives. Slavery was not basic to the economy. The English settlers did not see the Indian as being less than human and so unworthy of salvation—an attitude common among white planters toward non-white slave and servile populations in the West Indies.[97] Quite the contrary, those involved in the mission work in New England regarded the Indians as being free, if misguided and depraved, peoples who only needed instruction in Protestant civilization to be assimilated into church, state, and economy.[98] A common image of the Indian was of a remnant of one of the Lost Tribes of Israel whose ingathering and conversion would presage the Protestant millennium.[99]

These assumptions in turn dictated the techniques for conversion adopted by the missionaries, Eliot and Daniel Gookin in particular, and sponsored by the New England Company both before and after Boyle became governor. The Indians must be pried loose from their tribal ways before they could be effectively converted. They must give up what the missionaries regarded as idle and lecherous habits and apply themselves to a daily routine of hard work.[100] They must also shed their superstitions and listen to true men of God rather than resorting to tribal "Pauwau's" and "Pauwauings."[101] It was common practice for Eliot and Gookin to set up in small communities those Indians who were willing and to put them to work.[102] The preaching and catechizing could then go on in an atmosphere where tribal influences had broken down and where the subjects might be more susceptible to the Christian message. Indeed a part of that message, insofar as the missionaries were concerned, was the doctrine of the providential benefits of work. Work was not only essential to civilization, but, if combined with trust in God, it would also produce material advantage.[103] Nor did work mean enslavement; it was wage labor.[104] The missionaries do not seem to have regarded the Indians' economic position as being any different from that of the white settlers—or at least the poorer, more dependent and servile among them.[105] The religious instruction of the natives was the same as that of the settlers. The emphasis was upon the reading and close study of the Bible. So the Indians were taught to read and to grasp the proper interpretation of the biblical message.[106] And they were educated to virtually the same level as the whites. All would learn the rudiments, some would go to school, and a few would attend Harvard College.[107] Nor does there seem to have been any attempt to accommodate puritan Christianity to tribal rituals and beliefs in an effort to win more converts. The emphasis was on the genuineness of the conversion just as it was in the case of white believers, and in the case of the Indians this required full assimilation into white mores.[108] Protestant Christianity meant resettlement in communities based on the white model, a work schedule again based on the white model, wage labor, and the abandonment of tribal ways as far as possible. Whether any Indians ever went so far or what happened to those who tried are not questions we need ask here. The point is that this was the program sponsored by the New England Company to which Boyle as governor must have subscribed.

Nor is there any reason for him to have objected to this program. The work ethic Eliot and Gookin tried to inculcate was the same as that which Boyle had worked out for himself. Indeed this may have been another inducement for him to accept the governorship. Here was a way of spreading abroad the very morality he taught and hoped to see take root in England. The Indians might come to be model Christians. Certainly the Company under Boyle's leadership sponsored the printing of works written by Eliot for the Indians which intended to instill the work ethic as a basis of Christian life.[109] Boyle's devotion to Scripture-based religion also fitted with the work of the Company. Through most of Boyle's tenure as governor, the Company's major project was to support the translation, printing, and distribution of the Bible—the New Testament in the 1660s and, in the 1680s, the Old Testament. Eliot did the translating and Boyle was one of the mainstays of the work, giving money from his personal fortune and providing direction and inspiration as governor.[110] This is but one of many such undertakings that he patronized during the Restoration.[111]

Nor were the work ethic and Scripture-based religion all that Boyle sought to convey to the Indians. He also hoped to rid their minds "of the ridiculous Notions about" the workings of nature "and of the fond & superstitious practices those Errors ingag'd them to. . . ."[112] In their place he hoped that the missionaries and agents of the Company would plant better notions of nature deriving from the experimental philosophy which, at the time, Boyle was developing and which the Royal Society had been founded to promote.[113] Indeed Boyle hoped that his philosophy and that of the Royal Society would flourish in the colonies, especially New England, among settlers and natives alike. This could be expected to produce multiple beneficial effects. The Indians would be brought to correct belief, and the spiritual benefits apart, this would furnish a basis for peace between them and the whites. Not only could they live together, they could also learn to work together.

Experimental philosophy was, among other things, a tool for exploiting the riches of the colonies, and the work would go faster if the two races pooled their knowledge. The Indians, for example, might know of mineral resources which the whites in turn could use in building ships, tools, and weapons, and export abroad.[114] John Winthrop, Jr., moreover, suggested a scheme to Boyle which the company might sponsor. He proposed to use Indian labor in New England for the production of pitch vital to English shipping. There were secondary advantages to the plan: it would provide an outpost in a hitherto unsettled region of New England, and the Indians, having supplied a useful commodity, would constitute an equally useful market. The work the Indians did would not only serve the English, it would also civilize the workers themselves and prepare them to accept Christian teachings.[115] Once more the purposes of trade, empire, science, and religion would go hand in hand. The plan never materialized but it represented the ideal. Read in the light of Boyle's contemporary writings and those of his associate Peter Pett, Boyle's governorship of the Company becomes another expression of his largest goals, those of pansophical reformation.

To reinforce the point that Boyle's purposes in this regard after the Restoration were at one with his earlier thought, it is necessary to recall that the tracts he wrote in the 1650s where he is most explicit about his pansophy were first published in the early years of the Restoration—the *Style* in 1661 and "Part I" of the *Usefulness* in 1663. The publisher of the *Style,* by the way, was Peter Pett.[116] Boyle's writings after the Restoration, dealing with natural religion and philosophy as distinct from experiments, take up the same themes preoccupying him in the 1640s and 1650s. In *The Excellency of Theology* written in 1665,[117] for example, Boyle elaborates on his ethic,[118] his millenarianism,[119] his irenism, and his scripturalism.[120] Only the context has changed.

In the 1660s the latitudinarians emerged as an important intellectual movement within the church, and Boyle was one of their company. Other important representatives were Wilkins and Edward Stillingfleet.[121] Boyle had known the former since 1653 and had worked closely with him at Oxford in the 1650s. With Boyle he was one of the principal founders of the Royal Society. Boyle's ethical position as stated in *The Excellency of Theology*[122] is identical to that which Wilkins, like Boyle, had worked out for himself in the 1640s and 1650s[123] and to which he gave most systematic expression after the Restoration.[124] Stillingfleet and Boyle also shared the same latitudinarian views. Stillingfleet's greatest work, *Origines Sacrae,* first published in 1662, relied heavily upon Boyle's natural philosophy to support Stillingfleet's elaboration of his latitudinarian theology.[125] Boyle in turn approved of the book.[126] Pett's ecclesiastical position in *Liberty of Conscience* was the same as that which Stillingfleet put forward in his *Irenicum* (1659). Finally on October 6, 1662, he wrote to Boyle asking him "to communicate to the world those papers you are somewhere pleased to mention, in behalf of Christianity (against Hobbes. . .) that it may be seen yet further, that those great personages, who have courted nature so highly, that her cabinets are open to them, are far from looking on religion as mean and contemptible."[127]

Nor were the latitudinarians the only movement to emerge after the Restoration of which Boyle was a part. There was also, of course, the Royal Society. Wilkins and Boyle were fellows of the society and leading latitudinarians. There are other examples of the connection, including Oldenburg,[128] Pett,[129] Beale,[130] Evelyn,[131] John Wallis,[132] Thomas Sprat,[133] Joseph Glanvill,[134] and Sir Robert Moray.[135] The two movements were also bound together by a

common outlook. Barbara Shapiro has shown that the religion of
Wilkins and others whose meetings in London and Oxford in the
1640s and 1650s led to the founding of the Royal Society at the
Restoration was latitudinarian. She argues convincingly that
latitudinarians were attracted to science because they saw it as a
means to realizing their goals of religious moderation and ecclesiastical comprehension. The patient inquiry by which science proceeds
was a model of how men might behave and as such would serve as
a healthy corrective of the religious enthusiasm both generating
and generated by the civil wars. And the gradual revelation
through science of God's glory manifested in the creation would so
inspire men as to cause them to abandon their religious differences,
which make only for dissension and conflict, in favor of the peaceful and productive pursuit of more science. These affinities between the latitudinarians and the Royal Society are philosophical
ones, and make the case for the profound impact of establishment
science on latitudinarian religion. But these philosophical connections do not exhaust the whole range of interaction between science and religion after the Restoration. There is another set of relations which are not so much philosophical as they are ideological,
and in this case the influence runs in the opposite direction—from
religion to science.[136]

The latitudinarians and the Royal Society were equally devoted
to the same social vision, the joint purposes of science, trade, empire, and reformation. We have already argued this case for Boyle
and Pett. But the same vision animated the efforts of Wilkins, William, lord Brereton,[137] Sir Robert Moray, and Oldenburg, who
along with Boyle and Pett were all charter Fellows of the Royal Society, and Beale and Winthrop who became Fellows of the Society
soon after. The evidence for this connection between
latitudinarianism and the Royal Society comes from Sprat's *History*
and the record of the interest of the forenamed Fellows in the overseas empire, especially New England. Wilkins, as we have seen,
worked to devise a "universal character" to serve the purposes
equally of trade and religion overseas. Throughout the 1660s Lord
Brereton, Moray, Oldenburg, Boyle, and other Fellows continued
to press Winthrop for surveys of the natural wealth of New England with a view to its systematic exploitation.[138] On July 9, 1662,

Winthrop read to the Society his proposal for the manufacture of naval stores in New England and for the use of Indian labor in the project.[139] This is a classic example of how the purposes of trade, empire, science, and religion were wedded together in the minds of the Fellows.

Oldenburg and Beale shared Boyle's hope that the introduction into New England by Winthrop and his friends of the experimental philosophy of the Royal Society would further the joint causes of empire and reformation.[140] Not only would such science promote trade among the whites, it would also conduce to the subjugation and conversion of the red men. "I doubt not," Oldenburg wrote to Winthrop, "but the savage Indians themselves, when they shall see the Christians addicted, as to piety and vertue, so to all sorts of ingenuities, pleasing Experiments, usefull Inventions and Practices, will thereby insensibly and ye more cherefully subject themselves to you."[141] For Boyle and Oldenburg experimental philosophy was an instrument for the social control of native peoples within the empire.[142] Through science they could be peacefully won away from tribal ways and made to submit to the English regimen of work and prayer. Even before it was incorporated in 1662, the Royal Society was encouraged by the king to survey the riches of the empire.[143] And after it received its royal charter it spent much of its time attempting to promote industry, empire, and trade.[144] One of its major projects was the preparation of a history of trades, and in this regard as in so many others Boyle and his friends resumed their efforts after the Restoration.[145]

Besides the work of the Royal Society, Sprat's *History* reveals the same ideological affinities between latitudinarians and the Society. Sprat's book was the official history of the Society, receiving the approval of leading fellows, including Wilkins, Moray, and Evelyn before it was published in 1667.[146] It should also be read as a latitudinarian manifesto. Its content is largely the result of Wilkins' suggestions,[147] and those, of course, are latitudinarian. Through Sprat, Wilkins argues that the science of the Royal Society is a chief instrument of the Reformation. This forestalls those who said at the time that science is injurious to religion. But more interesting from our point of view, it gives science an ideological edge. According to Sprat and Wilkins, the cause of reformation is served by religious moderation, ecclesiastical comprehension, civil obedience, private enterprise, and profit. The prescription for the achievement of these mutually beneficial goals is experimental science. Its discipline tempers religious passion and helps men avoid two enemies of true religion, the enthusiasm of the sects and the wholesale submission of Catholics to papal authority and ecclesiastical tradition.[148] If this is not sufficient incentive, there are the material advantages of science. Men will bury their religious differences in favor of the opportunities for profit that science creates. And with business investment comes employment for those who might otherwise make trouble for church and state.[149] Science serves men's private interests and as such makes for the public good in the form of religious peace, civil order, and economic prosperity.[150] With these as its foundations the Reformation can spread abroad and ultimately defeat Catholicism.[151]

Indeed the new political economy which science can establish at home and abroad—a Protestant empire in place of the defeated Catholic ones of the past—is tantamount to a fulfillment of the Reformation. To confirm this one need only read the Bible. True religion is Scripture-based, and the Scriptures reveal a religion whose aims are exactly those of the Royal Society.[152] The Society itself is a model for the nation as a whole: it invites men of various religious persuasions,[153] talents,[154] and social backgrounds[155]—lords, gentlemen, merchants, tradesmen, and mechanics—to membership and submerges their religious differences, while drawing upon the variety of their skills in the pursuit of experimental science for the common good, as the Society defines it. Boyle himself provides an example of Sprat's point here. In 1665 Boyle helped Ralph Austen reissue his *Treatise of Fruit-Trees*. Austen was a sectary, and in 1653, when his book was first published, his observations on fruit trees were interspersed with sectarian comments. But a condition of Boyle's patronage was the removal of the offending passages.[156] The Royal Society might serve then as the basis of ecclesiastical comprehension, advantaging the material interests of all who subscribed to its ideology while ignoring or, as in Austen's case, quietly suppressing points of doctrinal conflict among them.

There is no evidence that Boyle was one of Sprat's advisers in the preparation of his *History* or that he read and approved the finished product before it was published; indeed the evidence suggests the reverse.[157] But this is not to say that he would have objected or been indifferent to its content. It is obvious that Boyle's views expressed by Pett and in his own *Usefulness* and *Style* were close and sometimes identical to those expressed by Wilkins and Sprat in the *History*. For all three there is a harmony between scriptural and natural truths—the Bible and the natural order—that in turn serves as a foundation for a philosophy of self-interest. God's word and his work properly studied authorize an ideology of work and acquisitiveness. It seems fair to say then that the leadership of the Royal Society shared Boyle's social vision in which science, trade, and empire were seen to work together to produce the Reformation. And this vision for Wilkins, Sprat, Wallis, and other Fellows was probably Comenian and pansophical in intellectual lineage just as it was for Boyle.[158] Benjamin De Mott has argued that Wilkins' universal character drew inspiration from Comenius.[159] Certainly Wallis was a Comenian in the 1640s.[150]

John Beale presents a perfect case for the linkage between Comenian pansophy and the Royal Society. In the 1650s, he was both corresponding with Comenius[161] and active in Hartlib's circle.[162] He became a Fellow of the Royal Society in 1663.[163] He devoted himself to every aspect of Comenian pansophy—irenic religion, utilitarian science,[164] propagation of the gospel,[165] and the reformation of the world.[166] Brereton seems to have shared Beale's pansophical vision both before and after the Restoration.[167] For both, its achievement would conduce to trade and empire.[168] Beale and Boyle were close friends after the Restoration. The latter sought Beale's advice about the theological aspects of the *Usefulness*,[169] and in their correspondence on the subject Beale betrays yet another link between Boyle's thought, Sprat's *History*, and hence the ideology of the Royal Society: Beale sees Boyle's *Usefulness* as bearing the same message as the *History*, as in fact a better apology for the Society even than the *History*.[170]

There is one final strain in Boyle's thought which he shared with some of his colleagues in the Royal Society, in particular Oldenburg,[171] Pett,[172] Beale,[173] and Winthrop.[174] This is his millenarianism. For all of them, millenarianism was connected to their idea of science. Some day God would teach men the complete

mastery of nature. For the moment they must be content to discover nature's secrets via experimental philosophy. This new science, however, did more than gradually increase man's command
of nature; it pointed the way to the order that would replace the
present one. They did not speculate about exactly when the change
would occur except to say that it might not be far away—whatever
that meant. To have gone further would have been to do as the
radical sectaries did. But if they never said precisely when it would
happen, they did sometimes suggest the nature of the new heaven
and earth, and it was a vision of the accomplishment of their reformation, when the purposes of trade, industry, empire, science,
and religion would have been achieved.[175] Everyone would be industrious, productive, and prosperous. The world would be
Protestant—whites, red men, reformed Catholics, and sectaries
alike committed to the Scripture-based religion of the Royal Society which authorized the virtues of capitalism. Indeed the world
would run on those virtues: self-interest would conduce to the
common good. As Pett said, "one kind of a *New Heaven* and a *New
Earth*, that perhaps we may shortly see in old *England*" will come
"when the necessary improvement of our Land by our numerous
People shall have enriched as many as deserve to be so, and when
to all, who are industrious, there will everywhere be *multiplex
praeda in medio posita*, and the effects of diligence fill all hands with
profit and eyes with pleasure."[176] It is not known when Pett wrote
this, but he did not publish it until 1688. It probably represents his
view at the Restoration because it is remarkably similar to the mil-
lennial vision Boyle adumbrated in the *Style*,[177] written in the early
1650s, which Pett published after the Restoration, first in English in
1661 and then in Latin in 1665.

Boyle's concern and the concern of some of his colleagues in the
Royal Society for empire, trade, and the millennium suggests that
we cannot accept the stereotype of the Royal Society, derived from
the accounts of its origins by Wallis[178] and Sprat,[179] that the men
whose meetings in London and Oxford in the 1640s and 1650s led
to its founding were devoted to pursuing a science divorced from
religion and politics. They may have forsworn conventional theology and politics—and this may have been Sprat and Wallis'
meaning—but their own ideology of science was neither apolitical

nor unrelated to religion. Instead, it was an aggressive, acquisitive, materialistic, imperialistic ideology justified in the name of the Reformation. This is not to say that those who put it forward were insincere about religion, but theirs was a religion of greed and self-aggrandizement. Given the circumstances, it seemed the best alternative. England was divided by deep religious and political cleavages and challenged by Catholic Europe. The ideology of the Royal Society would compose internal differences by committing every group and individual in the nation to experimental science and its material fruits. Both internal order and the pursuit of science, trade, and empire would make England strong enough to face and ultimately overcome the external threat posed by her Catholic enemies. The ideology of the Royal Society sprang then from a mixture of challenge and opportunity. It was the way to wealth and power. It was also a way of solving urgent domestic and international problems. Happily to its sponsors the pursuit of all of these aims was synonymous with planting God's kingdom. This is the ethic of Boyle's "Aretology" writ large.

## Magic, Miracles, and Mechanism

Boyle's natural philosophy as it evolved in the 1660s was, like the ideology of the Royal Society with which it merged, the product in part of some competing philosophies and theologies. Since he defined his own thought then in terms of these others, one of the best ways of understanding it and its origins would seem to be to study it in relation to this context of competing ideas—especially as this has never been done before. Nor was this a mere battle over philosophical and religious ideas; beneath the surface lay extreme ideological differences. The nature of society and government was at stake just as it was in Boyle's dialogue with the sects in the late 1640s and the 1650s. Indeed some of his opponents in the 1660s still represented positions against which he argued before the Restoration, and these are the ones we wish to consider here.

In 1665[180] or 1666[181] Boyle wrote *A Free Inquiry into the Vulgarly Received Notion of Nature*. By "the vulgarly received notion of nature" he means the conception deriving from ancient Greek philosophy, both Neoplatonic and Aristotelian,[182] that there is a governing agency in nature apart from God which cannot be reduced to the mechanical principles of matter and motion. This agency is called variously plastic nature, the astral spirits, or the soul of the world, and as Boyle says, is conceived by "the schools" as "a being that . . . does always that which is best."[183] Boyle's intention is to show that his own idea of nature is preferable to this Peripatetic and Platonic one because his goes further toward a proper understanding of the relations between Creator and creation. The criterion here for judging between natural philosophies is the degree to which they conform to religious doctrine; the grounds of truth are set by the tenets of Christian faith.

Boyle claims that his corpuscular philosophy is preferable on two counts to the theory of the soul of the world. First, it is a better explanation of God's acting in the world. The belief in a world-soul always working for the welfare of the universe makes it difficult to explain the natural disasters that befall some men at one time or another. This theory raises but does not answer the question of why nature does not benefit all men all of the time.[184] Boyle's corpuscular philosophy, on the other hand, answers this question in two ways. It maintains that God set matter in motion at the moment of creation in just that way in which he could accomplish many of his ends, "though that would infer the happening of seeming anomalies, and things really repugnant to the good or welfare of divers particular portions of the universe. . . ." These would be "seeming anomalies" because "God is a most free, as well as a most wise agent, and may in many things have ends unknown to us. . . ."[185] Among these unknowable ends is punishment of man's wickedness. This may be built into God's initial plan for the operation of the universe. The other way in which Boyle's philosophy answers the problem of evil is that God "sometimes purposely over-rules the regular" motions of matter "to execute his justice; and therefore plagues, earthquakes, inundations, and the like destructive calamities, though they are sometimes irregularities in nature, yet for that very reason they are designed by providence, which intends, by them, to deprive wicked men of that life, or of those blessings of life, whereof their sins have rendered them unworthy."[186] Boyle's theory explains the whole range of God's actings in the world, those things that injure man as well as those which profit him. The doctrine of a world-soul can account for only the latter and, because of this, might cause men to lose their faith in the face of calamity.

There is a second way in which Boyle's theory is preferable to "the vulgarly received" alternative. Boyle's position is supportive of orthodoxy; the alternative would tend to undermine it not only in time of calamity but by its very nature. Whereas Boyle's view stresses God's actings in the world, the other stresses natural processes. The implication in this latter view is to deny miraculous interventions[187] and to assert that nature is a closed system, that there is no need to seek supernatural explanations or divine assistance, that in fact it is more useful and proper to study and worship nature than God,[188] if indeed there is a God apart from nature and nature itself is not the only God.[189] This view of course is totally at odds with orthodox belief.

Why was Boyle so concerned to oppose his natural philosophy to the vulgarly received notion? Was Aristotelian and Platonic philosophy in 1666 tainted with heresy and atheism? If so, how could this be? For centuries Aristotle had been at the foundations of orthodox Christian thought. The answers to these questions lie in Boyle's treatise, A Free Inquiry, and in the context in which it was composed.

In his treatise Boyle says that the idea of a world-soul with its attendant heretical implications was not only current in early Christian times but has been revived by "a sect of men, as well professing Christianity, as pretending to philosophy, who (if I am not mis-informed of their doctrine) do very much symbolize with the antient Heathens, and talk much indeed of God, but mean such a one, as is not really distinct from the animated and intelligent universe; but is, on that account, very differing from the true God, that we Christians believe and worship."[190] Boyle does not identify these men, but there was a group who moved in court circles in the 1660s answering this description. Their leader was John Heydon, who had some connection with George Villiers, the second duke of Buckingham.[191] Others in the circle included the duke

of Richmond, the marquess of Worcester, the earl of Oxford, Sir
John Hanmer, Sir Ralph Freeman, Charles Potter, John Digby, and
Colonel Samuel Sandys.[192]

Heydon wrote and published several books in the early 1660s in
which he states his position. He believes that the soul of the world
"hath the beginning of motion";[193] that "the Sun, and Moon have
obtained the administration or ruling of the Heavens, and all
bodies under the Heavens"[194] and as such deserve to be wor-
shiped;[195] that "the world it self is immortal"; that "it is impossible
that any part of it can perish"; that "therefore we say a man dieth
when his soul and body are separated, not that anything of them
perisheth";[196] and that man through an understanding of nature
can see into the future and use such knowledge to his material advantage,[197] can "perform miraculous things,"[198] and can "ascend
to so great a perfection, that he is made the Son of God, and is
translated into that Image which is God, and is united with him;
which is not granted to Angels, the World, or any Creature, but to
man onely. . . ."[199] It is doctrines like these that Boyle opposes in
his *Free Inquiry*.[200]

Heydon and his circle claimed that they were brethren of "the
Rosie Cross,"[201] which was a movement of ideas in late sixteenth-
and seventeenth-century Europe whose adherents preached the reformation of the world through a reformation of learning.[202] Its
roots lay in the hermetic philosophy of the Florentine Neoplatonists,
and Heydon like other so-called Rosicrucians derived many of his
ideas and the general framework of his thinking directly or indi-
rectly from the natural magic of Marsilio Ficino.[203] Like Ficino he
hoped that through manipulation of celestial influences he could
gain mastery of nature. Astrology was central then to Heydon's
concern. He rewrote Bacon's *New Atlantis* and substituted for Solomon's House the Society of the Rosie Cross whose members were
devoted to the astrological study of the heavens for the purpose of
reforming the world.[204] Heydon's piece was published in 1662[205]
and may also have troubled Boyle because his own Royal Society
was founded on the Baconian model. Worst of all, in the 1640s and
1650s the whole tradition of natural magic deriving from Ficino and
the hermetic texts had come to be associated with radical sects.[206]
Boyle was at pains in this period to dissociate his Hermetism from

that of the sectaries. It did not help Heydon that there were millenarian overtones to his work.[207] Nor did it help that sectaries
were still active in the 1660s.

In 1663 and in late 1665 and early 1666 Roger Boyle, now earl of
Orrery, reported to the government that there were sectarian plots
on foot for rebellions in England and Ireland.[208] The plot among
sectaries to take Dublin Castle in 1663 was of major proportions.[209]
By 1665 and 1666 the situation had been exacerbated by the plague
during which the court retreated to Oxford and left London to the
nonconformists who entered the pulpits and preached sedition.[210]
The plague also probably helps to explain Boyle's argument in *A
Free Inquiry* in which he labors a preference for his own natural
philosophy to "the vulgarly received notion of nature" when it
comes to accounting for natural disasters. Heydon and his circle do
not seem to have been sectaries themselves. But Heydon was im-
prisoned in 1667 for plotting sedition and in his trial linked his
political activities during the previous three or four years with the
intrigues of Buckingham against the king.[211] Heydon says, moreover, in his most important work, *Theomagia*, that there are some
"Presbyterian Clergy" "who study this Art" of natural magic.[212].
Whether or not Heydon and company were involved directly in
nonconformist circles and sectarian plots, Samuel Parker, Anglican
priest and Fellow of the Royal Society,[213] made the connection in *A
Free and Impartial Censure of the Platonick Philosophie*. He wrote of
Heydon's group "that they directly Poison mens minds and dispose them to the wildest and most *Enthusiastick Fanaticisme*; for
there is so much Affinity between *Rosi-Crucianisme* and Enthusiasme, that whoever entertains the one, he may upon the same
reason embrace the other. . . ."[214] Nor did Parker stop there. Enthusiasm and, by implication, Rosicrucianism were tantamount to
sedition:

And what Pestilential Influences the Genius of *Enthusiasme* or
opinionative Zeal has upon the Publick Peace, is so evident
from Experience, that it needes not be prov'd from
Reason . . . . I am confident, that from the beginning . . . there has not been so great a Conjunction of Ignorance with Confidence, as in these Fellows [Heydon's circle],

which certainly . . . is . . . contrary and malignant to true knowledge.[215]

In a letter to Oldenburg in the spring of 1666 Beale commended "Parker's censure of ye Platonick Philosophy," and Oldenburg passed Beale's judgment on to Boyle in June of that year.[216]

The identification between Rosicrucianism and the radical sects established during the civil wars and interregnum persisted into the Restoration—and not without reason. In 1666, the very year of the publication of Parker's tract and the composition of Boyle's *Free Inquiry*, some conspirators, who based the timing of their plot on astrological prediction, were tried and executed.[217] It was for such reasons that in 1665 or 1666 Boyle wrote against "the vulgarly received notion of nature."

Nor is this by any means the sum of the evidence for the connection between Boyle's elaboration of his natural philosophy in *A Free Inquiry* and the world beyond his study window. Plague and fire were not all that visited London in 1665-66; there was also Valentine Greatrakes, the so-called Irish healer. He was an English Protestant whose family had settled in Munster, where during Cromwell's campaign he had served under Broghill for six years, rising to the rank of lieutenant.[218] Afterward in 1656 he settled down to his wife and farm in Affane, County Waterford.[219] But he writes that in 1662 "I had an Impulse, or a strange perswasion in my own mind (of which I am not able to give any rational account to another) which did very frequently suggest to me that there was bestowed on me the gift of curing the Kings-Evil. . . ."[220] Once he tested his "Impulse" and found that he did have such a "gift," he went on during the next four years, despite clerical disapproval, to cure not just the king's evil but other ills as well primarily by touching or stroking—which accounts no doubt for his reputation as "the Irish Stroker."[221] He stayed in Ireland but his fame spread, and in the summer of 1665 "two or three ships well fraighted out of England with all diseases" braved the Irish Sea for his cure and "most returned well home."[222]

One of those who read that summer of Greatrakes' success was Edward, viscount Conway. His wife, Lady Anne, had suffered for years from excruciating headaches. She had tried various remedies prescribed by a succession of doctors. All had failed. Lord Conway

now decided to seek the help of the Irish healer.[223] Through Orrery, Greatrakes' old commander, Conway persuaded him to visit
Ragley, Warwickshire, where Lady Conway was living.[224] He arrived in January 1666 but was unsuccessful in treating her. At Lord
Conway's insistence, however, he remained three or four weeks
for the sake of the neighbors who flocked to Ragley for the cure.[225]
He then went to Worcester[226] at the invitation of the mayor, where
he was saved from being "bruised to death" at the hands of the
crowds seeking his cure when an order came "from the Lord Ar-
lington, by command of his Majestie" to appear at court in
Whitehall.[227] The climax of his career as a healer was at hand. In
London that spring he drew "after him, some Noble-men, many
Courtiers, a few Clergy-men, several Magistrates, all sorts of Citizens, People of all ages, sexes and conditions. . . ."[228] Not only did
he work his cures but these became the subject of a popular furor
with ecclesiastical, political, and even social ramifications which
were not lost on the intellectuals.

According to Greatrakes, "Sir Heneage Finch [the Solicitor-
General] says that I have made the greatest faction and distraction
between clergy and laymen that any one has these 1000 years."[229]
To understand this "faction and distraction" several interrelated
factors must be taken into consideration. Throughout the period of
Greatrakes' notoriety from mid-1665 to mid-1666 the plague raged
at its greatest intensity. Not only did the physicians leave London,
but Charles II suspended his own public healings for the king's
evil.[230] David Lloyd, reader of the Charterhouse held in *Wonders No
Miracles* that Greatrakes' curing of that disease might be a plot inspired by republicans for undermining the monarchy.

Lloyd held that when the king's touch worked a cure it was not
miraculous but rather the result of "the power of Fancy" in the
lowly patient who is so excited by being in the royal presence and
subject to the royal ministrations that "his Spirits" rush "to assist
Nature with their utmost might, to encounter the Disease with
greater advantage."[231] One of Lloyd's theories is that Greatrakes
"with other cunning peoples suggestions" had caught on to the
trick and

> set up an Healing power, as well as the King; levelling his
> Gift, as well as they would his Office, with a design, that

when it appeared he could *do* no more than other men, he should *be* no more than other men: yea, and when parity of reason led them to attempt in other Diseases, what with some success they had begun in the *Kings Evil,* they might not only out-do his Majesty, but be in a fair way to give Laws to the world.[232]

Lloyd is not certain whether these seditious intentions are Catholic or sectarian,[233] or indeed whether Greatrakes is himself guilty of sedition or an innocent tool in other men's designs.[234] But of one thing he is certain—that Greatrakes and his followers are "dangerous, upon the two great accounts of letting in errors among the people, and upon the discovery of the pretenders, of letting out the people to Atheism,"[235] that is, disillusioning the people with religion. We shall return to what these errors might be.

Lloyd goes on to say that the threat posed by Greatrakes is exacerbated by two additional factors. First, there are "more subtle persons" than he who will see in his cures "the opportunity . . . to work upon an unstable people to more dangerous purposes."[236] Second, there are the times. He means not just the plague but, as he says, "it being a time of great Expectations among all men, and of strange Impressions upon very many; the very imagination of strange alterations in the world, makes strange alterations upon mens thoughts and spirits; it's no wonder, when all men look for a year of Miracles, that one man should attempt to begin it."[237] In Daniel and Revelations the number 666 bore apocalyptic significance. So the year 1666 raised the hopes of many, and especially sectaries, for the imminent fulfillment in one form or another of the biblical promises.[238] Lloyd himself, though not a sectary, thought that the world was in its "last daies"[239] before the apocalypse. In this light Greatrakes' career was "the praelude to the last Effort of Diabolical Illusions"[240] which was supposed to precede that event. Because of these millenarian expectations the masses were highly suggestible, and it would be all the easier for the "subtle" and "cunning" to turn Greatrakes' cures to seditious ends. But men must resist this diabolical "Essay made to try how far we are prepared . . . for the universal Apostacy, so much feared in the latter daies."[241]

Nor was Lloyd wrong to see the connections between Greatrakes, the millennium, and sedition. In England an anonymous pamphlet made explicit the connection between his cures and the coming millennium but left the nature of the imminent transformation unclear.[242] Greatrakes had been courted "by many parties but most highly . . . by ye Roman Catholicks,"[243] Daniel Coxe, a Fellow of the Royal Society, reported to Boyle on March 5, 1666. Some "adore him as an Apostle."[244] In Ireland he was suspected for "the society he most frequents who may have some ill designe to manadge under the countenance of his reputation. . . ."[245] The archbishop of Dublin would not charge Greatrakes himself "with any such seditious purposes." But he went on, "I will not undertake to acquit those who follow him for though he himselfe may be led onely by the conduct of a wilde fantasy, yet his prosilytes may propound . . . other use of his esteeme among the vulgar."[246] He left himself open to this "other use" by his own millenarian "dreames." [247] Another Dublin cleric was not so generous as his archbishop: he wrote "A dectection of the Imposture of Mr. Valentine Greatrakes: His pretended gift of healing."[248] And there was more than seditious writing and thinking; there was information about actual plots for sectarian risings against the government in England and Ireland in the spring of 1666—some of it reported by the earl of Orrery to the authorities.[249] Against this background Greatrakes' cures should be read.

Into this situation came Henry Stubbe, a physician at Stratford upon Avon, with the letter he published dated February 18, 1666, addressed to Boyle, and entitled *The Miraculous Conformist: Or an Account of Severall Marvailous Cures Performed by . . . Mr. Valentine Greatarick. . . .* Stubbe had observed Greatrakes' cures at Ragley. For Stubbe they were miracles,[250] but they were the result not of God's intervention in nature but rather of nature itself.[251] He also equates Greatrakes' cures with the miracles performed by "Christ and the Apostles,"[252] thereby implying that these too should be understood as natural rather than supernatural processes.

The reaction was immediate. Daniel Coxe, Boyle's close friend,[253] wrote to him on March 5, 1666. Coxe had learned

> by them who have reason to pretend to understand Dr Stubbs his designs . . . that Dr. S. intends to Dimonstrate from what Greaterex hath performed that ye miracles of our blessed

Savior were not derived from any extraordinary assistance of
a Divinity, much lesse from ye Union of ye divine nature with
Humanity; but that as G[reatrakes'] they might be meerly ye
result of his Constitution which same may bee affirmed of
others that have performed reall miracles (as wee simple
people stile them). And this hee intends to addresse to your
Honor. . . . But wee here have all such a strong persuasion of
Mr Boyles good will & unfained love to Christianity that wee
cannot imagine hee should Patronize any thing which hath
such a direct tendency to Atheisme & doth most positively
enervate ye very Basis of Christianity; & invalidate (att least
seemingly) the strongest motive to believe ye veracity of those
excellent Dictates which all that rightly improve their Reason
make ye rule of their present life & the foundation of their
hope for a future felicity exceeding imagination.[254]

Nor, according to Coxe, is Stubbe alone in his opinions. His "designe . . . will exceedingly oblidge those who like himself are so intent on ye gratifications of Sense or Evill Passions that they have
not will . . . to think of a Deity or immortall Soules or have so
much Philosophy as to reason themselves out of their Religion a
fond persuasion wherein a Company of pittifull superstitious cred-
ulous persons . . . are deluded."[255] Coxe has described a group
who have a "Religion" in which there is no belief in "a Deity or
immortall Soules." Judging from what we have quoted, the object
of worship is nature itself. Indeed there is nothing beyond the
natural order—and no life after death.[256] Here is an important
chapter in the origins of subversive deism in England more than a
decade before the publication of Charles Blount's deistical works.[257]

Four days later, on March 9, Boyle had read Stubbe's printed letter and written a private reply. Boyle too sees the atheistic tendency in Stubbe's remarks, though he claims that Stubbe may not
have intended it.[258] This aside, according to Boyle, Greatrakes'
cures are either not real miracles or, "if they have any thing in
them of a supernatural gift, it is . . . far short of the gifts of our
Saviour Christ and his apostles. . . ."[259] The logic of his case is that
if Greatrakes' cures have nothing supernatural in them at all and
hence are entirely physical and according to the ordinary processes

of nature or if his cures are miraculous but not to the same degree as those of Christ and the Apostles, then the exclusive divine origin of these latter and the credibility of the New Testament as divine revelation are preserved. What Boyle is most intent on denying is that opinion of "those enemies to Christianity . . . that granting the truth of the historical part of the New Testament, (which relates to miracles) have gone about to give an account of it by coelestial influences, or natural . . . complexions, or such conceits, which have quite lost them, in my thoughts, the title of knowing naturalists."[260]

Who are these "enemies to Christianity"? Stubbe spoke of natural complexions to explain Greatrakes' cures.[261] Heydon spoke of celestial influences. The threat they posed by these views was serious because they were not alone in holding them. Stubbe in particular represented a larger attack on the Bible as divine revelation in which lie the origins of English deism. The New Testament, argued its deistical critics, may have historical validity; it may even teach moral truths, but its origins are not divine. To prove this they sought to give natural explanations of the biblical miracles. The deists' attack by implication called into question the providence of God and Christ's divinity and hence his mission and power as the Redeemer; at issue were the foundations of Christianity.[262]

Boyle and his circle, especially Oldenburg, Lady Ranelagh,[263] and Dury,[264] had recognized this challenge by the late 1650s. Their intense scripturalism dictated that they see the deistical attack on revelation as especially menacing.[265] Before and after the Restoration they encouraged Adam Boreel, a Dutch scripturalist[266] and leader of the Collegiant movement in Amsterdam,[267] in his work designed to prove the divine origin of the New Testament, "Jesus Nazarenus Legislator." They pinned their hopes on Boreel's manuscript as supplying a definitive answer to the deists.[268] During the Greatrakes furor Boyle even contributed financially toward making a copy of the manuscript which could be circulated among friends in England.[269] It was never published, but Boyle must have got his copy because there is one among his papers in the Royal Society.[270] Thus when during the same period he wrote *A Free Inquiry into the Vulgarly Received Notion of Nature,* he probably had in mind not just Stubbe and Heydon but the subversive freethinkers whose views they represented. As he says in his letter to Stubbe on March 9, 1666, he could not regard such men as "knowing naturalists" because their natural philosophy tended to undermine Christian teaching by denying the divine origin of New Testament miracles.

Boyle's argument against "the vulgarly received notion of nature," the notion deriving from Plato and in particular from Aristotle, grew out of the deistical attack on Scripture based on explanations rooted in Aristotelian and Platonic conceptions of nature. There was an important tradition of the naturalistic interpretation of Plato and Aristotle in sixteenth- and seventeenth-century Europe upon which Stubbians and Heydonians could draw.[271] Boyle's corpuscular philosophy served as a defense of the faith against this opposition because it preserved the distinction between natural and supernatural phenomena and hence the divine origin of the events recorded in the New Testament on which rested the integrity of the religion.

The next volley lobbed at Stubbe came from David Lloyd's pen. His tract against Greatrakes, *Wonders No Miracles*, dated March 13, 1666, took account of Stubbe's *Miraculous Conformist*. Lloyd comes closer than anyone to suggesting the political radicalism implicit in Stubbe's explanation of Greatrakes' cures:

> it is the old Atheists obsolete cavil against Christs Miracles that he did that by the extraordinarily exact complexion of *his humane nature,* which all that saw, confessed done by the power of the *Divine;* either this complexion is the complexion of all men, and then every man could do feats . . . ; or *of some* [men], and then I wonder we have not yet been told, either by *God* or *Men,* what are those Individual qualifications that constitute this complexion . . . .[272]

If Greatrakes or, technically, nature as embodied in Greatrakes' "complexion" is capable of performing miracles equivalent to those performed by Christ and the Apostles, then this tends to subvert Christianity by challenging the doctrine of Christ's divine nature, the supernatural origins of the apostolic miracles, and the uniqueness and hence the force and credibility of Christian revelation. The cures also imply that some or all men have the same power within themselves, and this would tend to the subversion of all established authority, civil and ecclesiastical.

We have already seen that Lloyd drew certain subversive political implications from the cures. He argued that Greatrakes may be implicated, albeit unwittingly, in a plot with others to "set up an Healing power, as well as the King; levelling his Gift, as well as they would his Office, with a design, that when it appeared he could *do* no more than other men, he should *be* no more than other men. . . ."[273] The subversives Lloyd had in mind, given the language he used to describe them, could be no other than antimonarchists, Levellers, and republicans. He does not say that republicanism is the implication Stubbe draws from Greatrakes' career. But leveling is a possible implication to be drawn from Stubbe's interpretation of the cures: if an ordinary man like Greatrakes can do everything Christ or the king can, why should men have hereditary rulers set over them? The possibility that Stubbe intended his interpretation of the cures to be taken as an argument for republicanism is strengthened by the fact that before the Restoration Stubbe was a leading theorist and proponent of republicanism, especially in 1659, when the army restored the Rump, and republican sentiment was widespread in both Rump and army.[274]

If Stubbe's *Miraculous Conformist* is a cryptorepublican tract, Boyle would probably have read it as such. He must have been well acquainted with Stubbe's politics. They were both at Oxford in the late 1650s. From 1657 to the Restoration, Stubbe was "the second-keeper" of the Bodleian Library under Thomas Barlow, "the Head-Keeper" and Boyle's close friend.[275] As a republican polemicist in 1659 Stubbe was a defender of Sir Henry Vane against the attacks of Richard Baxter, who wrote in support of Richard Cromwell.[276] As we know, Baxter and Broghill were already close associates in the service of the Protectorate and scriptural religion against sectaries like Stubbe and Vane,[277] who preached popular sovereignty and unlimited toleration. As we know too, Boyle had on one occasion in the 1650s (probably in 1659) also crossed verbal swords with Vane over his misleading interpretation of Scrip-

ture.[278] Vane was an antinomian of sorts and as governor of Massachusetts Bay Colony in 1636 and 1637 had flirted, along with
Anne Hutchinson and John Cotton, with the antinomian doctrine
of the mortality of the soul.[279] Coxe's letter to Boyle in March 1666
suggests that Stubbe and his circle were mortalists too. This is
another link between *The Miraculous Conformist* and the radicalism
of the 1650s and would have made Boyle all the more anxious to
answer Stubbe and if possible to silence him. Mortalism was
anathema to Boyle—so much so that he initially justified his adoption of the corpuscular philosophy by arguing that it was a defense
against the mortalistic heresy.[280] Finally, it is almost certain that
Boyle and Barlow had the latter's subordinate at the Library in mind
when in 1659 they sponsored the publication of Sanderson's *Ten
Lectures* as an answer to the republicanism rampant at the time.[281]

Nor is this the end of the connections between Boyle, Stubbe,
and Greatrakes in terms of which Boyle would define his own position. In *The Miraculous Conformist* Stubbe suggests that the Royal
Society countenances his views on Greatrakes, "since," as he says
of the Society, "the Freedome, You allow me with you, permits me
to speak any thing, I shall, without derogating from the power of
God. . . ."[282] Lloyd's *Wonders No Miracles* also raised the question
of guilt by association but in a different form. He linked Greatrakes
to latitudinarianism, and the linkage was not complimentary to
either. "The man it seems being bred up in loose times, and a
more loose way, a *Souldier,* having prostituted *his understanding* to a
variety of Opinions and Errors, . . . he hath been in his time of
most of the Factions that were lately extant; and now pretends
himself a *Latitude-Man,* that is, one that *being of no Religion himself,
is indifferent what Religion others should be of. . . .*"[283]

Greatrakes, it is true, was a self-confessed latitudinarian. After
his career as a soldier he served as a Justice of the Peace for
County Cork[284] and conducted himself in that office as a model
latitudinarian. He prosecuted no one "for . . . Conscience barely;
so it led him not to do any thing to the disturbance of the civil
Peace. . . ."[285] And he made every effort to convert papists in his
neighborhood "for the good of their souls" and "the preservation
our own Bodies and Estates"[286]—a mixture of temporal and

spiritual motives which was at the core of latitudinarianism. His summary of his behavior in office is equally essential latitudinarianism: "I can truly say I never injured any man for his Conscience, conceiving that ought to be informed and not enforced."[287]

It is not surprising that the support for his healing mission in London came from leading latitudinarians—Wilkins, Benjamin Whichcote, Ralph Cudworth, George Rust, and Simon Patrick.[288] Boyle, too, during Greatrakes' London career in April 1666 was "a spectatour of at least 60 performances of his."[289] Indeed on Easter day 1666, Greatrakes performed his cures in Boyle's chamber.[290] Boyle and the other latitudinarians wrote testimonials as to the authenticity of the cures they observed, and these were appended to Greatrakes' *Brief Account.*[291] Greatrakes' career became a latitudinarian cause. His *Account* tells why. The record of his public service in Ireland appears there: his conduct in office was latitudinarian. His cures, moreover, are anything but irreligious. They are not acts of nature; neither are they wholly works of God. He writes:

> I have reason to believe that there is something in it of an extraordinary Gift of God. The Reasons and Arguments which incline me to this belief are, That I am very sensible of the particular time when this Gift was first bestowed on me, before which time I had it not; because, having my self for several years together been most violently troubled with the head-ach, though I have put my hand a thousand times to my head and held it, it would neither remove nor run out the pains but since God gave my hand this Gift, I have no sooner put it on my head where it was troubled, but I have removed and run it out.[292]

The same physical action which once did nothing now has a curative effect: the power comes not from nature but from God, and the proof of this lies in the fact that Greatrakes had not always possessed such power. But the healing action is not entirely supernatural either. "I suppose," as he says, "no man will question but that an extraordinary Gift may be exercised by natural means, or

that God may confer in an extraordinary manner such a temper of
Body upon a person as may, by a natural efficacy produce these
effects. . . .[293]

Why does Greatrakes insist that his gift is neither totally natural
nor totally supernatural? Here again the context alone can supply
the answer. By rejecting the supernatural explanation he avoids the
accusation that he is a pretender to the status of Christ, an Apostle
or great religious leader, when some of his followers saw him not
as an imposter but the genuine article.[294] And by dismissing a
wholly natural explanation he escapes the accusation of belonging
to Stubbe's camp. At the same time that he avoids both of these
pitfalls he can claim that his power, far from undermining religion
and society, gives support to both. Greatrakes stood the arguments
of his accusers on their heads.

> Give me leave to presuppose 2 or 3 Reasons why or where-
> fore God should now cure diseases in an extraordinary man-
> ner. The first is to convince this Age of Atheism, which (I am
> sorry to say it) many of our pretended Wits I fear are falling
> into, who make it their pastime to deride at Jesus and Chris-
> tianity, who cannot yet but believe Jesus to be God, when
> they see pains and diseases to vanish, and evil Spirits flye his
> Power. . . . Next the goodness of God, out of compassion to
> poor distressed man, may make use of never so worthless an
> Instrument to magnifie his own mercy and power, as he did
> of a brazen Serpent in the wilderness, that the glory and
> praise of all may be solely ascribed unto him, who by a little
> dust and clay can cure, and cause diseases to run through
> men, which no Physick could move. Next, God may, to abate
> the pride of the Papists (that make Miracles the undeniable
> Manifesto of the truth of their Church) make use of a Protes-
> tant to do such strange things in the face of the Sun, which
> they pretend to do in Cells.[295]

This last motive, the attack on papists, may have been in part a
reaction to the appearance in England at this time of several
Catholic healers,[296] at least one of whom performed not in public

but in the privacy of the queen's chapel in St. James', where his services aroused the antagonism of Anglican bishops.[297]

What is most interesting in connection with Greatrakes' explanation of his cures and the reason for it is that the explanation Boyle gives them in his answer to Stubbe is the same.

> I am not yet fully convinced, that there is in what . . . you . . . relate upon your own observations, . . . any thing that is purely supernatural (unless in the way, wherein he was made to take notice of his gift, and exercise it, there may be something of that kind) and therefore till the contrary doth appear, I hold it not unlawful to endeavour to give a physical account of his cures, and to enquire whether his touch be any more than a more noble specific, that reaches not to all diseases, or to most, but to more than the generality of specificks, whose operations are usually more confined.[298]

The fact that Boyle's explanation to Stubbe, dated March 9, 1666, is identical to Greatrakes' own account, dated May 10, 1666, suggests that the latitudinarians and especially Boyle had a hand in preparing Greatrakes' *Brief Account*. This suggestion is strengthened by the evidence already presented. Greatrakes is shown in his *Account* to be a latitudinarian; the reason he gives to explain why God has given him healing power—as a blow at once against atheists and papists—is consistent with latitudinarian purposes, and the latitudinarians are prominent among those whose testimonials to the cures are appended to the tract. *A Brief Account*, moreover, is in the form of a letter addressed to Boyle himself. Boyle never either publicly or privately, as far as the evidence allows, denounced or quibbled with the *Account*. Nor is it likely that he would have. His own testimonials appear among those of his latitudinarian friends at the end of the tract, and he must have been satisfied to find in it both the latitudinarian sentiments Greatrakes expressed and an explanation of the cures exactly like his own, if indeed his own explanation was not the direct source for the one in the tract.

It is in the light of the Greatrakes affair that Boyle's *Free Inquiry into the Vulgarly Received Notion of Nature* should be read. There he gives the same explanation of phenomena similar to Greatrakes' cures that appears in *A Brief Account* and his own letter to Stubbe.[299] And his reasons are the same: religion must be protected from an improper understanding of nature, and the corpuscular philosophy is the best way of doing so. *A Free Inquiry* represents his fullest expression of this philosophy,[300] and it is both interesting and significant that he undertakes to write it not for its own sake but as an attack on "the vulgarly received notion of nature." His quarrel here is less with Aristotle and his scholastic interpreters than with certain contemporaries. Aristotelianism was no longer the polite doctrine of the schools; it had been taken into the streets and was being discussed in the coffeehouses, and there it was being given new, alarming twists of meaning. The origins of Boyle's natural philosophy lie in part in the vulgarization, and radicalization, of Plato and Aristotle.[301]

Far from being irreligious in its effects, natural philosophy, properly understood and pursued, strengthens the faith. This is what Boyle had maintained against the mortalists, sectaries, and "Macchiavillians" in the 1640s and 1650s; it is what he continued to maintain against the likes of Heydon and Stubbe after the Restoration. The battle lines were the same. Only now the roles were reversed: sectaries and republicans were very much on the defensive, and it was Boyle who could at last publish the ideas he had once only circulated in manuscript among friends. The enemy was reduced to expressing their views in cryptic explanations of the cures of a rustic Irish stroker. Boyle, on the other hand, was now at the helm of the wider public with the full weight of the Royal Society and various imperial commissions backing his view of the relations between reason and faith, knowledge and society, science and power. With this support, he hoped to quell the dissidents and increase the ranks of the godly, to Christianize the world, and make the British empire strong and prosperous. This program would constitute the entering wedge in a reformation whereby his social vision, shared by his latitudinarian colleagues and the leadership of the Royal Society, would ultimately prevail everywhere.

# Chapter 5

# Science, Religion, and Revolution

In conclusion, I wish to point out how this study adds to the ongoing inquiry into the social relations of science in the seventeenth century. What is new derives from my attempt to explain the impact of the English revolution upon Boyle's thought. Other contributors to our understanding of the relations between Boyle's science and religion in this period have brought the contextual factor, if not the factor of revolution, into the picture. Professor Robert K. Merton, for example, in his stress on puritanism in the shaping of Boyle's science, acknowledges that puritan values did not remain fixed and constant but were themselves subject to influence by other factors,[1] and Professor Barbara J. Shapiro's trenchant critique of Merton recognizes the impact of war and politics upon science and intellect.[2] But neither has dealt with the interaction between Boyle's ideas and his experience of revolution in a sustained, precise, and analytical way. In this way I have integrated more aspects of his life and thought than had been done before—among others his pansophy; his Hermetism; his millenarianism; his scripturalism; his dialogue with the sects, "Macchiavillians," deists, mortalists and republicans; his government service; his family's fortunes. The list is long. And by this integration I have come to a deeper and more subtle understanding of the relationship between Boyle's own

177

science and faith and the social relations of science in revolutionary
England.

In particular Boyle's "puritanism," produced by revolution, is no
longer puritanism as Merton defines it. As a result, Merton's thesis
becomes subject to serious revision—at least when it comes to explaining Boyle, whose thought represented for Merton one of the
main evidences of the strength of his thesis. Boyle's childhood religious experiences bear the earmarks of Merton's puritanism—
anxiety about the state of one's soul with reference to the future
state and the expression of this anxiety in a compelling commitment to an ascetic life devoted to serving God.[3] More to this point
is the fact that Boyle spent his early adolescence in Calvinist
Geneva and was educated in the circle of one of its leading
ministerial families, the family Diodati.[4] But it is a long way from
Boyle's adolescent piety to the religious views he expresses in his
mature natural philosophy and the route is circuitous. He initially
expressed his adolescent puritanism, his commitment to a life
spent in God's service, in terms of an aristocratic ethic that limited
the outlets for such service to performance of the obligations traditionally expected of someone of Boyle's caste—namely, service to
family, peers, church, and king. These services suited the son of an
aristocrat, and they left no place for experiments and mechanics,
which were conventionally seen to be socially inferior employments. Yet Boyle was later to spend much of his life pursuing experimental science and mechanical philosophy and to see this endeavor as fulfilling his obligation to serve God. How is this discrepancy between the objects of his initial puritanism and those of his
mature belief to be explained?

The answer lies not in Merton's theory of the connection between a monolithic puritanism and science but in the dialectics of
revolution. What Boyle believed to be legitimate ways of satisfying
his compelling psychic need to serve God changed under the impact of events. When during the civil wars the paths to public and
godly service prescribed by the conventional wisdom were no
longer open to him, or when to have pursued them in the face of
circumstances would have been to invite ruin or at least to jeopar-
dize his fortune, he set off in a new direction. Gone were the aristocratic code and its assumptions. In their place stood an ethic em-

phasizing struggle against the odds and individual initiative in the pursuit of self-interest, an ethic that not only represented Boyle's predicament but also provided the psychic formulas for extricating himself from it. His success in the application of the new prescriptions mingled with his need to believe that he was doing God's will, and out of the resulting ferment came Boyle's particular kind of providentialism, the assumption that private interests piously pursued conduce in the long run to public good. Here was his new justification for public and godly service. So complete was his break with the old order that he put those gentlemen who still obeyed the traditional code in the camp of the ungodly.

After this moral and intellectual transformation Boyle's puritan emphasis on a godly life was still there but its forms and objects had changed. One of his new objects was natural philosophy. The study of nature for useful knowledge, scorned and disdained under the old aristocratic dispensation, became one of Boyle's chief preoccupations. He came to see it as constituting one of the principal means by which men, and especially gentlemen, could worship and serve God. He could claim as much because the natural philosophy he developed suited the purposes and satisfied the demands of his new ethic. In the private sphere the study of nature fostered industry and the fruits of industry—or profit. In the public sphere too the rewards were enormous: besides the obvious benefits to trade, empire, and Protestant power, there was in science, as applied to the strictly domestic scene, the formula for political stability, religious peace, and national prosperity. Science would create jobs and wealth, keeping men busy and making them too prosperous for religious dissension and political subversion. Experimental philosophy, the procedure of science, teaches religious truth by furnishing a model of how to live—soberly, industriously, temperately. And the mechanical philosophy, the content of science, does the same by confirming the doctrines of the immortality of the soul, of future rewards and punishments, and of the uniqueness and the divine origin and sanctity of Scripture, and so wins men back from the errors of heretics and radicals.

These public and private uses of science, moreover, are mutually beneficial: private profit conduces to stability and power, and they in turn increase security and the opportunity for profit. Science for

Boyle was the key to the connection between private interests and
the public good on the basis of which he legitimated his new ethic.
No longer socially, intellectually, and spiritually degrading or suspect, science or, more accurately, experimental and mechanical
philosophy had become supremely desirable at least to Boyle and
other founders of the Royal Society. The operative factor in the
case of Boyle's transformation was not puritanism, as Merton un-
derstands and applies it. It was the complicated dialectics of revolution as they worked upon Boyle's initial puritan compulsion to
serve God, a psychic need he shared with any Huguenot lord or
Genevan bourgeois of the late sixteenth and early seventeenth centuries but which led to the development and triumph of corpus-
cularianism as a result of the peculiar conditions at hand in mid-
seventeenth-century England.

# Abbreviations

# Abbreviations

| | |
|---|---|
| Add. | Additional |
| *AHR* | *The American Historical Review* |
| *AO* | Anthony Wood, *Athenae Oxonienses*, 2 vols. (London, 1691) |
| Birch, *History* | Thomas Birch, *The History of the Royal Society*, 4 vols. (London, 1756-1757) |
| Birch, *Life* in Works | Thomas Birch, *The Life of the Honourable Robert Boyle*, in Thomas Birch, ed., *The Works of the Honourable Robert Boyle*, 6 vols. (London, 1772), 1:v-ccxviii |
| BL | The Royal Society of London. Boyle Letters |
| B.M. | The British Museum |
| BP | The Royal Society of London. Boyle Papers |
| *Conway* | Marjorie H. Nicolson, ed., *Conway Letters* (New Haven, Conn., 1930) |
| *CSP, Col.* | *Calendar of State Papers, Colonial Series* |
| *DNB* | Sir Leslie Stephen and Sir Sidney Lee, eds., *The Dictionary of National Biography* |
| *EHR* | *The English Historical Review* |
| *HDC* | G. H. Turnbull, *Hartlib, Dury and Comenius* (Liverpool, England, 1947) |
| *HOC* | A. Rupert Hall and Marie Boas Hall, eds., *The Correspondence of Henry Oldenburg*, 7 vols. (Madison, Wis., 1965-1970) |
| *JHI* | *Journal of the History of Ideas* |

| | |
|---|---|
| Kellaway | William Kellaway, *The New England Company, 1649-1776* (New York, 1961) |
| *Lismore* | Alexander B. Grosart, ed., *The Lismore Papers,* 1st ser., 5 vols. (London, 1886); 2d ser., 5 vols. (London, 1887) |
| Maddison, *Life* | R. E. W. Maddison, *The Life of the Honourable Robert Boyle, F.R.S.* (London, 1969). |
| Maddison, "Studies" | R. E. W. Maddison, "Studies in the Life of Robert Boyle, F.R.S., Part VI. The Stalbridge Period, 1645-1655, and the Invisible College," *Notes and Records of the Royal Society of London* 18 (December 1963): 104-24 |
| *MHS* | *Massachusetts Historical Society* |
| *N&Q* | *Notes and Queries* |
| *N&R* | *Notes and Records of the Royal Society of London* |
| *P&P* | *Past and Present* |
| P.R.O. | **Public Record Office** |
| Pulsifer | David Pulsifer, ed., *Acts of the Commissioners of the United Colonies of New England, 1643-1679,* vols. 9-10, in *Records of the Colony of New Plymouth, in New England,* ed. Nathaniel B. Shurtleff, 12 vols. in 11, (Boston, 1855-1861) |
| r. | *recto* (for manuscript folios) |
| *Rawdon* | E. Berwick, ed., *The Rawdon Papers* (London, 1819). |
| *RB* | Richard Baxter, *Reliquiae Baxterianae . . .* (London, 1696) |
| *RBW* | Thomas Birch, ed., *The Works of the Honourable Robert Boyle,* 6 vols. (London, 1772) |
| R.S. | **The Royal Society of London** |
| *TRHS* | *Transactions of the Royal Historical Society* |
| v. | *verso* (for manuscript folios) |
| Vaughan | Robert Vaughan, ed., *The Protectorate of Oliver Cromwell,* 2 vols. (London, 1838) |

Westfall,
"Boyle Papers" R. S. Westfall, "Unpublished Boyle Papers Relating
to Scientific Method," *Annals of Science* 12 (March
1956): 63-73, and (June 1957): 103-17

Winthrop          Robert C. Winthrop, ed., *Correspondence of Hartlib,
Haak, Oldenburg and Others of the Founders of the
Royal Society with Governor Winthrop of Connecticut
1661-1672* (Boston, 1878)

*Worthington*      James Crossley, ed., *The Diary and Correspondence of
Dr John Worthington*, vol. 1 in vol. 13 (1847), vol. 2
in vol. 36 (1855), vol. 3 in vol. 114 (1886), of
*Chetham Society Remains*

# Notes

# Notes

## Notes to Preface

1. James B. Conant, ed., *Robert Boyle's Experiments in Pneumatics* (Cambridge, Mass., 1967); Marie Boas, "Boyle as Theoretical Scientist," *Isis* 40 (1950): 261-68; Marie Boas, "An Early Version of Boyle's Sceptical Chemist," *Isis* 45 (1954): 153-68; Marie Boas, "La Méthode Scientifique de Robert Boyle," *Revue d'histoire des Sciences* 9 (1956): 105-25; Marie Boas, *Robert Boyle and Seventeenth-Century Chemistry* (Cambridge, Mass., 1958); T. S. Kuhn, "Robert Boyle and Structural Chemistry in the Seventeenth Century," *Isis* 43 (April 1952): 12-36; R. S. Westfall, "Unpublished Boyle Papers Relating to Scientific Method," *Annals of Science* 12 (March 1956): 63-73, and (June 1957): 103-17; Henry G. Van Leeuwen, *The Problem of Certainty in English Thought 1630-1690* (The Hague, The Netherlands, 1963), pp. 90-106; Maurice Mandelbaum, *Philosophy, Science and Sense Perception* (Baltimore, 1964), pp. 88-117; R. H. Kargon, *Atomism in England from Harriot to Newton,* (Oxford, England, 1966), pp. 93-105; and L. Laudan, "The Clock Metaphor and Probabilism: the Impact of Descartes on English Methodological Thought, 1650-65," *Annals of Science* 22 (June 1966): 108-43.
2. L. T. More, *The Life and Works of the Honourable Robert Boyle* (New York, 1944); Mitchell S. Fisher, *Robert Boyle, Devout Naturalist* (Philadelphia, 1945); Richard S. Westfall, *Science and Religion in Seventeenth-Century England* (New Haven, Conn., 1958); and Kargon, *Atomism in England,* pp. 76, 93-105.
3. H. Fisch, "The Scientist as Priest: A Note on Robert Boyle's Natural Theology," *Isis* 40 (1953): 252-65; and J. E. McGuire, "Boyle's Conception of Nature," *JHI* 33 (October-December 1972): 523-42.
4. Robert K. Merton, *Science, Technology and Society in Seventeenth-Century England* (New York, 1970).
5. R. E. W. Maddison, *The Life of the Honourable Robert Boyle, F.R.S.* (London, 1969).

6. R. E. W. Maddison, "A Tentative Index of the Correspondence of the Honourable Robert Boyle, F.R.S., *N&R* 12 (November 1958): 128-201.

7. J. F. Fulton, *A Bibliography of the Honourable Robert Boyle, F.R.S.,* 2d ed. (Oxford, England, 1961).

8. Among works of this sort especially useful have been the following: Mary Douglas, *Natural Symbols* (Harmondsworth, England, 1973); Karl Mannheim, *Ideology and Utopia* (London, 1936); A. J. Krailsheimer, *Studies in Self-Interest* (Oxford, England, 1962); C. P. Macpherson, *The Political Theory of Possessive Individualism* (Oxford, England, 1962); T. S. Kuhn, *The Structure of Scientific Revolutions,* 2d ed. (Chicago, 1970); and David A. Hollinger, "T. S. Kuhn's Theory of Science and Its Implications for History," *AHR* 77 (April 1973): 370-93.

## Notes to Chapter 1

1. T. O. Ranger, "Richard Boyle and the Making of an Irish Fortune, 1588-1614," *Irish Historical Studies* 10 (1957): 257-97.

2. Chatsworth, Devonshire Collections; Richard, the earl of Cork, to Mr. Perkins, Dublin, June 2, 1635.

3. Ibid., Richard, the earl of Cork's Letter-Book, fol. 142, Lismore, January 6, 1636.

4. Quoted in Birch, *Life* in *Works,* p. xviii.

5. *Lismore,* 1st ser., 5: 108.

6. Quoted in Birch, *Life* in *Works,* p. xv.

7. Quoted in ibid.

8. For Marcombes see Maddison, *Life,* p. 21; and Maddison, "Studies in the Life of Robert Boyle, F.R.S. Part VII. The Grand Tour," *N&R* 20 (June 1965): 51-77 (cited hereafter as Maddison, "Tour").

9. Maddison, *Life,* p. 1.

10. Quoted in Birch, *Life* in *Works,* p. xxii.

11. Quoted in ibid., pp. xxii-xxiii.

12. Chatsworth, Devonshire Collections, November 16, 1640; see also *Lismore,* 2d ser., 5:114; Robert Boyle to his father, Lyons, May 15, 1642.

13. *Lismore,* 2d ser., 5: 19.

14. Ibid.

15. Ibid., p. 20.

16. Ibid., pp. 20-21.

17. Ibid., p. 22.

18. Ibid., p. 21.

19. Ibid., p. 22.

20. Ibid., p. 22.

21. Ibid., p. 21; Lyons, May 15, 1642.

22. Ibid., p. 72.
23. Ibid.
24. Ibid.; Robert Boyle to his father, Geneva, September 30, 1642.
25. Ibid.
26. Quoted in Birch, *Life* in *Works,* p. xxvii.
27. Lewis, Robert's older brother, was killed in battle.
28. Birch, *Life* in *Works,* p. xxvii.
29. Quoted in ibid. This passage suggests that Boyle would have fought on the side of the king. This is capable of two interpretations between which it is impossible to choose on the basis of the surviving evidence. First, Boyle may have been a royalist upon his returning from the Continent. If so there is no record of his championing the king's cause thereafter. As will later be clear, he tends not to read events from either the royalist or the parliamentary point of view but to invest them with a significance that transcends politics and is ultimately spiritual. Second, when he says he will serve under "the excellent king himself," he may mean that he will go to Ireland and help put down the rebellion against the crown. His older brothers were fighting there, and it is not unlikely that he was going to do likewise.
30. Ibid.
31. Ibid.
32. Dorothea Townshend, *The Life and Letters of the Great Earl of Cork* (London, 1904), p. 448.
33. Birch, *Life* in *Works,* p. xxvii.
34. C. Hill, *Reformation to Industrial Revolution* (Baltimore, 1969), p. 149.
35. Birch, *Life* in *Works,* p. xxvii; and *Calendar of Clarendon State Papers* (Oxford, England, 1872), p. 305.
36. Quoted in Birch, *Life* in *Works,* p. xxxiiii, London, October 22, 1646.
37. Quoted in ibid.
38. See, for example, John Wilkins, *The Beauty of Providence* (London, 1649); and James Stanley, seventh earl of Derby, *Private Devotions and Miscellanies,* ed. E. R. Raines. Part III: *The Stanley Papers,* in *Remains Historical and Literary Connected with the Palatine Counties of Lancaster and Chester* 70 (The Chetham Society, Manchester, 1867).
39. Quoted in Birch, *Life* in *Works,* pp. xxxiii-xxxiv.
40. Quoted in ibid., p. xxxiii.
41. Quoted in ibid., p. xxvii; and Mary Frear Keeler, *The Long Parliament 1640-1641* (Philadelphia, 1954), p. 239.
42. Quoted in Birch, *Life* in *Works,* p. xxvii.
43. Townshend, *Great Earl of Cork,* pp. 446-47; and Edward Hyde, earl of Clarendon, *State Papers* (Oxford, England, 1773) 2: 166-68.
44. Maddison, *Life,* pp. 61 and 63.
45. Only the briefest consideration of the careers of Dury and Hartlib is to be given here. For the context of their work see especially Hugh

Trevor-Roper, "Three Foreigners and the Philosophy of the English Revolution," *Encounter* 14 (1960): 3-20 (cited hereafter as Trevor-Roper, "Foreigners").

46. Charles Webster, "The Authorship and Significance of *Macaria*," *P&P*, no. 56 (August 1972): 36-42.

47. Ibid., pp. 42-43.

48. . . . *Macaria* . . . , in *The Harleian Miscellany* . . . 1 (London, 1808), p. 584.

49. Ibid., p. 582.

50. Ibid., pp. 583-84.

51. Ibid., p. 583.

52. Ibid.

53. Ibid., p. 582.

54. Ibid., p. 583.

55. Ibid., p. 584.

56. Ibid., p. 583.

57. Ibid., p. 584.

58. Ibid., pp. 584-85. "Secrets" refers here to chemical operations and more specifically to medicines and prescriptions or "receipts," as the word was then, for cures.

59. Birch, *Life* in *Works*, p. xxxi; Boyle to Marcombes, London, October 22, 1646.

60. Quoted in *ibid.*, p. xxix; Boyle to Lady Ranelagh, Stalbridge, March 30, 1646.

61. Quoted in ibid., p. xxxv; Boyle to Francis Tallents.

62. Quoted in ibid., pp. xxxii-xxxiii; Boyle to Marcombes, London, October 22, 1646.

63. Quoted in ibid., pp. xxxix-xl; Boyle to Dury, May 3, 1647.

64. Quoted in ibid., p. xxxv.

65. See note 43, this chapter.

66. Thomas Barlow, *Genuine Remains*, ed. Sir Peter Pett (London, 1693), p. 324.

67. *RBW* 6: 421; John Beale to Boyle, Yeovill, January 24, 1666.

68. E. de Budé, *Vie de Jean Diodati, Theologien Génevois 1574-1649* (Lausanne, 1869), pp. 31, 44-45.

69. Birch, *Life* in *Works*, p. xv.

70. *Lismore*, 1st ser., 4: 11, 200-201.

71. James C. Spalding and Maynard F. Brass, "Reduction of Episcopacy as a Means to Unity in England, 1640-1662," *Church History* 30 (December 1961): 414-32; and R. Buick Knox, *James Ussher* (Cardiff, Wales, 1967), pp. 115-16.

72. *HDC*, pp. 24, 156, 218, 225, 235.

73. Townshend, *Great Earl of Cork*, pp. 181, 188.

74. Maddison, *Life*, p. 21.

75. William Smith Clark, ed., *The Dramatic Works of Roger Boyle, Earl of Orrery* (Cambridge, Mass., 1937), 1: 5; and Budé, *Vie de Jean Diodati*, pp. 31, 44-45.

76. Clark, *Dramatic Works*, 1: 7.

77. Maddison, *Life*, p. 29.

78. *Lismore*, 1st ser., 5: 172.

79. BP 7, fol. 12.

80. Robert Boyle, *Some Considerations Touching the Style of the Holy Scriptures* (London, 1661), pp. 41-42, 76-78, 81-83. The unpublished "Essay of the Holy Scriptures" was begun sometime before January 25, 1650 (BP 36, fol. 36) and completed by 1651 or 1652 (*RBW* 2: 251; and Birch, *Life* in *Works*, p. xlvii).

81. Maddison, *Life*, p. 48; and Hugh Trevor-Roper, *The European Witch-Craze of the Sixteenth and Seventeenth Centuries and Other Essays* (New York, 1969), p. 209.

82. BP 8, fol. 133 r.; and Peter French, *John Dee* (London, 1972), pp. 155, 157-59 (cited hereafter as French, *Dee*).

83. For the dating of this passage see notes 57 and 66, chapter 3 below.

84. *Lismore*, 1st ser., 4: 217.

85. Quoted in Birch, *Life* in *Works*, p. xxxix, April 8, 1647.

86. Ibid., p. xli.

87. Quoted in ibid., p. xxxiv; Boyle to Tallents, London, February 20, 1647.

88. Ibid., p. xl.

89. Ibid., p. xxxiv.

90. Charles Webster has reviewed the scholarly literature dealing with the invisible college and offered a new hypothesis to explain it. See his "New Light on the Invisible College: the Social Relations of English Science in the Mid-Seventeenth Century," *TRHS* 5th ser., 24 (1974): 19-42. I am grateful to Mr. Webster for allowing me to read and use a prepublication typescript of this paper.

91. Quoted in Birch, *Life* in *Works*, p. xxxiv.

92. R.S., Robert Boyle, MS. 197, fol. 8. I assume that this manuscript dates from the mid-1640s because of the internal reference to "the Filosoficall Colledge." The handwriting is also that of other manuscripts dating from the 1640s and early 1650s and not afterward.

93. Ibid., fol. 19.

94. Ibid.

95. Ibid.

96. Ibid., fols. 20-21.

97. Ibid., fol. 8.

98. Ibid., fols. 7-8.

99. *RBW* 2: 323, 329-30.

100. Ibid., pp. 333-34.

101. Ibid., p. 342.

102. Boyle's later applications of the device will be brought out further on in the book.

103. *HDC;* R. F. Young, *Comenius in England* (Oxford, England, 1932); R. F. Young, *Comenius and the Indians of New England* (London, 1929); Trevor-Roper, "Foreigners"; and C. Webster, *Samuel Hartlib and the Advancement of Learning* (Cambridge, England, 1970).

104. J. A. Comenius, *The Way of Light,* trans. E. T. Campagnac (Liverpool, England, 1938), p. 4.

105. The original Latin edition was published in Amsterdam in 1668 and dedicated to the Royal Society of London. But the book had been written in England in 1641 and it was probably known to the Hartlib circle in the 1640s because Comenius' closest association while in England was with Hartlib and his colleagues and Comenius says that he left the manuscript of the book behind in England when he returned to the Continent (ibid., pp. 4-5).

106. Ibid., p. 7, for example.

107. Ibid., p. 5.

108. *RBW* 6: 132, Hartlib to Boyle, November 15, 1659.

109. Comenius, *Way of Light,* p. 81.

110. Ibid. The whole is grounded on this assumption.

111. Quoted in Birch, *Life* in *Works,* pp. xxxiv-xxxv.

112. Quoted in ibid., p. xxxviii, Boyle to Hartlib.

113. Margaret E. Rowbottom, "The Earliest Published Writing of Robert Boyle," *Annals of Science* 7 (November 21, 1950): 376-89; Marie Boas, *Robert Boyle and Seventeenth-Century Chemistry* (Cambridge, Mass., 1958), p. 17; and R. E. W. Maddison, "The Earliest Published Writing of Robert Boyle," *Annals of Science* 17 (1961): 165-73.

114. Rowbottom, "Writing of Robert Boyle," pp. 378-79.

115. See Walter E. Houghton, Jr., "The English Virtuoso in the Seventeenth Century," *JHI* 3 (January 1942): 51-73, and (April 1942): 190-219; and Lawrence Stone, *The Crisis of the Aristocracy 1558-1641* (Oxford, England, 1965), p. 717.

116. Francis Bacon, *Works,* eds. James Spedding, R. L. Ellis, and D. D. Heath (London, 1857-1874), 4: 78-79.

117. Rowbottom, "Writing of Robert Boyle," pp. 380-81.

118. Ibid., pp. 381-82.

119. Ibid., p. 382.

120. Ibid., p. 383.

121. Ibid.

122. Ibid.

123. J. A. Comenius, *The Reformation of Schools* (London, 1642), p. 31.

124. Ibid., p. 32.

125. Frances Yates, *The Rosicrucian Enlightenment* (London, 1972), pp. 155, 157, 161, 169-70 (cited hereafter as Yates, *Enlightenment*).

126. Birch, *Life* in *Works*, p. xxxviii.

127. Ibid.

128. Quoted in J. V. Andreae, *A Modell of a Christian Society,* reprinted in G. H. Turnbull, "Johann Valentin Andreaes Societas Christiana," *Zeitschrift für Deutsche Philologie* 74 (1955): 154.

129. Ibid., pp. 152, 153, 155, 157-59.

130. Birch, *Life* in *Works*, p. xxxviii, April 8, 1647.

131. BP 44, fol. 1r. "Diurnall Observations, Thoughts, & Collections. Begun at Stalbridge April 25th 1647."

132. Quoted in Birch, *Life* in *Works*, p. xxii.

133. Quoted in ibid.

134. Maddison, "Tour," p. 61.

135. "Philaretus" is the name by which Boyle refers to himself here and elsewhere.

136. Quoted in Birch, *Life* in *Works*, p. xxiii.

137. Quoted in ibid., p. xxii.

138. Quoted in ibid.

139. Maddison, *Life,* p. 1.


## Notes to Chapter 2

1. Quoted in Birch, *Life* in *Works*, p. xliii.

2. For the meanings attaching to the adjective "Machiavellian" in England in the 1640s, see Felix Raab, *The English Face of Machiavelli* (London, 1964), pp. 109-13.

3. R.S., MS. 196, fols. 54v.-55, "Of Piety." The content and handwriting of this manuscript suggest that it was written within several years of Boyle's return from Geneva. If this is so, it is contemporary with the period of Boyle's youth now being treated in the text.

4. R.S., "The Aretology or Ethicall Elements of Robert Boyle," MS. 195, fol. 170r. (hereafter cited as "Aretology").

5. Ibid., fol. 170.

6. Ibid., another manuscript in the same library—MS. 192, "The Ethicall Elements"—looks to be a draft of the first portion of MS. 195 (see note 4, this chapter).

7. Quoted in Birch, *Life* in *Works*, p. xxx.

8. Quoted in ibid., p. xxxiv.

9. Ibid., pp. xxxviii-xxxix, April 8, 1647.

10. B.M. Add. MS. 32093, fol. 293v., March 2, 1652.

11. Curtis Brown Watson, *Shakespeare and the Renaissance Concept of Honor* (Princeton, N.J., 1960), p. 67.

12. In this study little if any distinction is made between the aristocracy and the gentry. What the present writer chooses to call the aristocra-

tic ethic applied to both alike—and differently only in degree. This is not to say that there is no distinction to be drawn between aristocracy and gentry but only that it need not be made for the purposes of this study.

13. Robert Ashley, *Of Honour,* ed. Virgil B. Heltzel (San Marino, Calif., 1947), p. 35.
14. Ibid., pp. 28, 30.
15. Ruth Kelso, *The Doctrine of the English Gentleman in the Sixteenth Century* (Gloucester, Mass., 1964), p. 27.
16. Chatsworth, Devonshire Collections, Richard, the earl of Cork's Letter-Book, fol. 142, *Lismore,* January 6, 1636; Chatsworth, Devonshire Collections, Robert Boyle to Richard, the earl of Cork, November 16, 1640; and *Lismore,* 1st ser., 5: 114.
17. BP 37, "The Gentleman," fols. 1 and 4 (the folios in volume 37 are unnumbered; the folio numbers given here apply not to the folios of the volume but to the folios of this particular treatise, which is only a small part of the volume). For this tradition see Fritz Caspari, *Humanism and the Social Order in Tudor England* (New York, 1968), pp. 18-19, 189.
18. BP 37, "The Gentleman," fol. 1.
19. Ashley, *Of Honour,* p. 51; Kelso, *Doctrine,* pp. 22, 29-30; Watson, *Shakespeare,* p. 91; and Caspari, *Humanism,* pp. 18-20, 188-91.
20. BP 37, "The Gentleman," fol. 1.
21. Ibid., fols. 1-3.
22. Ibid., fol. 2.
23. Ibid.
24. Ibid., fol. 3.
25. Quoted in Birch, *Life* in *Works,* p. xii.
26. Quoted in ibid., pp. xii-xiii.
27. "Aretology," fol. 199.
28. *A Free Discourse Against Customary Swearing,* in *RBW* 6: 18. Birch (*Life* in *Works,* p. xliv) claims to have seen a finished or polished draft in Boyle's own script of this work dated 1647. This suggests that its composition was probably contemporary with "The Aretology."
29. *RBW* 6:19.
30. Watson, *Shakespeare,* p. 91; Ashley, *Of Honour,* p. 51; and Kelso, *Doctrine,* p. 22.
31. "Aretology," fols. 14v.-15 r.
32. Ibid.
33. Ibid., fol. 15r.
34. Ibid.
35. Ibid., fols. 22v-23r.
36. Ibid., fol. 23r.
37. Ibid., fol. 22v.
38. Ibid., fols. 23v.-24r.

39. Ibid.
40. R.S., MS. 196, fol. 38r., "Of Piety."
41. "Aretology," fols. 30v., 31v.-32r.
42. Ibid., fol. 14v.
43. Diogenes Laertius, *Lives of Eminent Philosophers,* trans. R. D. Hicks, 2 vols. (Cambridge, Mass., 1958), 2: 559.
44. "Aretology," fols. 13v. and 14v.
45. Birch claims that Boyle "read over the lives of the ancient philosophers with the utmost attention" sometime between September 1641 and May 1642 (see Birch, *Life* in *Works,* p. xxvi, and then ibid., pp. xxiv-xxvi). Whether Birch refers here to Diogenes' *Lives*— and his life of Epicurus in particular—is another question.
46. "Aretology," fol. 179r.
47. Ibid. There is a striking similarity between Boyle's sensibility in this regard and his contemporary's, Andrew Marvell.
48. Ibid., fol. 180v.
49. Ibid.
50. Ibid., fol. 177r.
51. Ibid.
52. Ibid.
53. Ibid., fol. 31v.
54. Ibid.
55. Ibid., fols. 31v.-32.
56. Ibid., fol. 32r.
57. R.S., MS. 196, fol. 63r., "Of Valour."
58. Ibid.
59. Ibid., fol. 63.
60. Ibid., fols. 63v.-64r.
61. Ibid., fol: 64r.
62. Ibid., fol. 63v.
63. Ibid., fols. 64v.-65r.
64. Ibid., fol. 65r.
65. For a similar transformation lived out and thought through by a French contemporary of Boyle's see F.E. Sutcliffe, *Guez de Balzac et Son Temps* (Paris, 1959), pp. 140-63.
66. "Aretology," fols. 211v.-212r.
67. Ibid., fol. 173r.; see also fol. 156.
68. Ibid., fol. 174r.
69. Ibid.
70. Ibid., fol. 174.
71. Ibid., fols. 174v.-175r.
72. Ibid., fol. 153v.
73. Ibid., fol. 155r.
74. Ibid., fol. 157r.
75. Ibid., fols. 23v.-24r.

76. Ibid., fol. 157r.
77. Ibid.
78. BP, "Of Time & Idleness" 14, fol. 20r. "Of Time & Idleness" is contemporary, or nearly so, with "The Aretology." (See BP 36.)
79. "Aretology," fols. 224v.-225r.
80. Ibid., fol. 197v.
81. Ibid., fol. 225r.
82. Ibid., fol. 225v.
83. Ibid., fols. 227v.-228r.
84. BP, "Of Time and Idleness," 14, Fol. 23r. The resemblance between Boyle's attitude toward time and the attitude expressed in Marvell's poetry is striking. See, for example, Marvell's "To His Coy Mistress."
85. BP, "Of Time & Idleness" 14, fol. 23r.
86. "Aretology," fol. 156r.
87. Boyle probably here meant by "Republickes" some form of elective monarchy.
88. "Aretology," fol. 156.
89. Ibid., fol. 29v.
90. Ibid., fol. 30r.
91. Ibid.
92. Ibid., fol. 25v.
93. Ibid., fol. 193r.
94. Ibid., fol. 26r.
95. Ibid., fol. 27r.
96. Ibid., fol. 17v.
97. This was written about 1647 (see Birch, Life in Works, p. xliv).
98. RBW 6: 18; see also R.S., MS. 196, fol. 38r., "Of Piety."
99. "Aretology," fol. 30v.
100. Ibid., fols. 205v.-206r.
101. Ibid., fol. 191.
102. Ibid., fol. 16.
103. Ibid., fol. 16v. "Our Knoledge," Boyle writes, "is like a paire of staires, at whose top we find our Coffin. Yet so much Knoledge may do, that tho it be not Happiness it selfe yet it may Discover it, & sho us the way to it."
104. Ibid., fol. 191r.
105. Ibid., fol. 191v.
106. Ibid.
107. Ibid., fol. 192r.
108. Ibid.
109. Ibid., fol. 192v.
110. Ibid.
111. C. Webster, "The Authorship and Significance of Macaria," P&P, no. 56 (August 1972): 42-43.

112. *RBW* 6: 132.
113. Quoted in Birch, *Life* in *Works,* pp. xxxviii-xxxix.
114. Quoted in ibid., p. xiii.
115. Ibid.


## Notes to Chapter 3

1. See note 19, this chapter.
2. *RBW* 1: 244.
3. Ibid., p. 255.
4. Ibid.
5. D. Underdown, *Pride's Purge* (Oxford, England, 1971), pp. 3, 14, 356; Leo Solt, *Saints in Arms* (Stanford, Calif., 1959), pp. 9-21; and J. S. Morrill, "Mutiny and Discontent in English Provincial Armies 1645-1647," *P&P,* no. 56 (August 1972): 49-74, especially 49-50, 52-53, 68, 73-74.
6. C. Hill, *The World Turned Upside Down* (London, 1972), pp. 132-33, for such views;·and C. H. Firth and R. S. Rait, eds., *Acts and Ordinances of the Interregnum* (London, 1911), 2: 409-12, for the law of August 9, 1650, against such views.
7. *RBW* 1: 254.
8. Ibid., pp. 254-55. For Boyle's anxiety about the contrary notions of the sects at the time see also ibid. 6: 45; Boyle to Lady Ranelagh, Stalbridge, May 13, 1648.
9. For the background and implications of this belief see Hill, *The World Turned Upside Down,* chap. 8.
10. *RBW* 1: 277-78.
11. Ibid., p. 279.
12. Ibid., pp. 277-78.
13. Ibid., pp. 254-55.
14. Ibid., p. 254.
15. K. Bottigheimer, *English Money and Irish Land* (Oxford, England, 1971), pp. 102-104, 108-109.
16. Thomas Carte, *An History of the Life of James Duke of Ormonde* (London, 1785-1786), 3: 589, the marquess of Ormonde to Broghill, Carrick, November 2, 1648; Edward Hyde, the earl of Clarendon, *State Papers* (Oxford, England, 1773) 2: 501, "The Lord Inchiquin to the Marquis of Ormond," Kilmallock, December 9, 1649; and Thomas Morrice, "The Life of the Earl of Orrery," in *A Collection of the State Letters of the Right Honourable Roger Boyle . . .* (London, 1742), p. 9.
17. Dorothea Townshend, *The Life and Letters of the Great Earl of Cork,* (London, 1904), p. 444; see also Morrice, "Earl of Orrery," pp. 10-11.

18. Maddison, "Studies," p. 113.
19. A pseudonum for Roger, baron Broghill.
20. Historical Library, Yale Medical Library, Yale University.
21. Morrice, "Earl of Orrery," p. 11.
22. Ibid.
23. Ibid.
24. BP 3, fol. 146r.
25. Morrice, "Earl of Orrery," p. 11.
26. Maddison, "Studies," p. 116.
27. Ibid., p. 117.
28. BP 3, 146r.
29. The best accounts are: A. Woolrych, "Oliver Cromwell and the Rule of the Saints," in *The English Civil War and After,* ed. R. H. Parry (London, 1970), pp. 59-77; Underdown, *Pride's Purge;* Hill, *The World Turned Upside Down;* and B. S. Capp, *The Fifth Monarchy Men* (London, 1972).
30. Hill, *The World Turned Upside Down,* p. 53; and Underdown, *Pride's Purge,* p. 5.
31. Ibid., p. 3.
32. Ibid., pp. 87, 174, and 267.
33. Hugh Kearney, *Scholars and Gentlemen* (Ithaca, N.Y., 1970), p. 10; and J. E. Farnell, "The Usurpation of Honest London Householders: Barebone's Parliament," EHR 82 (January 1967): 24-46.
34. *RBW* 5: 255-311.
35. For a summary and somewhat different but interesting analysis of the plot see Roger Pilkington, *Robert Boyle* (London, 1959), pp. 112-19.
36. *RBW* 5: 269, 276-77, 283-85, and 298-99.
37. BP 36.
38. *RBW,* 5: 285.
39. BP 36.
40. B.M. Add. MS. 32093, fol. 293, Robert Boyle to John Mallet, March 2, 1651; and B.M., Harley 7003, fol. 180r., same to same, Twitenham, November 1651.
41. *RBW* 2: 390.
42. Ibid., pp. 417-18, in a dialogue "which treats of Angling improved to spiritual uses" (ibid., p. 391).
43. Ibid. pp. 412-14. Boyle was not alone in this view of the masses; see Hill, *The World Turned Upside Down,* p. 58.
44. *RBW* 2: 412-14.
45. This too was not a unique view but current among social conservatives; see Roger Lockyer, *Tudor and Stuart Britain 1471-1714* (New York, 1964), p. 290; and Underdown, *Pride's Purge,* p. 264.
46. *RBW* 2: 414.
47. Ibid. pp. 412-14; and B.M. Add. MS. 4229, fol. 39. This may be why Boyle used the form of a dialogue to write about politics. As he says,

when he finally published the piece in 1665, the form allowed him "to speak of himself as of another person . . . to avoid being suspected" should the papers fall into the hands of the "usurping government, that then prevailed" (*RBW* 2: 390).

48. C. Hill, *The Century of Revolution 1603-1714* (London, 1964), pp. 132-39, 148-51, 153-54; and C. Hill, *God's Englishman* (New York, 1972), pp. 149-51.

49. Comparable in the sense that although the threat in 1648-49 was of revolution from below and that of 1687 was of revolution from above, either one would have subverted the gentry-dominated state brought into being in the course of the century.

50. Lucien Wolf (ed.), *Menasseh ben Israel. Mission to Cromwell* (London, 1901), p. xi–lxxvii.

51. M. James, *Social Problems and Policy during the Puritan Revolution 1640-1660* (London, 1930), pp. 189-90; and J. M. Batten, *John Dury* (Chicago, 1944), pp. 139-40 (cited hereafter as Batten, *Dury*).

52. B.M., Harley 7003, fol. 179; Boyle to Mallet, November 1651.

53. For instance, Richard Baxter, *The Unreasonableness of Infidelity* (London, 1655), "The Preface," and Part II, pp. 163-69, 176-77 (cited hereafter as Baxter, *Unreasonableness*); and Hill, *The World Turned Upside Down*, pp. 210-15.

54. B.M., Harley 7003, fol. 180r.

55. *RBW* 2: 309, and 6: 49; and B.M. Add. MS. 32093, fols. 293-94; Boyle to Mallet, March 2, 1651.

56. *RBW* 6: 49.

57. *Some Considerations Touching the Usefulness of Experimental Natural Philosophy*, Part I, in *RBW* 2: 19-20, 29-30 (cited hereafter as *Considerations*, Part I). These were written in large part between 1649 and 1654; see Westfall, "Boyle Papers," p. 65.

58. "Of Celestial Influences or Effluviums in the Air," in *RBW* 5: 638-42 (for dating see Westfall, "Boyle Papers," p. 65).

59. *RBW* 6: 46; Robert Boyle to Lady Elizabeth Hussey, June 6, 1648.

60. Besides the letter of August 31, 1649, see H. Fisch, "The Scientist as Priest: A Note on Robert Boyle's Natural Theology," *Isis* 40 (1953): 256, referring to certain of Boyle's *Occasional Reflections* pertaining to alchemy.

61. BP 8, fols. 123-38.

62. Ibid., fol. 123.

63. Ibid. 36.

64. Ibid. 8, fols. 127v. and 128v.

65. Westfall, "Boyle Papers," p. 65.

66. Compare, for instance, *RBW* 2: 6-7, 9-10, and BP 8, fol. 129; *RBW* 2: 15, and BP 8, fol. 124v.; *RBW* 2: 18-19, and BP 8, fol. 127v.; *RBW* 2: 19, 29, and BP 8, fol. 138r.; and *RBW* 2: 31-35, and BP 8, fols. 125r.-128v.

67. Ibid., fol. 123.
68. Ibid., fol. 138r.
69. Ibid.
70. Ibid.
71. Ibid.,
72. Ibid., 7, fol. 285r.
73. Ibid., fol. 272v.
74. *RBW* 6:50.
75. *Considerations,* Part I, in *RBW* 2: 8-9, 13-15, 30-35, 49-50.
76. Ibid., pp. 31-32; and BP 8, fol. 126r.
77. *Considerations,* Part I, in *RBW* 2: 53.
78. BP 8, fol. 126r.
79. *Considerations,* Part I, in *RBW* 2: 32.
80. Ibid., p. 62.
81. Ibid., pp. 32-33.
82. The history of this controversy has not been dealt with systematically
    as far as I know, but an illuminating treatment of some of the issues
    and participants is Paolo Rossi's "Nobility of Man and Plurality of
    Worlds," in *Science, Medicine and Society in the Renaissance,* ed. Allen
    Debus (New York, 1972), 2: 131-62.
83. Much of the argument outlined in this paragraph can be found in J.
    V. Andreae's *Christianopolis,* a work which Boyle knew and spoke
    favorably of to Hartlib. Andreae, like Boyle after him, argued that the
    study of nature, properly conducted, is at once a Christian duty and
    a source of moral and spiritual enlightenment. Andreae also said that
    man's contemplation of the creatures serves both of God's purposes
    in the creation at the same time. (*Christianopolis,* trans. Felix E. Held
    [New York, 1916], pp. 231-32). Here then are additional links be-
    tween the pansophical ideas that circulated among the Hartlib circle
    and the origins of Boyle's natural philosophy. But it would be unwise
    to think that Boyle's thought in this regard derived entirely from that
    circle. Boyle's unique experience also shaped his thinking and to
    some extent determined the meanings he read into ideas he picked
    up from Hartlib and company.
84. Frances Yates, *Giordano Bruno and the Hermetic Tradition* (London,
    1964), p. 2 (cited hereafter as Yates, *Bruno*).
85. Ibid., pp. 5-8.
86. Ibid., passim; J. E. McGuire and P. Rattansi, "Newton and the 'Pipes
    of Pan,' " *N&R* 21 (December 1966): 108-43; M. C. Jacob, "John To-
    land and the Newtonian Ideology," *Journal of the Courtauld and War-
    burg Institutes* 32 (1969): 307-31; and D. P. Walker, *The Ancient Theol-
    ogy* (London, 1972), passim.
87. Yates, *Bruno,* chap. 21.
88. See BP 8, fol. 128, for example.
89. Yates, *Enlightenment,* chaps. 11-13.

90. D. P. Walker, "The Prisca Theologia in France," *Journal of the Cour-tauld and Warburg Institutes* 17 (1954): 209, 211-12.

91. BP 8, fol. 127v., and *RBW* 2: 301, for references dating from 1649 or the early 1650s (see notes 57 and 66, this chapter, for dating) to Pico's Hermetism; for a reference to Mornay's see BP 8, fol. 133r., where Boyle cites the chief source for Mornay's Hermetism (cf. French, *Dee*, p. 158), "the third Chapter of that excellent Treatise of the Truth of Christian Religion . . . Penn'd & translated by the 2 greatest Favorites the two last Ages have afforded me Mr. Du Plessis & Sr Philip Sidney."

92. Yates, *Bruno*, pp. 35-36.

93. Allen Debus, ed. *Science and Education in the Seventeenth Century. The Webster-Ward Debate* (London, 1970), p. 9.

94. BP 8, fol. 128.

95. Ibid., fol. 128v.

96. *Considerations*, Part I, in *RBW* 2:9.

97. BP 8, fol. 125r.; and *Considerations*, Part I, in *RBW* 2: 33-34.

98. BP 8, fol. 125v.

99. Ibid., fol. 128.

100. *Considerations*, Part I, in *RBW* 2: 34; and BP 8, fol. 128.

101. *Considerations*, Part I, in *RBW* 2:6.

102. Ibid., p. 9.

103. Ibid., pp. 14-15.

104. BP 8, fol. 138r.

105. Baxter, *Unreasonableness*, "The Preface," and Part II, pp. 163-69, 176-77; and C. Hill, *Antichrist in Seventeenth-Century England* (Oxford, England, 1971), pp. 140-42 (cited hereafter as Hill, *Antichrist*).

106. H. R. Trevor-Roper, "Oliver Cromwell and His Parliaments," in *Religion, the Reformation and Social Change* (London, 1967), pp. 362-71; Austin Woolrych, "The Calling of Barebone's Parliament," *EHR* 316 (July 1965): 494-98, 512-13; William M. Lamont, *Godly Rule* (London, 1969), chaps. 6 and 7, especially pp. 136-40; Hill, *Antichrist*, pp. 94-145; and Capp, *Fifth Monarchy*, chaps. 1-4.

107. *Considerations*, Part I, in *RBW* 2: 6.

108. Fisch, "Scientist as Priest," pp. 252-65, treats of Boyle's appropriation of hermetic doctrines and claims that they served as the basis of "the integration" of his science and religion, to which his natural philosophy in turn "owes its dynamism . . ." (ibid., pp. 253-54). I agree about the integrating effect of Hermetism on Boyle's thought. But according to Fisch, Boyle's reasons for introducing hermetic doctrines into his thought were "metaphysical and psychological" (ibid., p. 254), whereas I am arguing that they were psychosocial or ideological.

109. Yates, *Bruno*, p. 6.

110. BP 8, fol. 127v.

111. *Considerations,* Part I, in *RBW* 2: 10.
112. Geoffrey Nuttall, " 'Unity with the Creation': George Fox and the Hermetic Tradition," in *The Puritan Spirit* (London, 1967), pp. 194-203; Hill, *The World Turned Upside Down,* pp. 231-35; and John Webster, *Academiarum Examen* (London, 1654), pp. 26-32.
113. For instance, Baxter, *Unreasonableness,* "The Preface," and Part II, pp. 163-69, 176-77; and *RB,* Book I, p. 76.
114. One of "the two leading mid-seventeenth century hermeticists," in K. Thomas, *Religion and the Decline of Magic* (London, 1971), p. 270; the other was Thomas Vaughan.
115. William Haller, *The Rise of Puritanism* (New York, 1938), pp. 211-12; and Serge Hutin, *Les Disciples Anglais de Jacob Boehme aux XVII^e et XVIII^e Siècles* (Paris, 1960), pp. 69-70.
116. Haller, *Puritanism,* p. 208.
117. Compare BP 8, fol. 127v., and Everard's translation, p. 2; and BP 8, fol. 128v., and Everard, p. 1, and "To the Reader"; see also *Considerations,* Part I, in *RBW* 2: 31.
118. The literature on Everard's career is considerable, but he lacks a systematic study: see among others R. M. Jones, *Mysticism and Democracy in the English Commonwealth* (Cambridge, Mass., 1932), p. 63ff.; G. Davies, "English Political Sermons, 1603-1640," *The Huntington Library Quarterly* 3 (October 1939): 9-10; W. K. Jordan, "Sectarian Thought and Its Relation to the Development of Religious Toleration, 1640-1660," *The Huntington Library Quarterly* 3 (January 1940): 214-19; Eirionnack, "Notes on Certain Theosophists and Mystics. Tauler and His School," *N&Q,* 4th ser., 1: 597-600; George Sabine, ed., *The Works of Gerrard Winstanley* (Ithaca, N. Y., 1941), pp. 29-31; and Nuttall, *The Puritan Spirit,* p. 195.
119. *Considerations,* Part I, in *RBW* 2: 61.
120. Ibid., p. 262; Maddison, "Studies"; and J. J. O'Brien, "Samuel Hartlib's Influence on Robert Boyle's Scientific Development. Part I. The Stalbridge Period," *Annals of Science* 21 (March 1965), pp. 1-14.
121. Webster, *Academiarum Examen,* pp. 74-76, 106–107; Baxter, *Unreasonableness,* Part IV, 146-149, 154-56; P. M. Rattansi, "Paracelsus and the Puritan Revolution," *Ambix* 11 (1964): 24-32; and P. M. Rattansi, "The Intellectual Origins of the Royal Society," *N&R* 23 (December 1968): 136-37.
122. Compare, for example, *Considerations,* Part I, in *RBW* 2: 61, and T. Vaughan, *Magia Adamica: Or the Ambiguitie of Magic,* in *The Magical Writings of Thomas Vaughan,* ed. A. E. Waite (London, 1888), pp. 103-104; see also G. H. Turnbull, "George Stirk, Philosopher by Fire (1628?-1665)," *Publications of the Colonial Society of Massachusetts* 38. *Transactions 1947-1951* (Boston, 1959), p. 238; R. S. Wilkinson, "The Hartlib Papers and Seventeenth-Century Chemistry. Part I," *Ambix* 15 (1968): 62-63; and Maddison, *Life,* p. 79.

123. T. Vaughan, *Anthroposophia Theomagia,* in Waite, ed., *Magical Writings,* p. 38.

124. *Conway,* p. 75.

125. *Considerations,* Part I, in *RBW* 2: 61.

126. Ibid., pp. 39, 45-46.

127. See note 1, in Preface.

128. *Considerations,* Part I, in *RBW* 2: 36.

129. Ibid., p. 37.

130. Ibid., pp. 37-38.

131. Ibid., pp. 38, 40.

132. Ibid., p. 40.

133. Baxter, *Unreasonableness,* "The Preface," p. (c3); Firth and Rait, *Acts and Ordinances of the Interregnum* 1: 1133-34; Nathaniel H. Henry, "Milton and Hobbes: Mortalism and the Intermediate State," *Studies in Philology* 48 (1951): 234-49; Joseph Frank, *The Levellers* (Cambridge, Mass., 1955), p. 299; and Hill, *The World Turned Upside Down,* pp. 133, 143-44.

134. Denis Saurat, *Milton, Man and Thinker* (London, 1944), p. 278; George Newton Conklin, *Biblical Criticism and Heresy in Milton* (New York, 1949), chap. 6; and Richard Overton, *Mans Mortalitie* (Amsterdam, 1644), pp. 27-29.

135. Hill, *The World Turned Upside Down,* pp. 111, 113-14, 143.

136. *Considerations,* Part I, in *RBW* 2: 38.

137. Ibid., p. 39.

138. Ibid., pp. 40-44, 47-49.

139. Ibid., p. 29.

140. Ibid., p. 19.

141. Ibid., p. 29.

142. Ibid., pp. 19-20.

143. Ibid., p. 19; BP 8, fol. 138r., written during the same period as the passages just quoted (note 56, this chapter), confirms the point of this paragraph and the following paragraph of the text.

144. *Considerations,* Part I, in *RBW* 2: 29.

145. Ibid.

146. Ibid., p. 14.

147. Ibid., pp. 56-57.

148. Ibid., p. 62.

149. *RBW,* 2: 251; cited hereafter as *Style;* this piece was begun before January 25, 1650 (BP 36) and first published in 1661.

150. *Considerations,* Part I, in *RBW* 2: 57-58.

151. Ibid., pp. 15-17, 19-20.

152. *Style,* in *RBW* 2: 291.

153. As Boyle says elsewhere, "The last and correctest edition of the law of Nature is the Gospel" (BP 5, fol. 96).

154. *Style,* in *RBW* 2: 275-76.

155. Ibid., p. 276; see also pp. 257-75.

156. Ibid., pp. 276-78, 290-91.

157. Ibid., p. 313.

158. Ibid., p. 312.

159. Ibid., p. 311.

160. See ibid., p. 275, where the connection seems implied.

161. Ibid., pp. 306-308, 312.

162. Ibid., pp. 306-307; see also *Considerations*, Part I, in *RBW* 2: 29; and BP 8, fol. 138r.

163. *Style*, in *RBW* 2: 308-309.

164. B.M., Harley 7003, fol. 180r.; and B.M. Add. MS. 32093 fol. 293.

165. *Style*, in *RBW* 2: 311; and *Considerations*, Part I, in *RBW* 2: 19-20.

166. *Style*, in *RBW* 2: 276-77, 290-91.

167. Ibid., p. 308; see also BP 8, fol. 128; and *Considerations*, Part I, in *RBW* 2: 32-33, 56-57, 62.

168. Antiscripturism was not uncommon among radical sectaries during the interregnum; Hill, *The World Turned Upside Down*, pp. 209-15. Boyle writes: "anti-scripturism grows . . . rife, and spreads . . . fast . . . " (*Style*, in *RBW* 2: 295), and he identifies this heresy with certain sectaries (ibid., p. 307).

169. *Style*, in *RBW* 2: 306, 307.

170. Ibid., p. 309.

171. B.M., Harley 7003, fol. 180r.

172. B.M., Add. MS. 32093, fol. 293.

173. B.M., Harley 7003, fol. 180r.; Boyle to Mallet, November 1651.

174. Ibid., fol. 179r.

175. B.M., Add. MS. 32093, fol. 293.

176. *Style*, in *RBW* 2: 247-48, 251.

177. Ibid., pp. 247-49.

178. *RBW* 6: 534; "K.R." to Robert Boyle, September 14.

179. Ibid., pp. 564-65; Mary E. Palgrave, *Mary Rich; Countess of Warwick (1625-1678)* (London, 1901), p. 137; and Mary Rich, countess of Warwick, *Autobiography*, ed. L. Crofton Croker (London, 1848), pp. 24-25.

180. *Style*, in *RBW* 2: 248.

181. George R. Abernathy, Jr., "The English Presbyterians and the Stuart Restoration, 1648-1663," in *Transactions of the American Philosophical Society*, N.S., 55, Part 2 (May 1965): 11-12.

182. *RB*, Book I, Part II, p. 197.

183. Ibid.

184. Geoffrey Nuttall, *Richard Baxter* (London, 1965), p. 79.

185. Ibid., pp. 79-80.

186. Baxter, *Unreasonableness*, "The Epistle Dedicatory" and "The Preface."

187. Ibid., "The Preface," and Part II, pp. 164-68.

188. Ibid.

189. Ibid., Part II, p. 176.

190. Ibid., "The Preface."

191. Ibid.
192. Ibid., Part IV, p. 148.
193. Ibid., "The Preface," and Part IV, pp. 148-49.
194. Ibid., "The Preface," and Part II, pp. 163-68, 176-77.
195. *Style,* in *RBW* 2: 276-77.
196. Ibid., p. 276.
197. *RB,* Book I, Part II, p. 197.
198. James D. Ogilvie, ed., *Diary of Sir Archibald Johnston of Wariston* 3, *1655-1660,* in *Publications of the Scottish Historical Society,* 3d ser., 34 (Edinburgh, 1940): xviii, xxvi; and H. R. Trevor-Roper, "Scotland and the Puritan Revolution," in *Religion, the Reformation and Social Change* (New York, 1968), pp. 433-36.
199. Abernathy, "The English Presbyterians," pp. 11-12.
200. Birch, *Life* in *Works,* pp. cxli-cxlii; and [Pete]r [Pet]t, *A Discourse Concerning Liberty of Conscience* (London, 1661), pp. 28, 51, 72-75 (cited hereafter as Pett, *Discourse*).
201. Birch, *Life* in *Works,* p. xlviii.
202. *Style,* in *RBW* 2: 248, 251-52.
203. Quoted in Birch, *Life* in *Works,* p. xlviii.
204. *Style,* in *RBW* 2: 275-77; and *HDC,* pp. 156, 218, 225, 321; and Richard Parr, *The Life of . . . James Usher* (London, 1684), pp. 557-58.
205. Birch, *Life* in *Works,* p. xlviii; and *RB,* Book I, Part II, p. 206.
206. *HOC* 1: xxx-xxxii.
207. Ibid., pp. 73-74.
208. Ibid., pp. 82-83.
209. Ibid., p. 117.
210. R.S., MS. 1, fols. 191v. and 192v.
211. Ibid., fols. 190, 191v.-192v.
212. Ibid., fols. 190v. and 191v.
213. Ibid., fol. 193r.
214. *HOC* 1:180.
215. Ibid., pp. 126 and 392; and Cecil Roth, *A Life of Menasseh ben Israel* (Philadelphia, 1934), p. 253.
216. *HOC* 1: 24.
217. Ibid., pp. 24, 180.
218. Ibid., p. 120; see also Hill, *God's Englishman,* p. 164.
219. *HOC* 1: 23-24, 28-29.
220. Batten, *Dury,* chap. 8; and Hill, *God's Englishman,* p. 165.
221. Batten, *Dury,* pp. 129, 139-40.
222. *HOC* 1: 24, 180.
223. Hill, *God's Englishman,* p. 155.
224. Hill, *The World Turned Upside Down.*
225. R.S., MS. 1, fol. 190v.
226. For Milton see his *Areopagitica,* in *Complete Prose Works of John Milton,* ed. Don Wolfe (New Haven, Conn., and London, 1959), 2: 565, 567-68; for the others see notes 53, 62, 123, 124, in chapter I, above.

227. R.S., MS. 1, fol. 190v.
228. Ibid., fol. 191v.
229. Ibid., fol. 190; and *Worthington* 1: 218.
230. R.S., MS. 1, fols. 190, 194; for Broghill's views see John Thurloe, *State Papers* 4: 558; for Boyle's position see notes 1-36, in chapter IV, below.
231. R.S., MS. 1, fols. 190, 194.
232. One of the others was John Beale who became one of Boyle's closest associates in the 1660s and who in the late 1650s corresponded with Comenius about the impending millennium (Vaughan, 2: 439, 443, 447, 450, 463, 464; and *HDC,* pp. 378-79).
233. J. J. O'Brien, "Commonwealth Schemes for the Advancement of Learning," *British Journal of Educational Studies* 16 (1968): 30-42, especially pp. 30-31, 37-38 (cited hereafter as O'Brien, "Commonwealth Schemes").
234. Hartlib and Beale, for instance, sought the pansophical goal of "the reformation of the world" (*RBW* 6: 131-32).
235. O'Brien, "Commonwealth Schemes," p. 38.
236. See, for instance, *Style* in *RBW* 2: 256ff.; and R. Boyle, *The Sceptical Chymist* (London, 1949), pp. 6-9, 230.
237. L. Laudan, "The Clock Metaphor and Probabilism: the Impact of Descartes on English Methodological Thought, 1650-65," *Annals of Science* 22 (June 1966): 73-104; and Henry G. Van Leeuwen, *The Problem of Certainty in English Thought 1630-1690* (The Hague, the Netherlands, 1963), pp. 91-106.
238. Maurice Mandelbaum, *Philosophy, Science and Sense Perception* (Baltimore, 1964), pp. 88-117.
239. BP 43, eight unnumbered consecutive folios; for this point see especially among the eight, fol. 3.
240. Ibid.
241. John E. Wilson, "Comment on 'Two Roads to the Puritan Millennium,' " *Church History* 32 (1963): 341; and Capp, *Fifth Monarchy,* chaps. 1-4.
242. Ibid., pp. 138, 142.
243. Ibid., pp. 132-33.
244. Ibid., p. 188.
245. BP 43; out of the eight folios altogether see fol. 2v.; and Capp, *Fifth Monarchy,* p. 75.
246. Hill, *God's Englishman,* p. 151; and Austin Woolrych, "Last Quests for a Settlement 1657-1660," in *The Interregnum,* ed. G. E. Aylmer (London, 1972), p. 187 (cited hereafter as Woolrych in Aylmer).
247. BP 43; out of the eight consecutive folios see fol. 1r.
248. Ibid., fol. 1v. and 4v.
249. Ibid., fols. 3-4.
250. Capp, *Fifth Monarchy,* p. 154.
251. BP 43; out of the eight folios altogether see fol. 4v.

252. Capp, *Fifth Monarchy,* p. 109.
253. Allhallows, London, where these sermons were delivered, was a center of this effort (ibid., p. 110).
254. Birch, *Life* in *Works,* p. cxli.
255. Ibid.
256. Woolrych in Aylmer, p. 187; Richard Schlatter, ed., *Richard Baxter and Puritan Politics* (New Brunswick, N. J., 1957), pp. 11-12; and T. C. Barnard, "Lord Broghill, Vincent Gookin and the Cork Elections of 1659," *EHR* 88 (April 1973): 354.
257. Robert Sanderson, *Several Cases of Conscience,* trans. Robert Codrington (London, 1660), "The Epistle Dedicatory"; *RBW* 6: 302; and I. Walton, *The Life of Dr. Sanderson* (London, 1678), pp. 04v.-05r.
258. Ibid.
259. RBW 6: 302; and Sanderson, *Cases of Conscience,* "To the Courteous Reader," pp. A3r.-A4v.
260. Woolrych in Aylmer, pp. 190-201.
261. See this chapter, note 4.
262. See, for instance, "An Agreement of the People . . ." (1647), reprinted in Don M. Wolfe, ed., *Leveller Manifestoes of the Puritan Revolution* (New York, 1944), pp. 226-27.
263. Sanderson, *Cases of Conscience,* pp. 253-54, 262.
264. Ibid., pp. 251-52.
265. Ibid., pp. 267-68.
266. Ibid.
267. Ibid., p. 268.
268. Ibid., "To the Courteous Reader," pp. A3r.-A4v. and 361.
269. Compare ibid., and *RBW* 6: 302.
270. *RBW* 6:302; and Walton, *Dr. Sanderson,* pp. 04v.-05.
271. Sanderson, *Cases of Conscience,* pp. 361-62.
272. Ibid., p. 361.
273. Ibid., p. 362.
274. Ibid.
275. *RBW* 6: 636-37.
276. O'Brien, "Commonwealth Schemes," pp. 34-42.
277. See, for instance, *RBW* 6: 131-32; and *HOC* 1: 384-85, 387.
278. See, for instance, *HOC* 1: 353-54.
279. See, for instance, ibid., pp. 125, 392, 406.

## Notes to Chapter 4

1. Pett, who became a fellow of All Souls in 1648, met Boyle at Oxford sometime after he went there and before Oliver Cromwell's death, and they subsequently became close friends (B.M. Add. MS. 4229, fol. 39).

2. Birch, *Life* in *Works*, pp. cxli-cxlii.
3. Ibid.
4. Ibid.
5. Wilbur C. Abbott, "English Conspiracy and Dissent, 1660-1674, I," *AHR* 14 (April 1909): 505 (cited hereafter as Abbott, "Conspiracy, I").
6. Barlow had been a friend of Pett's since at least 1654. W. Bray, ed., *The Diary and Correspondence of John Evelyn* (London, 1859), 3: 64; and Christ Church Library, Evelyn MSS, John Evelyn, Letter-Book, 1655-1679, Epistles 81, 89, 132, 133, 141.
7. Birch, *Life* in *Works*, pp. cxli-cxlii.
8. Ibid. That Barlow's fears were justified is suggested by evidence in *AO* 1: 364.
9. Birch, *Life* in *Works*, pp. cxli-cxlii.
10. Pett, *Discourse*, pp. 6-7.
11. Ibid., p. 8; and Thomas Barlow, *The Case of Toleration in Matters of Religion*, in *Several Miscellaneous and Weighty Cases of Conscience* by Thomas Barlow (London, 1692), pp. 12-13 (cited hereafter as Barlow, *Case*).
12. Barlow, *Case*, pp. 12-13.
13. Pett, *Discourse*, pp. 7-8, 10, 24.
14. Barlow, *Case*, pp. 22-27.
15. Pett, *Discourse*, p. 8.
16. Ibid., p. 9.
17. See, for example, Baxter, *Unreasonableness*, Part IV, pp. 146-49 and 154-56.
18. Pett, *Discourse*, pp. 21-22.
19. Ibid., pp. 51-56 and 71.
20. Ibid., p. 53.
21. Ibid., pp. 53-56.
22. Ibid., pp. 51 and 71.
23. Barlow too probably favored Usher's model and for similar reasons. Barlow was a friend and correspondent of Usher's until his death (The Bodleian Library, Tanner MS. 461.20b).
24. R. S. Bosher, *The Making of the Restoration Settlement* (Westminster, London, 1951), p. 45.
25. Ibid., p. 118.
26. Pett, *Discourse*, pp. 73-74.
27. Ibid., p. 74.
28. Ibid., pp. 74-75.
29. Ibid., p. 33.
30. Ibid., p. 37.
31. Ibid., p. 39.
32. Ibid.
33. Ibid., p. 9.
34. Ibid., pp. 28-29.

35. Ibid., pp. 33-36.
36. Ibid., pp. 61-63. Pett practiced what he preached. At the time he published these opinions he was persuading continental Protestants to settle in Ireland for what seem to be the purposes trade serves (*Rawdon*, pp. 142-43; Pett to John Bramhall, archbishop of Armagh, London, March 21, 1661).
37. Pett, *Discourse*, p. 69.
38. Ibid., pp. 37, 39, 47-49, 50-51, 71.
39. *RBW* 3: 395.
40. Ibid., p. 398.
41. Ibid., p. 402.
42. Ibid., p. 442.
43. Ibid., pp. 421-22.
44. Ibid., p. 442.
45. Ibid., pp. 446-48.
46. Walter E. Houghton, Jr., "The History of Trades: Its Relation to Seventeenth-Century Thought," *JHI* 2 (January 1941): 33-60 (cited hereafter as Houghton, "Trades").
47. Worsley was perhaps the most important influence on Boyle in this regard; C. Webster, "New Light on the Invisible College: The Social Relations of English Science in the Mid-Seventeenth Century," *TRHS* 5th ser., 24 (1974), 19-24. See also [B. Worsley], *The Advocate* (London, 1652), reprinted in *The Eastland Trade and the Commonweal in the Seventeenth Century* by R. W. K. Hinton (Cambridge, England, 1959), pp. 203-13. Andrews identifies Worsley as the author of *The Advocate*. Charles M. Andrews, *The Colonial Period in American History* (New Haven, Conn., 1938), 4: 23, 41, 60.
48. BP 8, fol. 1r. This is a draft outline of "Essay I" in "The Second Section" of "The Second Part" of *The Usefulness*. This outline was communicated by Boyle to Oldenburg on April 25, 1666 (BP 8, fol. 1r.), but it may have been written sometime before, perhaps even with the rest about 1658. In any case, it was not published with the rest but separately by Joseph Glanvill in *Plus Ultra . . .* (London, 1668), p. 104.
49. Pett, *Discourse*, pp. 33, 37, 39.
50. Webster, "New Light on the Invisible College"; and [Worsley] in Hinton, *Eastland Trade*, pp. 204-205, 209.
51. Pett, *Discourse*, p. 39.
52. Louis B. Wright, *Religion and Empire* (Chapel Hill, N. C., 1943), pp. 6, 26-28, 100-101, 107-108.
53. See, for instance, note 90, this chapter.
54. Quoted in R. F. Young, *Comenius in England* (Oxford, England, 1932), pp. 59-60.
55. Jonathan Cohen, "On the Project of a Universal Character," *Mind* 63 (1954): 49-63; Benjamin De Mott, "Comenius and the Real Character

in England," *Publications of the Modern Language Association* 70 (1955): 1068-81 (cited hereafter as De Mott, "Comenius"); and B. De Mott, "The Sources and Development of John Wilkins' Philosophical Language," *Journal of English and Germanic Philology* 57 (1958): 1-13 (cited hereafter as De Mott, "Sources").

56. Cave Beck, *The Universal Character* . . . (Ipswich, England, 1657).
57. George Dalgarno, *Ars signorum* . . . (London, 1661).
58. Vivian Salmon, ed., *The Works of Francis Lodwick* (London, 1972).
59. De Mott, "Sources," p. 5.
60. Vaughan 2: 435; and Dalgarno, *Ars signorum,* p. (A4)ff.
61. Wilkins, *An Essay Towards a Real Character and a Philosophical Language* (London, 1668), "The Epistle Dedicatory."
62. Dalgarno, *Ars signorum,* p. (A4)ff.
63. P.R.O., C.O. 1/14, fol. 112.
64. *CSP, Col., America and the West Indies, 1574-1660* 1: 492-93.
65. Richard S. Dunn, *Puritans and Yankees* (New York, 1971), pp. 137-38, 152, 162.
66. See note 35, chapter 1 above.
67. Winthrop, p. 13.
68. Andrews, *Colonial Period* 4: 54-55, 56.
69. J. E. Farnell, "The Navigation Act of 1651, the First Dutch War and the London Merchant Community," *Economic History Review,* 2d ser., 16 (1964): 441; and J. P. Cooper, "Social and Economic Policies under the Commonwealth," in *The Interregnum,* ed. G. E. Aylmer (London, 1972), p. 134.
70. Andrews, *Colonial Period* 4: 54.
71. P.R.O., C.O. 1/14, fols. 145v., 150v., 155r., 166v.; and *CSP, Col., America and the West Indies, 1661-1668* 5: 1-2.
72. Andrews, *Colonial Period* 4: 57.
73. Ibid., pp. 55 and 57.
74. B.M., Egerton 2395, fol. 296r.; Thomas Povey to Virginia, March 4, 1660.
75. P.R.O., C.O. 1/14, fols. 157v., 159r., 160r., 166v.; and, *CSP, Col. America & the West Indies, 1661-1668* 5: 49.
76. *CSP, Col.* 5:49.
77. P.R.O., C.O. 1/14, fols. 159r., 160r.
78. Ibid., fol. 160r.
79. *CSP, Col.* 5: 32; *MHS Proceedings,* 1st ser., 5: 376-77; and *MHS Collections,* 5th ser., 1: 400-403.
80. *MHS Collections,* 5th ser. 1: 400-403.
81. BP 39.
82. P.R.O., C.O. 1/14, fol. 169.
83. Kellaway, p. 45.
84. R. F. Young, *Comenius and the Indians of New England* (London, 1929), p. 25.

85. Edward Winslow, *The Glorious Progress of the Gospel, Amongst the Indians in New England* (London, 1649), in *MHS Collections*, 3d ser. (1834), 4: 69-99.

86. Thomas Shepard, *The Cleare Sun-Shine of the Gospell, Breaking Forth upon the Indians in New-England* (London, 1648), in *MHS Collections*, 3d ser. (1834), 4: 25-68.

87. John Eliot, *The Day-Breaking, If Not the Sun-Rising of the Gospell with the Indians in New-England* (London, 1647) in *MHS Collections*, 3d ser. (1834), 4: 1-23.

88. *HDC*, pp. 48, 270; Salmon, *Francis Lodwick*, p. 49; and Young, *Comenius and the Indians*, pp. 12, 17-18.

89. Young, pp. 23-24.

90. Batten, *Dury*, pp. 129, 139-40; and Peter Toon, "The Question of Jewish Immigration," in *Puritans, the Millennium and the Future of Israel*, ed. P. Toon (Cambridge, England, 1970), pp. 117-20. Also see note 173, this chapter.

91. BP 5, fol. 82; and Pulsifer, pp. 272-73, Boyle writing in behalf of the New England Company to their agents in America, the Commissioners of the United Colonies, London, May 15, 1662.

92. Kellaway, p. 42.

93. For Winthrop's role see *Some Correspondence Between the Governors and Treasurers of the New England Company in London and the Commissioners of the United Colonies in America, the Missionaries of the Company and Others Between the Years 1657 and 1712* (London, 1896), pp. 5-21, 30-33; and Pulsifer, pp. 290, 292-95, 318.

94. BL 1, fol. 31r.

95. BP 3, fols. 130, 131-33, and ibid., 5, fols. 75-90.

96. Lorenzo J. Greene, *The Negro in Colonial New England* (New York, 1969), pp. 257-63; and Marcus Jernegan, *Laboring and Dependent Classes in America 1607-1783* (Chicago, 1931), pp. 24-44.

97. BP 3, fols. 131-33.

98. Kellaway, p. 8; Alden T. Vaughan, *The New England Frontier: Puritans and Indians, 1620-1675* (Boston, 1965), pp. 260-76; and Shepard, *Sun-Shine of the Gospel*, p. 50.

99. Batten, *Dury*, pp. 139-40; and Toon, "Jewish Immigration," pp. 117-18.

100. Eliot, *Day-Breaking*, pp. 15, 20; and Shepard, *Sun-Shine of the Gospel*, p. 39.

101. John Eliot, *Indian Dialogues*, Cambridge, Mass. (1671), p. 20 (cited hereafter as Eliot, *Dialogues*).

102. G. D. Scull, ed., "Letters of the Reverend John Eliot, the Apostle to the Indians," *New England Historical and Genealogical Record* 36 (1882): 296; and Pulsifer, pp. 294, 314, 382.

103. Scull, "Letters," p. 295; and Eliot, *Dialogues*, pp. 3-4.

104. Scull, "Letters," p. 296.

105. Almon W. Lauber, *Indian Slavery in Colonial Times Within the Present Limits of the United States* (New York, 1913), pp. 293, 305.
106. Vaughan, *New England Frontier*, p. 293.
107. Young, *Comenius and the Indians*, pp. 14-17, 20-22; and Young, *Comenius in England*, pp. 90-95.
108. Alden Vaughan, *New England Frontier*, pp. 258-59.
109. Eliot, *Dialogues*, pp. 3-4.
110. Kellaway, chap. 6.
111. *HOC* 2: 214, 246, 603-604; Birch, *Life* in *Works, pp. cviii-cix;* and *RBW* 6: 323-25, 558-59, 562-79, 629-30.
112. BP 5, fol. 80.
113. Young, *Comenius in England*, p. 94.
114. Winthrop, pp. 30-31.
115. *MHS Collections*, 5th ser., 9: 45-47.
116. *RBW* 2: 251.
117. Ibid., 4:1, and ibid., 6: 525.
118. Ibid., 4: 11, 17, 19, 26, 39.
119. Ibid., pp. 11, 20-21.
120. Ibid., pp. 17-21.
121. *RB*, Book I, Part II, p. 388.
122. *RBW* 4: 39.
123. Barbara J. Shapiro, *John Wilkins* (Berkeley, Calif., 1969), p. 233.
124. John Wilkins, *Of the Principles and Duties of Natural Religion* (London) published posthumously in 1675.
125. *Origines Sacrae* (London, 1662), pp. 424-28, 458.
126. R.S., Robert Boyle, Commonplace Book 187, fol. 22v.
127. *RBW* 6: 462.
128. See chapter II above and this chapter below.
129. See, for instance, note 3ff., this chapter.
130. See notes 167 and 168, this chapter.
131. *HOC* 2: 320-21.
132. Shapiro, *John Wilkins*, p. 225.
133. Ibid., p. 227.
134. Ibid., pp. 226-29.
135. Ibid., pp. 226, 315.
136. For my extended critique of Shapiro's work see J. R. Jacob and M. C. Jacob, "Scientists and Society: the Saints Preserved," *Journal of European Studies* 1 (1971): 87-90.
137. For Brereton's latitudinarian sympathies see notes 166 and 168, this chapter.
138. Winthrop, pp. 25-27, 30-31, 34, 39, 47.
139. Birch, *History* 1: 88.
140. Winthrop, p. 28 for Oldenburg; and for Beale, Christ Church Library, Evelyn MSS, Letters 1-109, A-B, Letters 70 and 76.
141. Winthrop, pp. 42-43.

142. C. Hill, review of: *HOC* 5-8, in *EHR* 88 (April 1973): 384.
143. B.M. Egerton 2395, fol. 296r.
144. Robert K. Merton, *Science, Technology and Society in Seventeenth-Century England* (New York, 1970), pp. 148, 188, 239-61.
145. Houghton, "Trades," pp. 48-57.
146. *HOC* 2: 320-21.
147. Thomas Sprat, *A History of the Royal Society of London* (London, 1667), p. 94; and Birch, *History* 1: 85, 507; and ibid., 2: 6, 47, 138, 161, 163, 175.
148. Sprat, *Royal Society*, pp. 342-45, 370-75.
149. Ibid., pp. 343, 428.
150. Ibid., pp. 400, 408, 426-29.
151. Ibid., pp. 57, 371-74.
152. Ibid., pp. 22, 352, 368-69, 371, 377.
153. Ibid., pp. 63, 76.
154. Ibid., pp. 65-67, 130-31.
155. Ibid., pp. 67-76, 130-31.
156. *RBW* 6: 645-46; and *HOC* 2: 509.
157. *HOC*, 2: 320-21.
158. This view is contradictory to the notion put forward by Margery Purver that the Royal Society was not Comenian but Baconian in outlook and inspiration; see her *Royal Society: Concept and Creation* (London, 1967). For an extended critique of Dr. Purver's thesis see C. Webster, "The Origins of the Royal Society," *History of Science*, 6 (1967): 106-28. The question of the origins of the society is tangential to the present study except insofar as Boyle participated in its founding. My own view, however, is that the Royal Society was both Baconian and Comenian in origin—but only as these traditions were filtered through the English revolution down to 1662, as the founders of the society experienced it. This I have tried to suggest here in detail, however, only in the case of Robert Boyle.
159. De Mott, "Comenius," pp. 1068-81.
160. John Wallis, *Truth Tried . . .* (London, 1643), pp. 91 and 99.
161. Vaughan 2: 439, 443, 447, 450, 463, 464; and *HDC*, pp. 378, 379.
162. *RBW* 6: 96-97, 99, 105-107, 110-14, 130-32.
163. *DNB*.
164. *RBW* 6: 341; and R.S., Letter-Book—Supplement 1, fols. 399-400.
165. *RBW* 6: 131-32; *HOC* 1: 384; and *Worthington* 1: 156-58, 176.
166. *RBW* 6: 342, 442; and R.S., MS. B. 1. 15; Beale to William Brereton, March 25, 1663.
167. R.S., MS. B. 1. 15; and *RBW* 6: 96, 132.
168. For Beale see R.S., Letter-Book—Supplement 1, fols. 399-400; for Brereton see Winthrop, p. 47.
169. *RBW* 6: 342-43.
170. Ibid., p. 418.

171. *HOC* 1: 392, and ibid., 3: 446-47; also see notes 205-18, chapter 3 above.

172. Peter Pett, *The Happy Future State of England* (London, 1688), pp. 130, 275; Pett also published Boyle's chief millenarian statement, *Some Considerations Touching the Style of the Holy Scriptures* (*RBW* 2: 251).

173. *RBW* 6: 342, 442; Vaughan 2: 439, 443, 447, 450, 463, 464; R.S., MS. B. 1. 15; and Christ Church Library, Evelyn MSS, Letters 1-109. A-B. Letter 70.

174. G. H. Turnbull, "Some Correspondence of John Winthrop, Jr. and Samuel Hartlib," *MHS Proceedings* 72 (1961): 60.

175. See notes 171-74, this chapter.

176. Pett, *The Happy Future State of England,* p. 275.

177. See notes 149-80, chapter 3 above.

178. Thomas Hearne, *Works* (Oxford, England, 1725), 1: clxii-clxiii.

179. Sprat, *Royal Society,* pp. 53-56.

180. Birch, *Life* in *Works* 1: lxxxii.

181. *RBW* 5: 15.

182. Ibid., pp. 178, 184-85.

183. Ibid. p. 227.

184. Ibid., pp. 164, 198, 216, 226-27, 251-52.

185. Ibid., p. 164.

186. Ibid., p. 198.

187. Ibid., p. 164.

188. Ibid., pp. 182-83.

189. Ibid., pp. 250-51.

190. Ibid., p. 183.

191. John Heydon, *Theomagia* (London, 1663), Book III, pp. 36, 122, 134 (cited hereafter as Heydon, *Theomagia*).

192. Ibid., pp. 28, 36, 122, 134.

193. Ibid., "The Preface," f4.

194. Ibid., Book I, p. 168.

195. Ibid., "The Preface."

196. Ibid., Book III, p. 98.

197. Ibid., pp. 7, 23-25, 135-36.

198. John Heydon, *The Harmony of the World* (London, 1662), "The Preface."

199. Heydon, *Theomagia,* Book III, p. 101.

200. *RBW* 5: 164, 182-83, 186, 188, 250-51.

201. Heydon, *Theomagia,* Book I, p. 1.

202. Yates, *Enlightenment.*

203. Ibid., pp. xii, 79, 96, 128, 129; and Heydon, *Theomagia,* Book III, p. 101.

204. A. E. Waite, *The Real History of the Rosicrucians* (New York, 1888), pp. 348-86.

205. As the preface to Heydon's *Holy Guide* (London, 1662).

206. See note 120, chapter III above; and Samuel Parker, *A Free and Impartial Censure of the Platonick Philosophie* (Oxford, England, 1666), p. 75.

207. The rest of the title of Heydon's *Harmony of the World* (1662) runs *Whereunto is added, the state of the New Jerusalem, grounded upon the knowledge of Nature, Light of Reason, Phylosophy and Divinity.*

208. *CSP, Ireland, 1663-1665*, pp. 100-101, 662, 679; and *CSP, Ireland, 1666-1669*, pp. 25-26, 33-34, 93.

209. Abbott, "Conspiracy, I," pp. 518-28.

210. Walter George Bell, *The Great Plague in London in 1665*, rev. ed. (London, 1951), p. 223; and Wilbur C. Abbott, "English Conspiracy and Dissent, 1660-1674, II," *AHR* (July 1909): 699-700 (cited hereafter as Abbott, "Conspiracy, II").

211. *DNB.*

212. Heydon, *Theomagia*, Book III, p. 101.

213. *DNB.*

214. Parker, *Platonick Philosophie*, pp. 72–73.

215. Ibid.

216. *HOC* 3: 155.

217. *The London Gazette*, no. 48 (April 26-30, 1666).

218. Valentine Greatrakes, *A Brief Account of Mr. Valentine Greatraks, and Divers of the Strange Cures by Him Lately Performed* (London, 1666), pp. 15-18.

219. Ibid., p. 19.

220. Ibid., p. 22.

221. Ibid., pp. 22-23, 35-38.

222. Roger L'Estrange, ed., *The Newes*, no. 54 (July 13, 1665), p. 571.

223. *Rawdon*, pp. 204-207.

224. Greatrakes, *Brief Account*, p. 38.

225. Ibid., p. 39.

226. *N&Q*, 3d ser., 5 (June 11, 1864): 489.

227. Greatrakes, *Brief Account*, p. 39.

228. [David Lloyd], *Wonders No Miracles* (London, 1666), p. 32.

229. *Rawdon*, p. 211.

230. Raymund Crawfurd, *The King's Evil* (Oxford, England, 1911), p. 112.

231. [Lloyd], *Wonders*, p. 13.

232. Ibid., p. 14.

233. Ibid., p. 5.

234. Ibid., pp. 8-9.

235. Ibid., p. 8.

236. Ibid.

237. Ibid., pp. 11-12.

238. Hill, *Antichrist*, pp. 4-5, 28-29.

239. [Lloyd], *Wonders*, p. 8.

240. Ibid., p. 34.

241. Ibid., p. 35.

242. [Lyonell Beacher], *Wonders If Not Miracles* (London, 1665), pp. A2-A3.

243. BL 2, fol. 64r.

244. *Conway*, p. 274.

245. Ibid., p. 263; Michael Boyle, archbishop of Dublin, to Edward, lord Conway, Dublin, July 29, 1665.

246. Ibid.

247. Ibid., pp. 262-63.

248. B.M., Sloane 1926, fols. 1-10; see also Samuel Hayman, "Notes on the Family of Greatrakes Part I," *The Reliquary* 4 (October 1863): 88, for Dublin opinion about Greatrakes in the summer of 1665.

249. *CSP, Ireland, 1666-1669*, pp. 25-26, 33-34, 93; and Abbott, "Conspiracy, II," pp. 702-703.

250. Henry Stubbe, *The Miraculous Conformist* . . . (Oxford, England, 1666), p. 25.

251. Ibid., p. 14.

252. Ibid., p. 27.

253. BL 2, fols. 52-63.

254. Ibid., fol. 65v.

255. Ibid.

256. There may be a hint of this in Stubbe, *Miraculous Conformist*, p. 14.

257. *Anima Mundi* (1679?); and C. Blount, *Miracles, No Violations of the Law of Nature* (1683); and J. A. Redwood, "Blount, Deism and English Free Thought," *JHI* 35 (1974): 490-98.

258. Birch, *Life* in *Works*, pp. lxxix, lxxxv.

259. Ibid., p. lxxvii.

260. Ibid., p. lxxix.

261. Stubbe, *Miraculous Conformist*, p. 14; and [Lloyd], *Wonders*, p. 26.

262. *HOC* 1: 90-92, 116, 143-44, 382, 385-86, 391-92, 406.

263. Ibid.

264. *Worthington* 1: 199, 335.

265. See chapter 3.

266. *The New Schaff-Herzog Encyclopedia of Religious Knowledge*; and Leszek Kolakowski, *Chrétiens sans Église*, trans. Anna Posner (Paris, 1969), pp. 197-99.

267. *The Mennonite Encyclopedia*.

268. *HOC* 1: 90-92, 116, 143-44, 382, 385-86, 391-92, 406.

269. Ibid., 2: 404-405, 408, 509, 534, and ibid., 3: 18.

270. BP 12, 13, 15.

271. D. P. Walker, *Spiritual and Demonic Magic from Ficino to Campanella* (London, 1958), especially pp. 110-11; and Robert Lenoble, *Mersenne ou la Naissance du Mécanisme* (Paris, 1943).

272. [Lloyd], *Wonders*, p. 26.

273. See notes 231-41, this chapter.

274. Violet Rowe, *Sir Henry Vane the Younger* (London, 1970), p. 228; and Woolrych in Aylmer, p. 197.

275. *AO* 2: 413.
276. Perez Zagorin, *A History of Political Thought in the English Revolution* (London, 1954), p. 153; Richard Baxter, *A Holy Commonwealth* (London, 1659), "An Addition to the Preface, Being a Discussion of the Answer to the Healing Question"; Richard Baxter, *A Key for Catholicks* (London, 1659), pp. 330-31; and Henry Stubbe, *Malice Rebuked, or a Character of Mr. Richard Baxter's Abilities. And Vindication of the Honourable Sr. Henry Vane from His Aspersions in His Key for Catholicks* (London, 1659), pp. 37-60.
277. See notes 180-98, chapter 3 above.
278. See note 254, chapter 3 above.
279. Emery Battis, *Saints and Sectaries* (Chapel Hill, N. C., 1962), pp. 106, 269; Larzer Ziff, *The Career of John Cotton* (Princeton, N.J., 1962), pp. 115-16; and David Hall, ed., *The Antinomian Controversy, 1636-1638* (Middletown, Conn., 1968), pp. 7-10, 29, 317, 351-64.
280. See notes 132-36, chapter 3 above.
281. See notes 255-74, chapter 3 above.
282. Stubbe, *Miraculous Conformist*, p. 8.
283. [Lloyd], *Wonders*, p. 9; see also [Lloyd], p. 17.
284. Greatrakes, *Brief Account*, p. 19.
285. Ibid., p. 20.
286. Ibid.
287. Ibid., p. 21.
288. Ibid., pp. 56-63.
289. *Conway*, p. 273; Henry More to Lady Conway, Cambridge, April 28, [1666].
290. B.M. Add. MS. 4293, fol. 50.
291. Greatrakes, *Brief Account*, pp. 43-94.
292. Ibid., pp. 34-35.
293. Ibid., p. 35.
294. See notes 242 and 244, this chapter.
295. Greatrakes, *Brief Account*, pp. 30-31.
296. K. Thomas, *Religion and the Decline of Magic* (London, 1971), p. 202.
297. G. Hermant, *Mémoires sur l'Histoire Ecclésiastique du XVII^e Siècle (1630-1663)* (Paris, 1905), 6: 575-78.
298. Birch, *Life* in *Works*, p. lxxxi.
299. *RBW* 5: 216.
300. J. F. Fulton, *A Bibliography of the Honourable Robert Boyle, F. R. S.*, 2d ed. (Oxford, England, 1961), p. 112. R. S. Westfall, *Science and Religion in Seventeenth-Century England* (New Haven, Conn., 1958) p. 228; and J. E. McGuire, "Boyle's Conception of Nature," *JHI* 33 (October-December 1972): 525.
301. This is a chapter in a long story: see P. M. Rattansi, "The Social Interpretation of Science in the Seventeenth Century," in *Science and Society 1600-1900*, ed. Peter Mathias (Cambridge, England, 1972, pp.

1-32; and Yates, *Enlightenment*, pp. 111-17.

## Notes to Chapter 5

1. Robert K. Merton, *Science, Technology and Society in Seventeenth-Century England* (New York, 1970), pp. xxviii and 82.
2. Barbara J. Shapiro, *John Wilkins* (Berkeley, Calif., 1969).
3. Compare chapter 1 above and Merton, *Science*, chaps. 4 and 5.
4. See notes 77-80, chapter 1 above.

# Bibliography

# Bibliography

The following list includes only those works cited in the notes.

## Primary Sources

### Manuscripts

Bodleian Library, Oxford, England. Tanner MS. 461.20b.

The British Museum.
    Add. MS. 4229.
    Add. MS. 4293.
    Add. MS. 32093.
    Egerton 2395.
    Harley 7003.
    Sloane 1926.

Chatsworth, Derbyshire, England. Devonshire Collections.

Christ Church Library, Oxford, England. Evelyn MSS.

Public Record Office, London. C. O. 1/14.

The Royal Society of London.
    The Boyle Letters.
    The Boyle Papers.
    Boyle, Robert. Commonplace Book 187.
    Boyle, Robert. MSS. 192, 195, 196, and 197.
    Letter-Book—Supplement, I.
    MS. B.1.15.
    Oldenburg, Henry. Commonplace Book 187.

Historical Library, Yale Medical Library, Yale University. New Haven, Conn. Robert Boyle. A draft letter, dated March 26, 1649.

## Printed Sources

Andreae, J. V. *Christianopolis*. Translated by Felix E. Held. New York, 1916.

Andreae, J. V. *A Modell of a Christian Society*. In "Johann Valentin Andreaes Societas Christiana," by G. H. Turnbull. *Zeitschrift für Deutsche Philologie* 74 (1955).

Ashley, Robert. *Of Honour*. Edited by Virgil B. Heltzel. San Marino, Calif., 1947.

Bacon, Francis. *Works*. Edited by James Spedding, R. L. Ellis, and D. D. Heath. 14 vols. London, 1857-1874.

Barlow, Thomas. *Genuine Remains*. Edited by Sir Peter Pett. London, 1693.

Barlow, Thomas. *Several Miscellaneous and Weighty Cases of Conscience*. London, 1692.

Baxter, Richard. *A Holy Commonwealth*. London, 1659.

Baxter, Richard. *A Key for Catholicks*. London, 1659.

Baxter, Richard. *Reliquiae Baxterianae*. London, 1696.

Baxter, Richard. *The Unreasonableness of Infidelity*. London, 1655.

[Beacher, Lyonell.] *Wonders If Not Miracles*. London, 1665.

Beck, Cave. *The Universal Character . . . .* Ipswich, England, 1657.

Berwick, E., ed. *The Rawdon Papers*. London, 1819.

Birch, Thomas. *The History of the Royal Society . . .* 4 vols. London, 1756-1757.

Blount, Charles. *Anima Mundi*. [1679?]

Blount, Charles. *Miracles, No Violations of the Law of Nature.* London, 1683.

Boyle, Robert. *The Sceptical Chymist.* London, 1949.

Boyle, Robert. *The Works of the Honourable Robert Boyle.* Edited by Thomas Birch. 6 vols. London, 1772.

Bray, W., ed. *The Diary and Correspondence of John Evelyn.* 4 vols. London, 1859-1862.

*Calendar of Clarendon State Papers.* Oxford, England, 1872.

*Calendar of State Papers, Colonial Series.*

*Calendar of State Papers, Ireland, 1663-1669.*

Carte, Thomas. *An History of the Life of James Duke of Ormonde.* 3 vols. London, 1785-1786.

Clark, William S., ed. *The Dramatic Works of Roger Boyle, Earl of Orrery.* 2 vols. Cambridge, Mass., 1937.

Comenius, J. A. *The Reformation of Schools.* London, 1642.

Comenius, J. A. *The Way of Light.* Translated by E. F. Campagnac. Liverpool, England, 1938.

Crossley, James, ed. *The Diary and Correspondence of Dr. John Worthington.* Vol. 1, in vol. 13 (1847), vol. 2 in vol. 36 (1855), vol. 3 in vol. 114 (1886), of *Chetham Society Remains.*

Dalgarno, George. *Ars signorum* . . . . London, 1661.

Diogenes Laertius. *Lives of the Eminent Philosophers.* Translated by R. D. Hicks. 2 vols. Cambridge, Mass., 1958.

Eliot, John. *Indian Dialogues.* "Cambridge in New-England," 1671.

Eliot, John. *The Day-Breaking, If Not the Sun-Rising of the Gospell with the Indians in New-England.* London, 1647. In *MHS Collections,* 3d ser. (1834), 4: 1-23.

Everard, [John], trans. *The Divine Pymander of Hermes Mercurius Trismegistus*. London, 1650.

Firth, C. H., and Rait, R. S., eds. *Acts and Ordinances of the Interregnum*. London, 1911.

Glanvill, Joseph. *Plus Ultra* . . . . London, 1668.

*The Great Cures, and Strange Miracles, Performed by Mr. Valentine Gertrux*. . . . London, 1666. Copy in Osler Library, McGill University, Montreal, Canada.

Greatrakes, Valentine. *A Brief Account of Mr. Valentine Greatraks, and Divers of the Strange Cures by Him Lately Performed*. London, 1666.

Grosart, Alexander B., ed. *The Lisimore Papers*. 1st ser. 5 vols. London, 1886. 2d ser. 5 vols. London, 1887.

Hall, A. Rupert, and Hall, Marie Boas, eds. *The Correspondence of Henry Oldenburg*. 7 vols. Madison, Wis. 1965-1970.

Hall, David, ed. *The Antinomian Controversy, 1636-1638*. Middletown, Conn., 1968.

Hearne, Thomas. *Works*. 4 vols. Oxford, England, 1725.

Heydon, John. *The Harmony of the World*. London, 1662.

Heydon, John. *Holy Guide*. London, 1662.

Heydon, John. *Theomagia*. London, 1663.

Hyde, Edward, earl of Clarendon. *State Papers*. 3 vols. Oxford, England, 1767-1786.

L'Estrange, Roger, ed. *The Newes*, no. 54 (July 13, 1665).

[Lloyd, David.] *Wonders No Miracles*. London, 1666.

*The London Gazette*, no. 48 (April 26-30, 1666).

Maddison, R. E. W. "The Earliest Published Writing of Robert Boyle." *Annals of Science* 17 (1961): 165-73.

*MHS Collections*, 5th ser., 1: 400-403. Robert Boyle to John Endecott, London, March 17, 1665.

*MHS Proceedings*, 1st ser., 5: 376-77. Robert Boyle to John Winthrop, Jr., London, April 21, 1664.

Milton, John. *Areopagitica*. In *Complete Prose Works of John Milton*, vol. 2. Ed. Don Wolfe. New Haven, Conn., and London, 1959.

Morrice, Thomas, ed. *A Collection of the State Letters of the Right Honourable Roger Boyle*. London, 1742.

Nicolson, Marjorie H., ed. *Conway Letters*. New Haven, Conn., 1930.

Ogilvie, James D., ed. *Diary of Sir Archibald Johnston of Wariston*, vol. 3, 1655-1660. In *Publications of the Scottish Historical Society*, 3d ser., vol. 34. Edinburgh, 1940.

Overton, Richard. *Mans Mortalitie*. Amsterdam, 1644.

Parker, Samuel. *A Free and Impartial Censure of the Platonick Philosophie*. Oxford, England, 1666.

Parr, Richard. *The Life of . . . James Usher*. London, 1684.

Pett, Peter. *A Discourse Concerning Liberty of Conscience*. London, 1661.

Pett, Peter. *The Happy Future State of England*. London, 1688.

[Plattes, Gabriel.] . . . *Macaria* . . . . In *The Harleian Miscellany* . . . , vol. 1. London, 1808.

Pulsifer, David, ed. *Acts of the Commissioners of the United Colonies of New England, 1643-1679*. Vols. 9-10. In *Records of the Colony of New Plymouth, in New England*, edited by Nathaniel B. Shurtleff. 12 vols. in 11. Boston, 1855-1861.

Rich, Mary, countess of Warwick. *Autobiography*. Edited by L. Crofton Croker. London, 1848.

Rowbottom, Margaret E. "The Earliest Published Writing of Robert Boyle." *Annals of Science* 6 (November 1950): 376-89.

Sabine, George, ed. *The Works of Gerrard Winstanley.* Ithaca, N.Y., 1941.

Salmon, Vivian, ed. *The Works of Francis Lodwick.* London, 1972.

Sanderson, Robert. *Several Cases of Conscience.* Translated by Robert Codrington. London, 1660.

Scull, G. D., ed. "Letters of the Reverend John Eliot, the Apostle to the Indians." *New England Historical and Genealogical Record* 36 (1882).

Shepard, Thomas. *The Cleare Sun-Shine of the Gospell, Breaking Forth upon the Indians in New-England.* London, 1648. In *MHS Collections,* 3d ser. (1834), 4: 25-68.

*Some Correspondence Between the Governors and Treasurers of the New England Company in London and the Commissioners of the United Colonies in America, the Missionaries of the Company and Others Between the Years 1657 and 1712.* London, 1896.

Stanley, James, seventh earl of Derby. *Private Devotions and Miscellanies.* Edited by E. R. Raines. Part III, *The Stanley Papers.* In *Remains Historical and Literary Connected with the Palatine Counties of Lancaster and Chester,* vol. 70. The Chetham Society, Manchester, 1867.

Sprat, Thomas. *A History of the Royal Society of London.* London, 1667.

Stillingfleet, Edward. *Origines Sacrae.* London, 1662.

Stubbe, Henry. *Malice Rebuked, or a Character of Mr. Richard Baxter's Abilities.* London, 1659.

Stubbe, Henry. *The Miraculous Conformist . . . .* Oxford, England, 1666.

Thurloe, John. *A Collection of the State Papers of John Thurloe.* 7 vols. London, 1742.

*The Trumbull Papers. MHS Collections,* 5th ser. (1885), 9: 45-47, John Winthrop, "Proposals concerning the employing the Indians in New England."

Turnbull, G. H. *Hartlib, Dury and Comenius.* Liverpool, England, 1947.

Turnbull, G. H. "Some Correspondence of John Winthrop, Jr. and Samuel Hartlib." *MHS Proceedings* 72 (1961).

Vaughan, Robert, ed. *The Protectorate of Oliver Cromwell.* 2 vols. London, 1838.

Waite, A. E., ed. *The Magical Writings of Thomas Vaughan.* London, 1888.

Wallis, John. *Truth Tried . . . .* London, 1643.

Walton, I. *The Life of Dr. Sanderson.* London, 1678.

Webster, John. *Academiarum Examen.* London, 1654.

Wilkins, John. *The Beauty of Providence.* London, 1649.

Wilkins, John. *An Essay Towards a Real Character and a Philosophical Language.* London, 1668.

Wilkins, John. *Of the Principles and Duties of Natural Religion.* London, 1675.

Winslow, Edward. *The Glorious Progress of the Gospel, Amongst the Indians in New England.* London, 1649. In *MHS Collections,* 3d ser. (1834), 4: 69-99.

Winthrop, Robert C., ed. *Correspondence of Hartlib, Haak, Oldenburg and Others of the Founders of the Royal Society with Governor Winthrop of Connecticut 1661-1672.* Boston, 1878.

Wolfe, Don M., ed. *Leveller Manifestoes of the Puritan Revolution.* New York, 1944.

Wood, Anthony. *Athenae Oxonienses.* 2 vols. London, 1691.

## Secondary Works

Abernathy, George R. "The English Presbyterians and the Stuart Restoration, 1648-1663." In *Transactions of the American Philosophical Society,* N.S. 55, Part 2 (May 1965).

Abernathy, George R. "Richard Baxter and the Cromwellian Church." *Huntington Library Quarterly* 24 (1961).

Abbott, Wilbur C. "English Conspiracy and Dissent, 1660-1674, I." *AHR* 14 (April 1909). "English Conspiracy and Dissent, 1660-1674, II," *AHR* (July 1909).

Andrews, Charles M. *The Colonial Period in American History.* 4 vols. New Haven, Conn., 1938.

Aylmer, G. E., ed. *The Interregnum.* London, 1972.

Barnard, T. C. "Lord Broghill, Vincent Gookin and the Cork Elections of 1659." *EHR* 88 (April 1973).

Barnard, T. C. "Planters and Policies in Cromwellian Ireland." *P&P*, no. 61 (November 1973): 31-69.

Batten, J. M. *John Dury.* Chicago, 1944.

Battis, Emery. *Saints and Sectaries.* Chapel Hill, N. C., 1962.

Bell, Walter George. *The Great Plague in London in 1665.* Rev. ed. London, 1951.

Boas, Marie. "Boyle as Theoretical Scientist." *Isis* 15 (1950): 261-68.

Boas, Marie. "An Early Version of Boyle's Sceptical Chemist." *Isis* 45 (1954): 153-68.

Boas, Marie. "La Méthode Scientifique de Robert Boyle." *Revue d'Histoire des Sciences* 9 (1956): 105-25.

Boas, Marie. *Robert Boyle and Seventeenth-Century Chemistry.* Cambridge, England, 1958.

Bosher, R. S. *The Making of the Restoration Settlement.* Westminster, England, 1951.

Bottigheimer, Karl. *English Money and Irish Land.* Oxford, England, 1971.

Budé, E. de. *Vie de Jean Diodati, Theologien Génevois 1574-1649.* Lausanne, Switzerland, 1869.

Capp, B. S. *The Fifth Monarchy Men.* London, 1972.

Caspari, Fritz. *Humanism and the Social Order in Tudor England.* New York, 1968.

Cohen, Jonathan. "On the Project of a Universal Character." *Mind* 63 (1954): 49-63.

Conant, James B., ed. *Robert Boyle's Experiments in Pneumatics.* Cambridge, Mass., 1967.

Conklin, George Newton. *Biblical Criticism and Heresy in Milton.* New York, 1949.

Crawfurd, Raymund. *The King's Evil.* Oxford, England, 1911.

Davies, G. "English Political Sermons, 1603-1640." *The Huntington Library Quarterly* 3 (October 1939).

Debus, Allen, ed. *Science and Education in the Seventeeth Century. The Webster-Ward Debate.* London, 1970.

Debus, Allen, ed. *Science, Medicine and Society in the Renaissance.* 2 vols. New York, 1972.

De Mott, Benjamin. "Comenius and the Real Character in England." *Publications of the Modern Language Association* 70 (1955): 1068-81.

De Mott, Benjamin. "The Sources and Development of John Wilkins' Philosophical Language." *Journal of English and Germanic Philology* 57 (1958): 1-13.

*DNB.*

Douglas, Mary. *Natural Symbols.* Harmondsworth, England, 1973.

Dunn, Richard S. *Puritans and Yankees.* New York, 1971.

Eirionnack. "Notes on Certain Theosophists and Mystics. Tauler and His School," *N&Q,* 4th ser., 1: 597-600.

Farnell, J. E. "The Navigation Act of 1651, the First Dutch War and the London Merchant Community." *Economic History Review,* 2d ser., 16 (1964).

Farnell, J. E. "The Usurpation of Honest London Householders: Barebone's Parliament," *EHR* 82 (January 1967): 24-46.

Fisch, H. "The Scientist as Priest: a Note on Robert Boyle's Natural Theology," *Isis* 15 (1953): 252-65.

Fisher, Mitchell S. *Robert Boyle, Devout Naturalist.* Philadelphia, 1945.

Frank, Joseph. *The Levellers.* Cambridge, Mass., 1955.

French, Peter. *John Dee.* London, 1972.

Fulton, J. F. *A Bibliography of the Honourable Robert Boyle, F.R.S.* 2d ed. Oxford, England, 1961.

Greene, Lorenzo J. *The Negro in Colonial New England.* New York, 1969.

Haller, William. *The Rise of Puritanism.* New York, 1938.

Hayman, Samuel. "Notes on the Family of Greatrakes Part I." *The Reliquary* 4 (October 1863).

Henry, Nathaniel H. "Milton and Hobbes: Mortalism and the Intermediate State." *Studies in Philology* 48 (1951): 234-49.

Hermant, G. *Mémoires sur l'Histoire Ecclésiastique du XVIIᵉ Siècle (1630-1663).* 6 vols. Paris, 1905.

Hill, C. *Antichrist in Seventeenth-Century England.* Oxford, England, 1971.

Hill, C. *The Century of Revolution 1603-1714.* London, 1964.

Hill, C. *God's Englishman.* New York, 1972.

Hill, C. *Reformation to Industrial Revolution.* Baltimore, 1969.

Hill, C. Review of *HOC* 5-8, in *EHR* 88 (April 1973): 384.

Hill, C. *The World Turned Upside Down.* London, 1972.

Hinton, R. W. K. *The Eastland Trade and the Commonweal in the Seventeenth Century.* Cambridge, England, 1959.

Hollinger, David A. "T. S. Kuhn's Theory of Science and Its Implications for History." *AHR* 78 (April 1973): 370-93.

Houghton, Walter E. "The English Virtuoso in the Seventeenth

Century," *JHI* 3 (January 1942): 51-73, and (April 1942): 190-219.

Houghton, Walter E. "The History of Trades: Its Relation to Seventeenth Century Thought," *JHI* 2 (January 1941).

Hutin, Serge. *Les Disciples Anglais de Jacob Boehme aux XVII^e et XVIII^e Siècles*. Paris, 1960.

Jacob, J. R. "The Ideological Origins of Robert Boyle's Natural Philosophy." *Journal of European Studies* 2 (March 1972): 1-21.

Jacob, J. R., and Jacob, M. C. "Scientists and Society: the Saints Preserved." *Journal of European Studies* 1 (1971): 87-90.

Jacob, M. C. "John Toland and the Newtonian Ideology." *Journal of the Courtauld and Warburg Institutes* 32 (1969): 307-31.

James, M. *Social Problems and Policy during the Puritan Revolution 1640-1660*. London, 1930.

Jernegan, Marcus. *Laboring and Dependent Classes in America 1607-1783*. Chicago, 1931.

Jones, R. M. *Mysticism and Democracy in the English Commonwealth*. Cambridge, Mass., 1932.

Jordan, W. K. "Sectarian Thought and Its Relation to the Development of Religious Toleration, 1640-1660." *The Huntington Library Quarterly* 3 (January 1940): 214-19.

Kargon, R. H. *Atomism in England from Harriot to Newton*. Oxford, England, 1966.

Kearney, Hugh. *Scholars and Gentlemen*. Ithaca, N. Y., 1970.

Keeler, Mary Frear. *The Long Parliament 1640-1641*. Philadelphia, 1954.

Kellaway, William. *The New England Company, 1649-1776*. New York, 1961.

Kelso, Ruth. *The Doctrine of the English Gentleman in the Sixteenth Century*. Gloucester, Mass., 1964.

Knox, R. Buick. *James Ussher*. Cardiff, Wales, 1967.

Kolakowski, Leszek. *Chrétiens sans Église*. Translated by Anna Posner. Paris, 1969.

Krailsheimer, A. J. *Studies in Self-interest*. Oxford, England, 1962.

Kuhn, T. S. "Robert Boyle and Structural Chemistry in the Seventeenth Century." *Isis* 43 (April 1952): 12-36.

Kuhn, T. S. *The Structure of Scientific Revolutions*. 2d ed. Chicago, 1970.

Lamont, William M. *Godly Rule*. London, 1969.

Lauber, Almon W. *Indian Slavery in Colonial Times Within the Present Limits of the United States*. New York, 1913.

Laudan, L. "The Clock Metaphor and Probabilism: the Impact of Descartes on English Methodological Thought, 1650-65." *Annals of Science* 22 (June 1966): 108-43.

Lenoble, Robert. *Mersenne ou la Naissance du Mécanisme*. Paris, 1943.

Lockyer, Roger. *Tudor and Stuart Britain 1471-1714*. New York, 1964.

McGuire, J. E. "Boyle's Conception of Nature." *JHI* 33 (October-December 1972): 523-42.

McGuire, J. E., and Rattansi, P. "Newton and the 'Pipes of Pan.' " *N&R* 21 (December 1966): 108-43.

Macpherson, C. P. *The Political Theory of Possessive Individualism*. Oxford, England, 1962.

Maddison, R. E. W. *The Life of the Honourable Robert Boyle, F.R.S.* London, 1969.

Maddison, R. E. W. "Studies in the Life of Robert Boyle, F.R.S., Part VI. The Stalbridge Period, 1645-1655, and the Invisible College." *N&R* 18 (December 1963): 104-24.

Maddison, R. E. W. "Studies in the Life of Robert Boyle, F.R.S. Part VII. The Grand Tour," *N&R* 20 (June 1965): 51-77.

Maddison, R. E. W. "A Tentative Index of the Correspondence of the Honourable Robert Boyle, F.R.S.," *N&R* 12 (November 1958): 128-201.

Mandelbaum, Maurice. *Philosophy, Science and Sense Perception.* Baltimore, 1964.

Mannheim, Karl. *Ideology and Utopia.* London, 1936.

Mathias, Peter, ed. *Science and Society 1600-1900.* Cambridge, England, 1972.

*The Mennonite Encyclopedia.*

Merton, Robert K. *Science, Technology and Society in Seventeenth-Century England.* New York, 1970.

More, L. T. *The Life and Works of the Honourable Robert Boyle.* New York, 1944.

Morrill, J. S. "Mutiny and Discontent in English Provincial Armies 1645-1647." *P&P*, no. 56 (August 1972): 49-74.

*The New Schaff-Herzog Encyclopedia of Religious Knowledge.*

Nuttall, Geoffrey. *The Puritan Spirit.* London, 1967.

Nuttall, Geoffrey. *Richard Baxter.* London, 1965.

O'Brien, J. J. "Commonwealth Schemes for the Advancement of Learning." *British Journal of Educational Studies* 16 (1968).

O'Brien, J. J. "Samuel Hartlib's Influence on Robert Boyle's Scientific Development. Part I. The Stalbridge Period." *Annals of Science* 21 (March 1965): 1-14.

Palgrave, Mary E. *Mary Rich, Countess of Warwick* (1625-1678). London, 1901.

Parry, R. H., ed. *The English Civil War and After.* London, 1970.

Pilkington, Roger. *Robert Boyle.* London, 1959.

Purver, Margery. *Royal Society: Concept and Creation.* London, 1967.

R. W. *N&Q,* 3d ser., 5 (June 11, 1864): 489.

Raab, Felix. *The English Face of Machiavelli.* London, 1964.

Ranger, T. O. "Richard Boyle and the Making of an Irish Fortune, 1588-1614." *Irish Historical Studies* 10 (1957):
257-97.

Rattansi, P. M. "The Intellectual Origins of the Royal Society."
*N&R* 23 (December 1968).

Rattansi, P. M. "Paracelsus and the Puritan Revolution," *Ambix*
11 (1964): 24-32.

Redwood, J. A. "Blount, Deism and English Free Thought." *JHI*
35 (1974): 490-498.

Trevor-Roper, H. R. *The European Witch-Craze of the Sixteenth and
Seventeenth Centuries and Other Essays.* New York,
1969.

Trevor-Roper, H. R. *Religion, the Reformation, and Social Change.*
London, 1967.

Trevor-Roper, H. R. "Three Foreigners and the Philosophy of
the English Revolution," *Encounter* 14 (1960): 3-20.

Roth, Cecil. *A Life of Menasseh ben Israel.* Philadelphia, 1934.

Rowe, Violet. *Sir Henry Vane the Younger.* London, 1970.

Saurat, Denis. *Milton, Man and Thinker.* London, 1944.

Schlatter, Richard, ed. *Richard Baxter and Puritan Politics.* New
Brunswick, N. J., 1957.

Shapiro, Barbara J. *John Wilkins.* Berkeley, Calif., 1969.

Solt, Leo. *Saints in Arms.* Stanford, Calif., 1959.

Spalding, James C., and Brass, Maynard F. "Reduction of Episcopacy as a Means to Unity in England, 1640-1662."
*Church History* 30 (December 1961): 414-32.

Stone, Lawrence. *The Crisis of the Aristocracy 1558-1641.* Oxford,
England, 1965.

Sutcliffe, F. E. *Guez de Balzac et Son Temps.* Paris, 1959.

Thomas, Keith. *Religion and the Decline of Magic.* London, 1971.

Toon, Peter, ed. *Puritans, the Millennium and the Future of Israel.* Cambridge, England, 1970.

Townshend, Dorothea. *The Life and Letters of the Great Earl of Cork.* London, 1904.

Turnbull, G. H. "George Stirk, Philosopher by Fire (1628?-1665)." *Publications of the Colonial Society of Massachusetts.* Vol. 38. *Transactions 1947-1951.* Boston, 1959.

Underdown, David. *Pride's Purge.* Oxford, England, 1971.

Van Leeuwen, Henry G. *The Problem of Certainty in English Thought 1630-1690.* The Hague, the Netherlands, 1963.

Vaughan, Alden T. *The New England Frontier: Puritans and Indians, 1620-1675.* Boston, 1965.

Waite, A. E. *The Real History of the Rosicrucians.* New York, 1888.

Walker, D. P. *The Ancient Theology.* London, 1972.

Walker, D. P. "The Prisca Theologia in France." *Journal of the Courtauld and Warburg Institutes* 17 (1954).

Walker, D. P. *Spiritual and Demonic Magic from Ficino to Campanella.* London, 1958.

Watson, Curtis Brown. *Shakespeare and the Renaissance Concept of Honor.* Princeton, N. J., 1960.

Webster, Charles. "The Authorship and Significance of *Macaria.*" *P&P,* no. 56 (August 1972): 36-42.

Webster, Charles. "New Light on the Invisible College: the Social Relations of English Science in the Mid-Seventeenth Century," *TRHS,* 5th ser., 24 (1974): 19-42.

Webster, Charles. "The Origins of the Royal Society," *History of Science* 6 (1967): 106–28.

Webster, Charles. *Samuel Hartlib and the Advancement of Learning.* Cambridge, England, 1970.

Westfall, R. S. *Science and Religion in Seventeenth-Century England.* New Haven, Conn., 1958.

Westfall, R. S. "Unpublished Boyle Papers Relating to Scientific Method." *Annals of Science* 12 (March 1956): 63-73, and (June 1957): 103-17.

Wilkinson, R. S. "The Hartlib Papers and Seventeenth-century Chemistry. Part I." *Ambix* 15 (1968).

Wilson, John E. "Comment on 'Two Roads to the Puritan Millennium.' " *Church History* 32 (1963).

Wolf, Lucien, ed. *Menasseh ben Israel. Mission to Cromwell.* London, 1901.

Woolrych, Austin. "The Calling of Barebone's Parliament." *EHR* 316 (July 1965).

Wright, Louis B. *Religion and Empire.* Chapel Hill, N. C., 1943.

Yates, Frances. *Giordano Bruno and the Hermetic Tradition.* London, 1964.

Yates, Frances. *The Rosicrucian Enlightenment.* London, 1972.

Young, R. E. *Comenius and the Indians of New England.* London, 1929.

Young, R. E. *Comenius in England.* Oxford, England, 1932.

Zagorin, Perez. *A History of Political Thought in the English Revolution.* London, 1954.

Ziff, Larzer. *The Career of John Cotton.* Princeton, N. J., 1962.

# Index

# Index